Filibusters and Expansionists

Filibusters and Expansionists

JEFFERSONIAN MANIFEST DESTINY, 1800–1821

Frank Lawrence Owsley, Jr.
and Gene A. Smith

The University of
Alabama
Press

Tuscaloosa and
London

∞

The paper on which this book is printed
meets the minimum requirements of
American National Standard
for Information Science–Permanence of Paper
for Printed Library Materials,
ANSI Z39.48-1984.

Library of Congress Cataloging-in-Publication Data

Owsley, Frank Lawrence, 1928–
Filibusters and expansionists : Jeffersonian manifest destiny,
1800–1821 / Frank Lawrence Owsley, Jr., and
Gene A. Smith
p. cm.
Includes bibliographical references and index.
ISBN 0-8173-0880-6
1. Gulf Coast Region (U.S.)—History. 2. United States—
Territorial expansion. 3. Filibusters. 4. Florida—History—
Spanish colony, 1784–1821. 5. Texas—History—1810–1821.
6. Jefferson, Thomas, 1743–1826. 7. Madison, James, 1751–1836.
8. Monroe, James, 1758–1831. I. Smith, Gene A., 1963– .
II. Title.
F296.094 1997
976´.03—dc21   96-51196

British Library Cataloguing-in-Publication Data available

To DOROTHY SELLERS OWSLEY
who has helped in immeasurable ways
and to
MABLE ANN JONES
for her constant encouragement

CONTENTS

Preface   ix

Introduction   1

1. "A Special Kind of State Making":
   Jeffersonian Manifest Destiny   7

2. "To Conquer without War": The
   Philosophy of Jeffersonian Expansion   16

3. Followers of the Green Flag:
   Revolution in the Texas Borderlands   32

4. The First Spanish-American War:
   Patriot Efforts to Annex Florida   61

5. "Pacified by Paternal Solitude": Indian
   Wars as an Expansionist Movement   82

6. A Leftover of War: Negro Fort   103

7. "A Set of Desperate and Bloody Dogs":
   The Acquisition of Amelia Island   118

8. Destiny Becomes Manifest:
   Andrew Jackson Invades Florida   141

9. "Taking Advantage of Propitious
   Circumstances": The Struggle for Texas   164

10. A Jeffersonian Leviathan:
    Manifest Destiny Succeeds   181

Notes   193

Bibliography   223

Index   235

ILLUSTRATIONS

Thomas Jefferson   18
James Madison   28
James Wilkinson   33
William C. C. Claiborne   45
James Monroe   72
David Mitchell   75
Juan Ruíz Apodaca   93
Edmund P. Gaines   107
Gregor MacGregor   123
Daniel Todd Patterson   135
Andrew Jackson   143
John Quincy Adams   162
Jean Joseph Amable Humbert   168
Jean Laffite   171
Francisco Xavier Mina   174

MAPS

Texas Borderlands, 1803–1813   35
East Florida, 1804–1813   65
The Gulf Coast, 1810–1815   90
East Florida, 1816–1818   120
The Gulf Coast, 1816–1818   148
Texas Borderlands, 1815–1821   165

PREFACE

THOSE WHO HAVE written of U.S. history have long been selective in their choice of topics. Few people schooled in the subject have not heard of the Battle of Bunker Hill, the Boston Tea Party, the Lewis and Clark expedition, the Battle of New Orleans, the Alamo, or even Custer's Last Stand. Little, however, has been written—with the exception of the acquisition of Louisiana and Florida—about the movement in this country to expand into the South and Southwest during the first two decades of the nineteenth century. This early expansion movement ultimately freed the United States from French and Spanish domination and changed the map of the country forever. This book explores the motives of those presidents in office during that time, and also the successful and unsuccessful intrigues and episodes of the entire movement. What may have appeared to be nameless frontiersmen or adventurers simply seeking new lands was, in fact, part of a grand plan, whose designers—Jefferson, Madison, and Monroe—intended to expand the boundaries of the United States in almost any manner. But this story cannot be told without giving some attention to the Northeastern detractors of expansion, for in all great struggles there are winners and losers. This story was no exception. The public and private intrigues in these twenty-odd years give the whole story a flavor of mystery not often known. It is our hope that this study will provide not only knowledge of these diverse actions but also continuity to the events, thereby illustrating that there was always either planning or, at best, tacit approval of the Jeffersonians for land acquisition during this time.

We have incurred many debts in writing this book. Our colleagues in the profession have been very generous with their time and advice. We have profited from the reading done by Robert E. May, John M. Belohlavek, Robert V. Remini, Don Coerver, Ken Stevens, Donald E. Worcester, and Spencer Tucker. On numerous occasions H. David Williams helped us track down seemingly elusive bibliographic entries. We are also deeply indebted to Auburn University, Texas Christian University, and Montana State University at Billings (formerly Eastern Montana College) for time released from teaching and for other support. Without blocks of time and generous financial support, we could not have finished this book, particularly the research.

Many public and private institutions have been very gracious in allowing us to use their records and in affording us very welcomed assistance. Those staffs outside the United States that were particularly helpful were at the National Maritime Museum of Greenwich, the Public Record Office in London, and the National Library of Scotland in Edinburgh, and we appreciate the two latter institutions' permission to use material having the Crown copyright. We wish to offer considerable thanks to the staff members at the National Archives, the National Historical Publications and Records Commission, and the Manuscript Division of the Library of Congress, all in Washington, D.C.

Many departments of archives and history on the state level offered us invaluable assistance: Alabama, Georgia, Mississippi, Tennessee, and Texas, in particular. The Mobile Public Library was especially important, allowing us to use the John Forbes Papers. We are also in the debt of those staff members at the university libraries at Alabama, Auburn, Georgia, Florida, South Florida (Tampa), Indiana, Louisiana State, Montana State at Billings, Texas Christian, Oklahoma, Virginia, and the University of New Orleans. The Henry H. Huntington Library in San Marino, California, the Houghton Library at Harvard, the Howard Tilton Memorial Library at Tulane, the Louisiana State Museum, the Virginia Historical Society, the New York Public Library, and the

State Historical Society of Wisconsin deserve special thanks. The Georgia Department of History and Archives, the Historic New Orleans Collection, the Filson Club, the Naval Historical Center, and the National Archives have graciously allowed us to use illustrative materials. Cartographer/historian Dr. Donald S. Frazier designed the excellent maps.

We are greatly appreciative of the interest of Nicole Mitchell, Malcolm MacDonald, and the staff members of The University of Alabama Press. We owe thanks to Jonathan Lawrence for much-needed lessons in copyediting. We are most indebted to our families for their support of our arduous task. Without their help and encouragement this project would never have been accomplished.

Filibusters and Expansionists

Introduction

WITH THE FIRST European–Native American contact early in the sixteenth century, North America became a theater for far-removed imperial powers seeking to subjugate the land and peoples for their own advantage. Throughout the remainder of the sixteenth, seventeenth, and eighteenth centuries, England, France, Spain, and other, minor powers jostled one another to gain supremacy of the North American continent, usually at the expense of Native Americans. Yet by the end of the eighteenth century the cast of actors had changed as the fledgling republic of the United States replaced France as a leader in the international North American power struggle. Moreover, the setting had changed as the British were removed to lands north of the St. Lawrence River and the Great Lakes. Spain had been reduced to lands west of the Mississippi River and to the Florida peninsula. The United States emerged from the Revolutionary War as an independent nation occupying lands between the Atlantic Ocean and the Mississippi River, from the St. Lawrence River to the thirty-first parallel. An embryonic country imbued with a spirited nationalism had been forged from a collection of diverse colonial entities.

During the first generation of this nation's history (1790–1820), nationalism thrived at the expense of, and sometimes even transgressed the rights of, the continent's other inhabitants,

1

be they English, Spanish, or Native American. That nationalism became the means, as historian Albert Weinberg argues, for the ultimate end: expansion at the expense of others.[1] Explaining American history in this fashion began in Chicago on 12 July 1893, with historian Frederick Jackson Turner's essay, "The Significance of the Frontier in American History." In it he remarked that "American history has been in a large degree the history of the colonization of the Great West." And, he contended, it was the conquest of the frontier that created the American identity.[2]

Turner's arguments have to this day created a historiographical debate that may never be settled. This book does not intend either to support Turner's critics or to bolster his argument, but rather proposes to enlarge the body of knowledge about the expansionist movement. Since the appearance of Turner's essay, several generations of historians have tried to tackle the same question, albeit through different avenues. Many of the resulting works have attempted to explain expansion through the nebulous concept of "Manifest Destiny," and although they offer different definitions of Manifest Destiny, their conclusions seem to be somewhat congruent. Our book hopes to contribute to this larger historiographical debate.

The names Thomas Jefferson, James Madison, and James Monroe conjure images of pristine founding fathers and great contributors to early American history. They are associated with the Declaration of Independence, the Constitution, and the Monroe Doctrine, respectively. Schoolchildren from the earliest age have been saturated with the glorious exploits of these well-known icons. As well, Americans have learned that the founding fathers sacrificed to offer a visionary course for their nation and subsequently became immortalized for their selfless efforts. But it is their "selfless" role in the saga of Gulf Coast territorial expansion and Manifest Destiny that has not been examined, much less understood. Yet, when one examines territorial aggrandizement, the three Jeffersonians were anything but altruistic. They were fervent expansionists willing to go to almost any length to secure additional territory in the South and Southwest.

2

The literature of westward expansion and Manifest Destiny is filled with the names of Jefferson, Madison, and Monroe, as if to lend legitimacy to the subjects explored. Yet seldom in such works do these names appear in conjunction with the Gulf South. In fact, the Gulf South is seldom mentioned at all. Turner's book-length study of territorial expansion, *The Frontier in American History* (1921), presents the importance of the Mississippi Valley (broadly defined) but ignores the Gulf of Mexico region. Herbert Eugene Bolton's *The Spanish Borderlands* (1921) examines Spain's North American empire, including the Gulf Coast, but for an earlier period, while his *Wider Horizons of American History* (1939) only introduces this book's subject in a few brief pages. Other similar studies, including Ray Allen Billington's *Westward Expansion: A History of the American Frontier* (1949), Frederick Merk's *History of the Westward Movement* (1978), Bernard DeVoto's *The Course of Empire* (1952), and Francis S. Philbrick's *The Rise of the West, 1754–1830* (1965), provide only cursory treatment of expansion into Louisiana and Florida. Even Reginald Horsman's *The Frontier in the Formative Years, 1783–1815* (1970), while attempting to give a survey of the country's frontier growth during the period, offers little detail about the Gulf Coast. None of these authors has provided an explanation of the Gulf South's importance to the development of the young republic, nor has any presented an interpretation of the role the Jeffersonians played in acquiring the region.

Some of the above-mentioned authors have defined expansion as a belligerent predilection for acquiring territory, prompted by concerns over settlement, commerce, and security. Others intimate that American expansion meant more than the simple desire for concrete material gains, as it offered individuality, liberty, democracy, and fulfillment of the republican vision. Gulf Coast expansion, however, cannot be explained within the confines of this black-and-white dichotomy, because it embodies elements of both groups. Perhaps for this reason, or simply because the episodes this study recounts are not shaped by great men or great events, a comprehensive study of Gulf Coast expansion during the critical Jeffersonian era has not appeared.

3

Introduction

Although it seems that the episodes or operations against the Spanish in the South have been neglected, that assumption is far from the truth. Most of the events chronicled in the following chapters have been examined, but they have not been intricately interwoven and systematically explored as parts of a collective whole. The Baton Rouge revolution of 1810, mentioned in chapter 1, has been recounted in Stanley Clisby Arthur's *The Story of the West Florida Rebellion* (1935) and Isaac Joslin Cox's *The West Florida Controversy, 1798–1813* (1918). Julia K. Garrett's *Green Flag Over Texas* (1939) and Harris Gaylord Warren's *The Sword Was Their Passport* (1943) discuss the subject of chapter 3, the 1810 revolution in the Texas borderlands. The operations against Spanish Florida and Amelia Island in 1812, the topic of chapter 4, have been covered by Rembert W. Patrick's *Florida Fiasco: Rampant Rebels on the Georgia-Florida Border, 1810–1815* (1954) and in an earlier work by Julius W. Pratt, *Expansionists of 1812* (1925). The Creek Indian War reviewed in chapter 5 and Jackson's invasion of Florida presented in chapter 8 have been chronicled by many sources. In *Andrew Jackson and the Course of American Empire, 1767–1821* (1977), Robert V. Remini has presented Jackson himself as a principal character. The destruction of Negro Fort, described in chapter 6, is the one part of this work that has not merited a book-length study, probably because many consider it a by-product of the War of 1812. The 1817 conquest of Amelia Island by privateers, examined in chapter 7, has been investigated by T. Frederick Davis in *MacGregor's Invasion of Florida* (1928). The attempt to liberate Texas following the War of 1812, discussed in chapter 9, has been unfolded in Warren's *The Sword Was Their Passport*. Later accounts of filibusters and Manifest Destiny such as Charles H. Brown's *Agents of Manifest Destiny: The Lives and Times of the Filibusters* (1980) appear to ignore these earlier activities and dwell on actions that occurred considerably later in the century. One final work worthy of mention is William E. Dodd's *Expansion and Conflict* (1915). Although Dodd covers the politics of expansion as a source of sectional conflict, much of his book deals with a later period.

Obviously, the importance of this study is not that these incidents have not been examined. Each of these episodes has been chronicled, although some of the studies are dated and lack detail or cohesion, and the discovery of new material warrants additional scholarship on the subject. This study's value and originality are that it assimilates the various episodes into a whole, showing how each one relates to the others to describe the manner in which American expansion or Manifest Destiny occurred during the Jeffersonian period. This has not been done heretofore. This work also demonstrates that Jefferson, Madison, and Monroe were passionately interested in securing the Gulf Coast, their preoccupation in acquisition of this land revealed through relentless official and "unofficial" federally sponsored efforts— what in the middle of the nineteenth century were called filibustering expeditions—to seize lands in the Gulf South from Spain, Native Americans, and mulatto communities. The result was that the United States easily wrested land along the Gulf Coast from less powerful foes and in so doing expanded Jefferson's precious empire of liberty. As such, the study embodies the crux of Manifest Destiny, for as historian Norman Graebner maintains, the natural right of expansion unquestionably lay in the right to gain territory from powerless neighbors.[3]

One last reason to value this study is that it examines the roots of sectionalism. The Constitution was designed to divide the power in this country in two ways in Congress. Each state—large or small, densely or sparsely populated—had the same number of representatives in the Senate. Members of the House of Representatives, on the other hand, were apportioned according to the size of the state's population. The urban Northeast had been able to retain a considerable amount of power up until the emergence of a dedicated expansionist movement, but as each new state in the South and Southwest entered the union, the Northeast saw its sphere of influence diluted tremendously. A knowledge of this desire for new land and an understanding of the reasons for expansion are necessary if one is to study sectional disputes. Much has been written about the New England states and their way of life to support that area's desire to remain the same. Little has been researched, however, about how the decisions made during this period brought about the bitter sectional strife later. These efforts are significant in themselves, but even more significant is the impact that expansion and the idea of Manifest Destiny had on the whole nation. All of these episodes, most of which were not publicly known at the time, shed light on the operation of the Jeffersonian administrations during this critical formative period. Moreover, this study offers information on the young nation's diplomatic maneuvers, adding insight into the relationship between the country's distinctly different political regions. In so doing, it broadens the understanding of the political development of the United States and offers a foundation for further study of the events leading ultimately to the sectional conflict and the American Civil War.

We have found this work to be not only valuable but interesting as well. Few historical characters are more intriguing than Gregor MacGregor, Augustus William Magee, George Mathews, Luis Aury, Jean Laffite, John Hamilton Robinson, and even the shady James Wilkinson—and this is only the beginning of the list. Although the actions of many of these characters overlap, the authors have endeavored to weave them into one expansionist picture as much as possible within the term of each president and secretary of state in the Jeffersonian period.

CHAPTER ONE

"A Special Kind of State Making": Jeffersonian Manifest Destiny

AT FOUR O'CLOCK on Sunday morning, 23 September 1810, eighty armed Americans commanded by Philemon Thomas stormed the dilapidated Spanish fort in Baton Rouge, West Florida. As the invaders streamed through the undefended gate and gaps in the stockade and past the unloaded cannon, they demanded that Spanish troops surrender their weapons. Don Louis Antonio de Grand-Pré, commander of the bastion, bravely resisted as his few ill-equipped and invalid soldiers conceded. Other than the brave young leader and Manuel Matamoros (one of his soldiers), who died defending their honor and the Spanish flag, there were no casualties. Governor Carlos De Lassus, abruptly awakened by the screaming and gunshots, quickly dressed and hurried toward the fort. But before he had traveled the block from his house to the scene of activity, rebel horsemen overwhelmed and captured him. With the governor's apprehension, the conquest of Spanish Baton Rouge had ended in a matter of minutes.[1]

After the conquest, the Americans called a convention of delegates representing the region and, on 26 September, issued a Declaration of Independence for West Florida. Soon thereafter the convention delivered a copy of the document to Governor David Holmes of the Mississippi Territory and Governor William C. C. Claiborne of the Orleans Territory, insisting they forward

7

it to the government in Washington. They also requested annexation into the United States and protection against Spanish retribution.[2]

Republican President James Madison faced a quandary. He wanted to annex Baton Rouge immediately, but he knew that he could not use military forces for such a venture without congressional approval, and that body would not meet until early December. Moreover, military occupation of Spanish territory would incur the wrath of not only Spain but perhaps even England and France. Madison feared that should the government not aid West Florida, there would "be danger of its passing into the hands of a third and dangerous party." Britain, the president had written to his friend Thomas Jefferson, had a "propensity to fish in troubled waters," and Madison realized that the moment would be lost should the United States not cast its line.[3]

Rumors of the impending arrival of Spanish troops from Cuba or Veracruz, combined with fabricated accounts of a British landing at Pensacola and stories of American adventurers seizing additional Spanish territory, forced Madison to take action before Congress convened. On 27 October 1810 he issued a proclamation instructing American officials to take possession of West Florida, based on the Louisiana Purchase of 1803. The United States, the president declared, had not previously exercised its title to the territory, not because of any doubt of its legitimacy, but rather because of "events over which [the country] had no control." He announced that the time had arrived; "the tranquility and security of our adjoining territories are endangered," and the country's revenue and commercial laws as well as slave importation statutes were being violated. Although Madison made no reference to the Baton Rouge revolution in that message, he did admit that "a crisis has at length arrived subversive of the order of things under the Spanish authorities," and should the United States not act immediately it "may lead to events ultimately contravening the views of both parties."[4]

In conclusion, Madison instructed Governor Claiborne to take possession of the territory for the United States. The message also directed the inhabitants to obey the laws, to maintain order, and to cherish the harmony and protection of their life, property, and religion. The president had by executive order incorporated Spanish Baton Rouge into the American territory of Orleans; this claim included all of West Florida except the city of Mobile.[5]

The annexation of the Baton Rouge district provided the most successful example of the covert Jeffersonian idea of expansion during the early years of the republic. It also established a pattern future filibusters would be eager to imitate. Jefferson, Madison, and Monroe all wanted American expansion, yet without embroiling the nation in a war; the Baton Rouge incident easily accomplished that goal. The government encouraged American citizens to emigrate into Spanish-held territory along the Gulf of Mexico. Once Americans saturated those provinces, the government covertly encouraged them to overthrow Spanish rule and, subsequently, to invite protection and ultimately annexation into the United States.[6]

This type of operation was well suited to the goals of the young republic. The filibusters, many of whom were citizens of American descent operating within the boundaries of Spanish colonies, did not violate neutrality laws. They seized power at Spain's expense not only because they wanted an efficient, responsible local government to protect their rights, but also because they hoped to acquire land and/or wealth. Spain's archaic administrative system could not provide those securities, nor could it defend its North American colonies from lawless adventurers who threatened stability. Therefore, the patriots/filibusters acted for themselves; they revolted, seized power, and requested American protection of their cherished rights. The republican government of the United States, favoring continued expansion, accepted such invitations as long as those lands could be held short of war.

American expansionism such as the Baton Rouge incident has inextricably become linked to the term "Manifest Destiny," coined by John L. O'Sullivan in 1845. Yet discussion of that process generally centers not on the act of extension itself but around the concept of "destiny." By the 1840s the idea was widely accepted that Providence had destined the United States to continued growth and that expansion was a civilizing process based on moral progress rather than military might.*

The "natural right" of expansion, however, unquestionably lay in the power to conquer. What ultimately made expansion not only possible but apparently inevitable was not some transcendent destiny but rather the absence of a powerful neighbor to check its progress. Earlier in the nineteenth century, the Jeffersonian presidents (Jefferson, Madison, and Monroe) benefited from the lack of powerful neighbors: a neglectful British empire ruled over Canada, and a disintegrating Spanish empire controlled the Gulf region.[7]

This definition of Manifest Destiny provides the framework to study land expansion along the Gulf Coast during the Jeffersonian period. It also indicates that this process may in fact be "the first whisperings of Manifest Destiny."[8] In any case, it certainly substantiates the premise that the concept embodied in Manifest Destiny emerged, not in the 1840s, but perhaps as early as Anglo-European contact in the seventeenth century. Throughout the seventeenth and eighteenth centuries, American colonials moved westward searching for new lands at the Native Americans' expense. The European wars for empire fought in North America during the eighteenth century only slowed their expansive desires. After independence, those former colonists found western territory controlled by Native Americans who did not understand white land hunger; Americans also discovered artificial boundaries separating the United States from British Canada and Spanish Florida and Louisiana.

The American Revolution demonstrated the ideological importance of natural rights, and paramount for Americans was the

---

*Even as early as 1814, the term "destiny" could be found as relating to expansionist ideas. Andrew Jackson received a letter from his friend Matthew Lyon, a member of Congress from Vermont and, later, Kentucky, using the term in this way. "This Nation are destined to civilize and Govern this Continent." Although the word "manifest" is missing, clearly the thought is there. Matthew Lyon to Andrew Jackson, 2 June 1814, *The Papers of Andrew Jackson*, ed. David D. Moser et al. (Knoxville: University of Tennessee Press, 1994), 4:78–79.

right of land ownership. Yet with a growing population and limited territory, those opportunities would be restricted unless the country continued to expand. And a study of Jeffersonian expansion indicates that the idea flourished early—if not in name, certainly as a part of government policy during the first two decades of the nineteenth century.[9]

At the beginning of the century, many members of the Republican party supported expansion as a means of continuing the nation's growth and development; expansion also displayed to the world the country's faith in human freedom and republican government.[10] Jefferson remarked in his first inaugural address that his United States was "a chosen country, with room enough for our descendants to the hundredth and thousandth generation."[11] Yet in 1801 his United States was a country confined by the Great Lakes to the north, the Mississippi River to the west, and the thirty-first parallel to the south. Foreign powers surrounded the United States and threatened its security. The presence in Canada of English forces who were allied with Native Americans in the Northwest jeopardized the aspirations espoused in the American Declaration of Independence. Spanish control of the Gulf Coast and lands west of the Mississippi stymied fulfillment of Americans' natural rights. Jefferson and his immediate successors believed the only way to ensure the nation's survival was by removing the obstacles prohibiting future growth, whether they were Spanish or British, Native American or even African American.[12]

Not all agreed with this vision of growth. The Northeast, especially New England, wanted no territorial expansion. Federalist opposition had manifested itself during the debates over the Louisiana Purchase as well as during attempts to acquire Canada and the Floridas. Generally, this group feared that each new southern or western state that entered into the Union diminished the influence and political power of the Northeast while enhancing the largely Republican South and West. Those fears were not unfounded. The balance of political power shifted during the first three decades of the nation's existence because of the admission of six new states, five of which were western or

11

southern. The opening of vast areas of Indian lands for white settlement also strengthened the growing Republican party.[13]

Despite the opposition, Jefferson, Madison, and Monroe worked openly and covertly to incorporate neighboring regions into the United States. Louisiana, Texas, the Floridas, and even Canada interested those who wanted to extend the nation's boundaries. Republicans would use diplomacy, purchase, or, as a last resort, carry out clandestine activities to acquire these territories. The turmoil of the Napoleonic Wars preoccupied Europe while allowing Americans to strengthen their expansionist claims. England's struggle with France absorbed its energies and left Canada to fend for itself. Napoleon's invasion of Spain and the resultant Peninsula War only fostered an already disintegrating Spanish authority in North America. In fact, the population of Spanish Louisiana and Florida amounted to about fifty thousand people, with a mere fifteen hundred troops available to garrison the entire region. Further, U.S. commerce at New Orleans doubled Spanish trade, and the influx of Americans into the territory steadily increased.[14] It was these weaknesses within Spain's North American colonies, as historian Frederick Merk has commented, that tempted Americans "to experiment with a special kind of state making—state making at the expense of a foreign power."[15] In reality, Americans were filibustering in the hopes of state making, and their success depended upon taking advantage of and exploiting their superior position.[16]

The United States quickly took advantage of the unrest in Europe, as well as Spain's weaknesses in North America. In 1802 Jefferson authorized Robert R. Livingston, minister to France, and James Monroe, minister extraordinary to that country, to negotiate the purchase of territory east of the Mississippi River, including New Orleans. While negotiations occurred, the president secured appropriations for Meriwether Lewis and William Clark to explore lands west of the Mississippi. Although publicly extolling the scientific purposes of the mission, Jefferson wanted a military reconnaissance to appraise the strength of Native Americans within the territory, to determine the region's commercial value, and, more importantly, to indicate the area's suitability for future American expansion. The Lewis and Clark expedition did not occur until after the Louisiana Purchase, but it nonetheless indicated Jefferson's desire to utilize covert operations to reconnoiter the area; it was but one of a series of incursions into Louisiana and Spanish territory under the guise of exploration.[17]

Jefferson's successor, James Madison, more actively supported covert operations and filibustering attempts as a means of promoting territorial expansion. The beginnings of the Hidalgo Revolution in Mexico in 1810 provided the opportunity for the United States to strengthen its claim on Texas, an area Republicans believed to be part of the Louisiana Purchase. Madison's State Department unofficially provided financial and military assistance to Bernardo Gutiérrez de Lara, José Alvarez de Toledo, and Augustus William Magee in their attempts to overthrow Spanish rule in the isolated Texas province. The Texas insurrection, coinciding with the previously mentioned revolution in Baton Rouge that created the original "lone star" republic, ultimately failed because of factors beyond the American government's control. Nonetheless, it indicated the administration's position on "local" revolutions and the desire to bring those like-minded movements into the American fold.[18]

In East Florida in 1812, American "patriots" instigated a revolution similar to the one in Baton Rouge. Composed of both settlers and adventurers, these filibusters seized the settlement of Fernandina on St. Mary's Island, East Florida. After capturing the town, the movement, led by American Army General George Mathews, formed the "Republic of Florida," organized a provisional government, and thereafter laid siege to the Spanish fort at St. Augustine. The Madison administration initially supported the "patriots" and provided them with military assistance, but these activities soon threatened to drag the United States into a conflict with Spain. An impending war with England also created the possibility of having to fight both nations simultaneously. The young republic could not afford to jeopardize its freedom in such a manner, so Madison's administration disavowed Mathews's activities and withdrew support for the operation. The Republic of Florida failed and East Florida remained a Spanish colony.[19]

During the War of 1812 the U.S. government strengthened its claim to southern lands by waging Indian wars to promote expansion. The administration sent General Andrew Jackson south to prosecute the war against those Creeks hostile to the United States. Although this did not represent a covert or filibustering operation, it nonetheless demonstrated the government's policy of expanding against weaker neighbors. The resultant war destroyed the buffer zone for Spain's Florida colonies and opened additional lands to white settlers, who flooded into the territory. Most of the defeated Indians who remained hostile to the United States fled to Spanish Florida, where they were joined by runaway slaves. These groups soon became a threat to peace and stability in the region as they began raiding the southern American frontier; this prompted the U.S. government to take decisive action.

Shortly before Madison's second term ended, American army and naval forces reduced Negro Fort at Prospect Bluff on the Apalachicola River. Abandoned by the British, the position had become a refuge for Indians and runaway slaves who were a threat to peace in the region. The position also represented a visible sign of opposition that jeopardized the southern plantation economy and endangered future American expansion. Military forces responded and destroyed the bastion to remove this obstacle. Although the Madison administration did not have prior knowledge of the operation and the attack was not authorized by the U.S. government, its results could not be ignored.[20]

In 1817, James Monroe, Madison's successor, provided unofficial support for Scotsman Gregor MacGregor and his plan to seize Amelia Island, East Florida (in the mouth of the St. Mary's River), as an operational base for Venezuelan revolutionaries. MacGregor's revolt succeeded, and soon thereafter the island became a haven for pirates, smugglers, and slave traders. As long as the Monroe administration believed the filibusters could seize Florida from Spain without embroiling the United States in war, they waited. But Monroe saw no advantage to continuing covert operations once law and order deteriorated on Amelia Island and threatened the stability of the entire region. The U.S. government took action when that occurred; in the spring of 1818 the War Department instructed General Edmund P. Gaines to seize the island. Gaines dispatched Colonel James Bankhead, who accomplished the task without firing a shot.[21]

Andrew Jackson's invasion of Florida during the spring of 1818 provided the last impetus of Jeffersonian expansion. The aftermath of the War of 1812 left Florida in an unsettled state. The existence of Negro Fort, as well as the MacGregor expedition, demonstrated Spain's inability to maintain control. In an attempt to restore peace to the region, the Monroe administration authorized Jackson to pursue unfriendly Indians into Spanish Florida (chapter 5 includes more detail concerning the Indians). The general, broadly interpreting his orders, proceeded to capture Spanish positions at St. Mark's and Pensacola, claiming they were bases of operation for Indian attacks against the United States. He also executed two British subjects whom he accused of fostering Indian violence. Though the general would be criticized for exceeding his orders, his actions vividly indicated that Spain could not hold Florida. In fact, less than a year after Jackson's invasion, the Spanish government agreed to the Transcontinental Treaty, relinquishing Florida to the United States.[22]

With the acquisition of Florida, southern Manifest Destiny was complete. All the lands east of the Mississippi River, in addition to the Louisiana Purchase, had been acquired without war. Afterward expansion focused westward, and within the next thirty years the nation would encompass the lands between the Atlantic and the Pacific, as Republicans had prophesied. Jefferson's purchase of Louisiana, combined with the covert operations of the Madison and Monroe administrations and the eventual cession of Florida, removed the immediate threat of European influences from America's borders. The War of 1812, the military operation against Negro Fort, and Jackson's invasion of Florida destroyed the threat of the southern Indians and free black settlements. With the destruction of America's weaker neighbors, whether Spanish, Native Americans, or African Americans, the ideas inherent in Manifest Destiny would have the opportunity to flourish robustly.

15

CHAPTER TWO

"To Conquer without War":
The Philosophy of
Jeffersonian Expansion

NINETEENTH-CENTURY Manifest Destiny meant expansion, ordained by divine will, over an unspecified area that could include North America, or even the entire Western Hemisphere.[1] Thomas Jefferson, writing in 1786, had expressed that same hope: "Our continent must be viewed as the nest from which all America, North and South is to be peopled."[2] Just as the 1840s view of destiny held that the American peopling of the continent or hemisphere would happen in due time, as if God had sanctioned it, so did the Jeffersonians believe some three decades earlier. Shortly before the War of 1812, Jefferson informed John Jacob Astor that he "looked forward with gratification to the time when" the entirety of the Pacific Coast would be populated "with free and independent Americans."[3] Earlier he had offered a hemispherical view: "It is impossible not to look forward to distant times, when our rapid multiplication will expand itself . . . and cover the whole northern, if not the southern continent."[4] For Republicans, expanding throughout the continent and hemisphere provided for an "empire of liberty," which would preserve the young republic's cherished beliefs from European destruction.[5]

Expansion throughout the Western Hemisphere had to begin with the settlement and development of lands across the Appalachian Mountains. Moreover, navigation of the Mississippi River, the lifeline of the West, would definitely need to remain open for successful expansion. The river had become the mainstay of transportation and communication for farmers and frontiersmen west of the Appalachians, and as long as that thoroughfare remained open, all were satisfied. Yet when there appeared a possibility of closing the Mississippi, tempers flared. In 1785–86, during the Confederation period, American Secretary of Foreign Affairs John Jay negotiated a treaty with Spanish Foreign Minister Don Diego de Gardoqui proposing to close the Mississippi for at least twenty-five years in return for favorable commercial concessions. Once Jay learned of the opposition to the agreement, his better judgment prevailed and he did not submit the Jay-Gardoqui Treaty to the American Confederation Congress; the river remained open.[6]

Spain's control of the Mississippi River and the Gulf Coast had blocked outlets for American commerce, threatened the security of the young nation, and infringed on the United States's "pursuit of happiness."[7] Despite these encroachments, possession of those lands could not "be in better hands," Jefferson wrote in 1788. His only apprehension was that Spain was "too feeble to hold them till our population can be sufficiently advanced to gain it from them piece by piece."[8] Understanding the river's importance both to western development and to the future prosperity and harmony of the United States, Jefferson had notified Madison in January 1787 from Paris that "the act which abandons the navigation of the Mississippi is an act of separation between the eastern and western country." It would split the country and relinquish more than half of the nation's territory to a new western entity. Should that be done, Jefferson professed that the inhabitants of the new region would be ready "to rescue the navigation of the Mississippi out of the hands of Spain, and to add New Orleans to their own territory."[9] The western interests, he therefore concluded, must not be sacrificed to those of the maritime states lest it bring disunion and the failure of the republican experiment.[10] "The navigation of the Mississippi was," Jefferson believed, "perhaps, the strongest trial to which the . . . federal government could be put."[11]

Thomas Jefferson. Portrait by Asher B. Durand after Gilbert Stuart (Courtesy of the National Archives)

While serving as secretary of state during Washington's presidency, Jefferson had worked diligently to gain free access to the Mississippi. He wanted to employ diplomacy to acquire rightful use of the river, but he would not stop at extortion should Spain be unwilling to relinquish that right. Using the threat of a European war in August 1790 over the Nootka Sound dispute, Jefferson wrote to William Short that the country would be among Spain's enemies should the United States not be given access to the Mississippi. This right included not only that of navigation, but also a port of deposit near the mouth of the river. If Spain did not concede these to the United States, Jefferson believed it would bring the two nations to war. "Nature has decided what shall be the geography of . . . the Island of New Orleans," and the cession of this to the United States "could not be hazarded to Spain."[12] For the first time, Jefferson was expressing that America's right to sovereign possession of a port or land acquisition on the Mississippi River was intrinsic to its natural right of navigation.[13]

Writing again to Short and also to William Carmichael in March 1793, Jefferson elaborated on his argument concerning America's natural right to navigation and to a port of deposit on the river. His argument, based on "the law of nature and nations," contended that the segment of the Mississippi controlled by Spain should not be considered as part of a river, but instead as "a streight [*sic*] of the sea," and just as "the Ocean is free to all men, . . . the Rivers [are] to all their inhabitants." Nature granted to the United States and its citizens the right to navigate the Mississippi River, and with that privilege came the right to use the river's shores for deposit.[14] Jefferson's argument, while showing ingenuity and persuasiveness, did not sway the Spanish government. Only the Jay Treaty pressured Spain into making a settlement on the Mississippi question. In 1795 Thomas Pinckney negotiated with the Spanish government a treaty giving the United States free navigation of the Mississippi and the right of deposit at New Orleans for three years, and thereafter at another designated point. Most believed this settled the Mississippi question and removed the major obstacle to the growth and prosperity of the United States and to harmonious Spanish-American relations.[15]

The Mississippi problem emerged again during Jefferson's presidency, but this time there were other characters involved. Revolution on the Caribbean island of San Domang (Haiti) threatened the stability of Louisiana and the Mississippi River. The Treaty of San Ildefonso of 1 October 1800, drawn up between France and Spain according to Napoleon Bonaparte's wishes, underscored the uncertainty by making Louisiana the breadbasket for what appeared to be a western French empire.

The formal transfer of Louisiana from Spain to France, however, did not occur until after the Peace of Amiens in 1802, which left ample time for other complications.[16]

Spain's cession of Louisiana and the Floridas to France, Jefferson believed, "works most sorely on the United States," because it threatened the American right of navigation as well as the country's security. France, he acknowledged, was "our natural friend, . . . one which we never could have an occasion of difference." But despite the bonds of friendship and the historic ties that linked the two together, he knew, "there is on the globe one single spot, the possessor of which is our natural and habitual enemy." "It is New Orleans," he professed, "through which the produce of three-eighths of our territory must pass to market, and from its fertility it will ere long yield more than half of our whole produce, and contain more than half of our inhabitants."[17] Should France remain obstinate in its attitude concerning possession of Louisiana, Jefferson predicted that "this speck which now appears as an almost invisible point in the horizon, [will become] the embryo of a tornado which will burst on the countries on both sides of the Atlantic."[18] That tornado would mean war, for he had written in 1786 that the United States must have "the navigation of the Mississippi."[19]

Before France could take possession of Louisiana, a more critical event occurred. On 16 October 1802, Juan Ventura Morales, Spanish intendant at New Orleans, closed the port to all American commerce descending the river, blatantly violating the 1795 Pinckney Treaty.[20] Jefferson claimed that Morales's action "has thrown the country into such a flame of hostile disposition as can scarcely be described." It brought the countries to the brink of war, even though Jefferson believed peaceful means would be the most speedy and effective way to solve the problem.[21] The president responded by appointing James Monroe as minister extraordinary, empowered to negotiate with both France and Spain to settle the Mississippi question. Should Monroe fail, the nation's only alternative was "to get entangled in European politics," which could mean war.[22]

Because Jefferson's attentions had not been "confined to the

Eastern states alone, but . . . to the western states also," war became a possible solution for the Mississippi question.[23] If Monroe's mission failed, Jefferson understood that "war cannot be distant" and as such the nation should immediately prepare for that course.[24] Secretary of the Navy Robert Smith asked Congress to begin those preparations by constructing a gunboat flotilla in early 1803.[25] Fortunately, the difficulties with Spain were short lived. By the spring of 1803, King Charles IV disavowed Morales's act and renewed the right of deposit. But this magnanimous gesture really made little difference, because France and Napoleon already controlled the region's destiny. Even so, Jefferson took steps to ensure that such an event did not recur. Monroe traveled to Europe to purchase the entire territory east of the Mississippi River, including New Orleans. The president hoped that negotiations would produce the desired results. "Peace," he claimed, "is our passion," but if peaceful negotiations failed the United States would resort to war.[26]

While Congress prepared for the possibility of war, Robert R. Livingston, minister to France, negotiated one of the nation's greatest diplomatic coups, the Louisiana Purchase. Jefferson received news on 3 July 1803 that the Louisiana question had been settled by Livingston, Monroe, and François Barbé-Marbois, French minister of finance. In the settlement the United States agreed to buy the Louisiana region for $15 million, thereby bringing an end to the Mississippi saga. Historian Henry Adams asserted that no other treaty gave the United States so much for so little in return. "It was unparalleled, because it cost almost nothing." True, it represented a diplomatic victory, but the entire episode demonstrated that Jefferson strongly supported westward expansion and that he understood the Mississippi River's importance to this development. It also proved that security and expansion were synonymous for the United States, and that the country would, if necessary, threaten to go to war to defend both.[27]

Once the Mississippi question was settled, Jefferson remarked that "this removes from us the greatest source of danger to our peace."[28] But this prophetic statement was unfounded, for navigation of the country's other southern rivers would also become issues of contention. Although the Louisiana Purchase settled the American claim to the Mississippi River, it did not provide the right to navigate, nor a right of deposit for the other river systems flowing into the Gulf of Mexico. The Pearl River, Pascagoula River, Perdido River, the Alabama River system, the Escambia River, and the Apalachicola River were not included in the Louisiana Purchase and thus became sources of controversy between the United States and Spain during the first two decades of the nineteenth century.

These rivers flowing through West Florida remained issues of contention in Spanish-American relations until the Monroe administration formally acquired Florida in 1821. Although the Mississippi system embodied the great watershed for lands between the Appalachian and Rocky Mountains, other rivers flowing into the Gulf were similarly important. The Alabama River system, including the Mobile and Tombigbee Rivers, and the Apalachicola River system became essential transportation and communication routes for the southwestern territories of the United States. Those rivers became as important to the settlers of the Mississippi Territory and Tennessee as was the Mississippi to inhabitants of Ohio, Kentucky, and western Pennsylvania. Just as westerners had demanded that the Mississippi remain open, American frontiersmen in the Gulf Southwest insisted that these river systems, too, be opened to American trade.

James Madison, Jefferson's secretary of state, contended that navigation of the southwestern rivers was necessary for maximizing the use of the Gulf of Mexico.[29] Moreover, the congressional committee that recommended the appropriations for the Louisiana Purchase foresaw the importance of the Gulf Coast to continued American expansion and concurred with Madison: "If we look forward to the free use of the Mississippi, the Apalachicola, and the other rivers of the West by ourselves and our posterity, . . . the Floridas must become a part of the United States, either by purchase or by conquest."[30]

Just as Jefferson wanted access to the Mississippi River, he also wanted to bring within the American fold the Floridas, which controlled the rivers of the Gulf South.[31] In April 1791, Jefferson had informed President Washington that Governor Juan Nepomuceno de Quesada y Barnuevo had invited Americans to settle in Spanish Florida. This offered a blessing in disguise, and Jefferson remarked that he wished one hundred thousand Americans would accept this invitation. Washington's secretary of state believed this would deliver to the United States "peaceably what may otherwise cost us a war."[32]

In 1803 Jefferson wished to acquire New Orleans and West Florida, in that order, and had instructed Livingston and Monroe to attempt to purchase land east, not west, of the Mississippi River in the hopes of settling the problems experienced by frontiersmen along the Gulf. To that end, the United States acquired New Orleans in the Louisiana Purchase, but the status of West Florida remained ambiguous. The eastern boundaries for the territory seemed unclear, leaving room for doubt and confusion. Monroe, who had helped negotiate the Purchase, was not confused by the provisions of the treaty at all. In fact, he insisted that the deal included Mobile as well as West Florida.[33] Livingston concurred with Monroe, arguing that the United States should take possession of West Florida as a part of the Louisiana Purchase.[34]

Even though the status of West Florida remained doubtful, Jefferson and Congress took steps to prove conclusively that it belonged to the United States as part of the Louisiana Purchase. At Jefferson's behest, Congress in February 1804 passed the Mobile Act, which gave the United States legal control over part of the region. The act proclaimed the annexation of all navigable rivers and streams within the United States that flowed into the Gulf of Mexico. It also created a separate customs district at Fort Stoddert (north of the thirty-first parallel) to collect duties.[35]

The Marquis de Casa Yrujo, Spanish minister to the United States, protested the American claim under the Mobile Act. Jefferson's proclamation of 20 May 1804, asserting that the Mobile revenue district included only those waters within the boundaries of the United States, momentarily mollified Spain's protest. Although Jefferson had been willing to risk war for the right to use the Mississippi, he was reluctant to take such action over West Florida. Perhaps his belief that American settlers would eventually seize the West Florida lands that they believed were rightfully theirs made him realize that war was unnecessary.[36]

Jeffersonian Republicans recognized the importance of both East and West Florida, but for more than reasons of navigation. True, the Floridas commanded the rivers of the Southwest, but the area was also important for security reasons. As long as a foreign nation possessed the Floridas, that country threatened Jefferson's domain because the peninsula could be used as an operational base against the southern United States. Exactly this had been done during the colonial and revolutionary periods. The area could also be used as a refuge for Indians and runaway slaves. Confusion in the Floridas had been further exacerbated when the territory changed from British to Spanish control. Moreover, the region's multinational inhabitants reluctantly swore loyalty to a government that could not retain the peninsula or protect their interests. Problems such as these along the frontier created a general atmosphere of lawlessness and insecurity that threatened American existence.[37]

The disintegration of the Spanish empire created unforeseen problems for the United States. Jefferson had remarked that Spanish control over the Floridas did not threaten the United States, because Americans could wrest the lands from Spain in due time. Also, Spain's weakness did not imperil American independence. But should France or Great Britain gain command of Florida, American independence or control over and access to the Mississippi River and Gulf Coast could be threatened.[38] Jefferson had expressed this concern in 1793 when he remarked that Great Britain would seize Florida and "thus completely encircle us with her colonies and fleets."[39] In 1815 Monroe reiterated the same sentiments when he declared that "East-Florida in itself is comparatively nothing but as a post in the hands of Great Britain it is of the highest importance." If the British gained control over Florida, Monroe contended, they would command the Gulf of Mexico and all its waters, including the Mississippi. Furthermore, the United States would lose "a vast proportion of the

24

most fertile and productive parts of this Union, on which the navigation and commerce so essentially depend."[40]

The Spanish loss of Florida remained a constant threat during the first two decades of the nineteenth century. The uncertainties of the Napoleonic Wars in Europe only fostered those fears. Florida resembled a pawn waiting to change European hands, and it appeared that the only way to prevent such a catastrophe was for the United States to use any method to seize the moment, just as Louisiana had been procured. Thus, during his administration Jefferson tried gentle persuasion, diplomacy, blustering, and even the threat of war to secure Florida—all to no avail.[41]

As war with Great Britain drew closer, fears over losing Florida intensified. Jefferson believed in 1811, after the American seizure of Baton Rouge, that the event would prompt the English to seize East Florida on Spain's behalf; in order to prevent British involvement, the United States "should take it with a declaration." Not only should the United States take East Florida, but Jefferson also advocated military occupation of West Florida to prevent England or any other European power from seizing the peninsula.[42]

Foreign possession of Florida meant not only control over territory adjacent to the United States, but also influence over Indians in the region. That possibility disturbed Americans who lived in the area bordering Spanish West Florida, because "the plundering spirit of the savages" threatened their very existence. Fear of belligerent Creeks and Seminoles in Florida left many American settlers feeling as if they were already under the yoke of foreign oppressors.[43] Spain had for decades used the natives in Florida to buffer American expansion and to strengthen its tenuous hold over the region. Spanish policy, aimed at keeping the Indians strong enough to defend themselves and Spanish territory but not so strong that they would provoke a war with the United States, created a "force in being" that discouraged American expansion into, or attempted conquest of, Florida.[44]

According to southern plantation owners, runaway slaves embodied an equally dangerous lawless group. Spanish Florida had become a sanctuary for slaves fleeing the Mississippi Territory,

Georgia, and even the Carolinas. After the fugitives arrived in Florida they could own property, including cattle and farms; they generally were not encumbered by white control or by the Spanish government. This situation set a dangerous example, because southern slaveholders believed it provoked slave rebellions on nearby American plantations. The presence of this group in the borderlands contributed to American fears about security and convinced them of the need to acquire Florida. Jefferson, Madison, and Monroe—all three southern slaveholders—could surely understand the anxiety of those confronted by this situation.[45]

Another concern over Spanish infringement on natural rights regarded the American belief in the "pursuit of happiness." This highly nebulous expression has a meaning as broad as its assertion in the Declaration of Independence and as narrow as the interests of the individual. The framework to the pursuit of happiness came in the form of the Declaration, but its expression with regard to land expansion is much more pertinent and realistic. Moreover, it concerned more than just navigation of the rivers and acquisition of East and West Florida. It also included westward expansion to Texas and the Pacific coast of North America, as well as Cuba and South America.

Spanish lands in the Gulf region presented the only realistic interest to expansionist-minded Republicans. Possession of the Mississippi River and surrounding lands provided the right to navigation and deposit while simultaneously satisfying the American right to economic prosperity. Procuring Florida, Jefferson believed, "will fill the American mind with joy" because doing so would remove the possibility of war with either Spain or France. It would also complete the territorial integrity of the eastern United States.[46] Possession of Florida would allow American attentions to focus on Spanish-held Cuba and Texas as the next areas believed to be within the realm of American acquisition.[47]

Jefferson's belief in the pursuit of happiness involved the egalitarian right of people to freedom and liberty. His "empire of liberty" embodied that concept and called for expansion that would result in the creation of new states of approximately "thirty-thousand square miles" each. This would satisfy "the energetic nature of our governments" and allow the people "a just share in their own" rule.[48] Additional territory also allowed yeoman farmers to purchase lands at minimal prices, thus creating the basis of Jefferson's agrarian democracy. Furthermore, these sales permitted the country to extinguish much of its national debt, thereby providing future fiscal security for the republican government.[49] Jefferson wrote that a "duplication of area for the extending a government so free and economical as ours [is] a great achievement to the mass of happiness."[50] He believed, contrary to Montesquieu, that a large "republican" country "founded, not on conquest, but [on] principles of compact and equality," will produce "the most wonderful work of wisdom and disinterested patriotism that has ever yet appeared on the globe."[51]

For Jefferson personally, the acquisition of additional lands provided the opportunity to increase the sum total of human knowledge. His desire to learn more of the geography, natural history, and inhabitants of the Louisiana Purchase prompted him to authorize Meriwether Lewis and William Clark to explore and report on that area.[52] The administration also commissioned the Dunbar-Hunter, Sibley, Freeman, and Pike expeditions to acquire further knowledge of the region's geographical and scientific attributes.[53]

Perhaps Jefferson used these expeditions to gauge the region's potential for settlement or to solidify the American claim to the territory, but given his interest in science, his support probably represented an earnest desire to learn more about the Purchase. As Jefferson informed his secretary of war, Henry Dearborn, "the field of knowledge is the common property of all mankind," and any discoveries will benefit this and every other nation; exploration and the advancement of scientific knowledge logically fulfilled Jefferson's pursuit of happiness.[54]

Madison's pursuit of happiness in some respects mirrored Jefferson's, but in other ways it was quite different. Just as Jefferson wanted access to southern rivers, so did Madison. Both believed that the right to the Mississippi River was essential to the country's economic development, but Madison carried it further.

James Madison. Portrait by Asher B. Durand after Gilbert Stuart (Courtesy of the National Archives)

If the country controlled the trans-Appalachian West and access to it via the rivers of the region, American industrial development would be postponed. Ostensibly, Europeans would then benefit. The United States would not become a manufacturing competitor, and Europeans could support the growth of the agrarian republic. But should the Mississippi River be denied to us, Madison argued, "many of our supernumerary hands who in the former case would [be] husbandmen on the waters of the Missipi [*sic*] will on the other supposition be manufacturers."[55]

Westward expansion fulfilled another aspect of Madison's pursuit of happiness. Profitable lands in the southwestern territories, including those held by the Spanish, could serve as a haven for a growing population that might otherwise become involved in manufacturing. If the population did become industrially oriented, according to Madison, this would threaten both Europeans and the republican character of the United States. Land acquisition or right to land in the West ensured the survival of the agrarian republic by providing the growing American population with the opportunity for landownership. Moreover, cheap fertile lands, and the right to acquire and use those lands, confirmed the right to pursue and obtain happiness.[56]

Madison equated successful expansion with the pursuit of happiness only if farmers could transport their produce to market. Without access to markets, the industrious American farmer had no reason to migrate. But after the acquisition of the Mississippi River, the trans-Appalachian West became interconnected with the commercial world. Free access to navigation, whether the Mississippi or the rivers of the Spanish Gulf Coast, meant the opportunity to market products and develop western lands. This was central to Madison's concept of the pursuit of happiness, as free trade benefited western frontier expansion because the productivity of those lands made American farmers industrious, self-sustaining republicans.[57]

James Monroe, the last of the true Jeffersonians, viewed the pursuit of happiness in much the same way as Jefferson and Madison. He believed that Americans were entitled to the freedom and liberty Jefferson had advocated, but he also believed that economic development was essential to happiness, as did Madison. His view of happiness emphasized security to ensure the visions of both Jefferson and Madison. Monroe thought that the United States remained in constant danger from European powers. Those nations—and England in particular—he contended, remained hostile to the United States. If the United States survived as a nation, it served as an example for other colonies, thereby providing an impetus for revolution throughout the Western Hemisphere. But as long as Europe remained preoccupied with continental affairs, the United States would survive and could pursue security and happiness through territorial expansion.[58]

Monroe believed that the continuation of the European wars provided Americans with the "liberty to pursue their interior arrangements without apprehending . . . interferences." The acquisition of Spanish-held lands would for the immediate future give the United States the territory to satisfy its growing population. Monroe also thought expansion would afford harmony between the United States and Spain by removing the "cause of jealousy" and the "points of collision"; the result would be perpetual friendship and peace.[59]

Monroe argued that American acquisition of Spanish-held lands would benefit not only the United States but also Spain, and even England. Such a situation presupposed the removal of any powerful enemy of Britain from the region. This provided security for the United States while simultaneously opening such territories as markets for British industries. Both the United States and Great Britain would benefit from such an arrangement, because Americans would win territory and security while the British would have access to markets that might otherwise be denied.[60]

Although Jefferson, Madison, and Monroe did not entirely concur on their ideas of the pursuit of happiness, they all agreed that expansion was necessary to fulfill that natural right. Whether the pursuit of happiness involved the creation of new republics or states for Jefferson's empire of liberty, or whether it was concerned with becoming interrelated with the world economic system, or whether security provided the opportunity for both new states and economic prosperity, one theme remained constant: happiness meant the acquisition of new lands, and Americans pursued that goal.

Obviously, all three Republican presidents strongly supported expansion. They also wanted to acquire Spanish-held North American lands without war, which could endanger the survival of the United States. Although the threat of war could be used to influence events, all three preferred to allow natural immigration to ensure American superiority over a disintegrating Spanish empire. All three understood that a growing United States needed more land and that Spanish weaknesses meant that those

lands could be taken at will. Central to this belief was the con-
viction that Americans had a natural right to fulfill their expansionist aims. The revolutionary generation could understand
strong arguments based on navigation, security, and the pursuit
of happiness. Expansion into the Mississippi watershed, Florida,
Texas, and even Cuba and South America could be accomplished
without sacrificing American independence. Natural population
pressure, combined with freedom and liberty, encouraged
Americans to express their dreams, of which landownership remained paramount. Jefferson, Madison, and Monroe all philosophically supported Manifest Destiny and purposely tried to realize it. General Louis Marie Turreau, Napoleon's minister to the
United States in 1805, succinctly described that commitment to
American expansion when he declared that the "first fact" of Jeffersonian politics was "to conquer without war." General Turreau,
though thoroughly disliked by Jefferson, was undoubtedly correct in his assessment. The weaknesses of the Spanish North
American empire and the presence of the early impulses of Manifest Destiny allowed that approach to succeed.[61]

CHAPTER THREE

Followers of the Green Flag:
Revolution in the Texas Borderlands

THE VOLATILITY OF the Southwest was almost beyond belief in
the first decade of the nineteenth century. Much of what happened there reflected existing dissension over the issue of expansion in the United States. The well-known story of Aaron Burr
sets the background for years of intrigue. Burr, running for
governor of the state of New York while he was still vice president of the United States, mixed himself in politics and agreed,
should he win the election, to deliver New York to Federalists who
wished to secede from the Union over expansionism. But his loss
and the politically motivated duel in which he killed Alexander
Hamilton all but ended his career in politics. After his vice presidential term concluded, he amassed a large force and headed for
New Orleans in 1806. His partner in this venture was General
James Wilkinson, territorial governor of Louisiana. Burr never
revealed his ultimate plan for the area, and opinion remains divided as to whether he intended to have his own country or share
his spoils with the United States. This latter action would have
been an about-face from his earlier public stance in New York.
As Burr traveled South, General Wilkinson apparently thought
better of his part in the venture and apprised President Jefferson
of the situation. Although Burr was tried for treason but never
convicted, his actions set the stage for a sectional tug-of-war over
expansion. And Spain became the ultimate loser.[1]

James Wilkinson. Portrait by John Wesley Jarvis (Courtesy of The Filson Club Historical Society, Louisville, Kentucky)

Prior to the Louisiana Purchase in 1803, the United States probably offered no real threat to Texas, even though Spanish officials believed otherwise. The few American trappers and traders who traveled to Texas before the Purchase presented no serious problems, yet Spain's fear of American influence bordered on paranoia. The killing of Philip Nolan and the imprisonment of his followers in March 1801 offers an excellent example of this great fear. Nolan, an Irish adventurer and a friend of General Wilkinson, was primarily a horse hunter who had operated with his men in Texas for several years. He might have been an agent working for Wilkinson, who was said to have accepted money to spy for Spain, or perhaps for some other aggressive American official, but his small party represented no real threat

33

to Spanish Texas, and certainly no immediate threat. It was true that Nolan had close association with Wilkinson and even made trips to Texas for the general. Nolan was well known as a horse trader to many politically important Americans, including Thomas Jefferson. The correspondence of Nolan and others reveals that Americans did want information about Texas; Nolan responded by mapping and exploring the territory. As such, he could have been considered an explorer and perhaps even a spy. Spanish Commandant-General Pedro de Nava dispatched a force of 150 troops to capture Nolan and his party of 5 or 6 men. Though Nolan was likely scouting Texas for the United States, Nava certainly overreacted, probably because he believed that the American intended to make some sort of alliance with the Indians. This notion, never proven as a matter of fact, was pure speculation based on mistrust and panic. Spain was nervous enough, however, to believe anything.[2]

The Louisiana Purchase had created a more dangerous climate for Spanish Texas than it did for West Florida. Not only did Americans congregate in large numbers on the Louisiana-Texas border, but there was even clear disagreement as to the exact location of that border. The situation worsened as Americans began to believe that the Louisiana Purchase also included Texas. The boundary between Texas and Louisiana, long in dispute, had not been settled by France and Spain prior to 1763, when the area changed hands. After the United States bought Louisiana, the location of the boundary became a major concern. Spanish officials in Texas, naturally wanting to protect their border, tried to put as much distance as possible between the aggressive Americans to the east and their valuable holdings farther west.[3]

The first real problem along the Texas-Louisiana border concerned a number of Louisianians of French and Spanish descent who wanted to immigrate to Texas rather than become citizens of the United States. Spanish officials expressed differing opinions on whether these foreigners should be allowed to migrate into the area. Governor Juan Bautista de Elguezabal preferred to admit all these immigrants, settling them in Texas. They would serve as a buffer to expansionist Americans, providing the

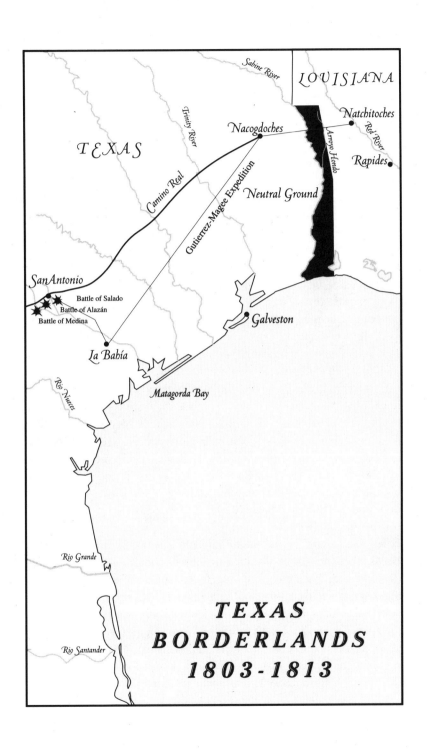

LOUISIANA

Sabine River

Natchitoches

Trinity River

Nacogdoches

Red River

Arroyo Hondo

Rapides

T E X A S

Camino Real

Gutierrez-Magee Expedition

Neutral Ground

25

San Antonio

Battle of Salado
Battle of Alazán
Battle of Medina

Galveston

La Bahía

Rio Nueces

Matagorda Bay

Rio Grande

TEXAS
BORDERLANDS
1803-1813

Rio Santander

best possible method of defending the province. Commandant-General Nemesio Salcedo disagreed, believing that these new American and French immigrants would not remain loyal to Spanish interests. In fact, he was convinced that many were spies for the United States, Napoleon, or the Bonapartist government in Spain. If permitted to enter Texas at all, he argued, they should be settled well into the interior, as far as possible from the border.[4]

Don Nemesio's distrust prevented Governor Elguezabal from implementing his plan to settle a thousand families from Louisiana in a new colony at the mouth of the Trinity River; it was at first delayed and then eventually abandoned because of widespread suspicion. One can only wonder of the ultimate effect on Anglo-American westward expansion had East Texas received a large population of non-English-speaking people. Indeed, American expansion into that region might have been permanently thwarted. Certainly Governor Elguezabal's plan represented the best possible defense available to Spain at that time.

The border dispute represented an inevitable conflict between U.S. and Spanish forces. It was surprising, however, that it did not happen sooner. Perhaps both sides' desire for peaceful relations delayed actual confrontation. The three years after the American occupation of Louisiana witnessed posturing between border posts, although no actual attacks occurred. In one instance an American expedition repulsed a Spanish force without bloodshed; this ultimately resulted in Spanish troops withdrawing from posts claimed by the United States. But this calm could not last forever.

In 1805 Don Nemesio began increasing Spanish forces in Texas, posting a large number of men at the mouth of the Trinity River and at Nacogdoches. By the year's end he had expanded the Texas garrison to some 700 men, with 141 stationed at Nacogdoches.[5] Although these numbers were by no means overwhelming, they do reinforce the idea that Don Nemesio was exercising all possible options to strengthen his position in Texas and to support the border claims, especially considering the threat to the Spanish homeland and the war in Europe.[6]

The increase in Spanish forces resulted in more and larger patrols crossing the Sabine and aggressively moving well east of that point. Officials at Natchitoches, Louisiana, complained to the Spanish commander at Nacogdoches, Texas, that troops illegally crossed the Sabine boundary into American territory. Needless to say, the Spanish denied these allegations, claiming their patrols were only intercepting horse thieves and smugglers. Moreover, these Spanish moves resulted in similar American actions. For example, on 5 February 1806, about 150 armed Americans, acting unofficially, approached Spanish posts east of the Sabine and demanded they withdraw. Greatly outnumbered, the Spanish left without a fight.

From these actions it appeared that war was inevitable. Don Nemesio ordered Lieutenant Colonel Simón de Herrera, governor of Nuevo León, to assume command of Spanish forces in East Texas. As he arrived in the border area in June 1806, he was greeted with news that war was imminent and probably unavoidable. Continuing their military buildup, the Spanish amassed 1,368 soldiers in East Texas, with 883 of these awaiting Herrera at Nacogdoches. This force probably represented the largest Spanish detachment ever in East Texas. Rumors circulated, however, that American General James Wilkinson commanded as many as 15,000 men at Natchitoches. In reality, Wilkinson's army was probably no larger than that of the Spanish, and the general certainly had no more regular troops. The rumors of such a large force were not lost on the Spanish.[7]

No one actually wanted a conflict. Nonetheless, Captain John Shaw, commander of the New Orleans naval station, instructed his gunboat commanders "to act entirely on the defensive" when encountering foreign troops. The commander also reminded his officers that, though they were to "defend [themselves] in the best possible manner," they should not allow "an indignity to their flag." Shaw skeptically reported to Secretary of the Navy Robert Smith that although his forces were proceeding to Natchitoches to join General Wilkinson, he expected that *"one action was to deside [sic]"* the fate of the country. Should the Spanish be victorious, he predicted "there was nothing preventing their marching to New Orleans," where they would find "numerous . . . followers of a victorious flag."[8]

The Spanish certainly neither wanted nor could afford war. In fact, Herrera did not have the stomach for committing his "lazy, half-mutinous, barefooted soldiers" to a conflict that could be settled diplomatically. Although there were many bellicose leaders in the United States, it is highly unlikely that any of them sought military action. The two nations ultimately avoided hostilities when General Wilkinson informed the Spanish on 29 October 1806 that he would withdraw American troops east of the Arroyo Hondo, a tributary of the Red River, if the Spanish would withdraw west of the Sabine. The territory between the rivers would be neutral ground until diplomats settled the boundary.[9]

On 4 November Herrera agreed to Wilkinson's proposal, even though he had been ordered to attack should the Americans advance beyond the Arroyo Hondo. This agreement, often referred to as the Treaty of the Neutral Ground, is incorrectly designated, since neither side ever approved it. At any rate, though neither side ratified the agreement, both accepted its provisions, as it allowed each to avoid conflict honorably. Although Herrera may have violated his orders, he received high praise from his superiors. Likewise, Wilkinson, though ordered to seize the disputed territory to the Sabine River, was also commended by the U.S. War Department. Again, what could have been a serious dispute was settled peaceably.

Wilkinson agreed to a settlement at this time because the Burr conspiracy threatened the territory, and the nation needed American troops to protect Louisiana itself. In retrospect, Wilkinson's real or alleged interest in this conspiracy does bring an element of truth to this story. More likely, however, the United States did not want a war with Spain. American authorities were certainly pleased with Wilkinson's compromise.[10] Soon after the agreement, the neutral ground became a lawless center for adventurers, filibusters, and an assortment of other undesirables who caused endless trouble on both sides of the border. Still, the existence of this buffer zone prevented any serious conflict between the two countries for several more years.[11]

The expedition of Captain Zebulon Pike in 1806–7 and the Embargo Act of 1808 would provide the only other serious disputes concerning the United States and Spain in Texas during the next few years. The Pike expedition, supposedly an exploration of what is present-day Colorado, greatly alarmed Spanish officials, who believed the captain was searching for lands favorable for American expansion. Acting on their suspicions, they arrested Pike and his men and carried them to Santa Fe and later to Chihuahua City, where they met with Don Nemesio. They eventually escorted the Americans back through Texas to Nacogdoches and released them.[12] Whether or not Pike's mission represented a reconnaissance expedition, he saw much of Texas and gained considerable knowledge of the area. The Spanish apparently concluded that Pike planned to recruit the Comanches to the American cause. Although this was pure speculation, the Spanish did send a large expedition into Indian territory, possibly to impress the tribes with their power. In the end, it is doubtful whether either Pike or the Spanish wielded much influence on the Indians.[13]

The Embargo Act of 1808 had a deleterious effect on Spanish-Indian relations. Spanish control of the Indians in Texas (the Caddo Indians in East Texas and the Apaches and Comanches in West and North Central Texas, respectively) and what became in 1821 the province of New Mexico depended heavily on the distribution of presents. The embargo, unfortunately for Spain, greatly impeded its efforts to obtain the goods needed for trade, since most of the gifts came from the United States. These obstacles, along with constant army desertions and the influx of runaway slaves, strained any Spanish-American alliance. The situation was further exacerbated by the presence of illegal American immigrants and by unending disturbances caused by an unruly population in the neutral ground. Despite this, the border remained peaceful until Father Miguel Hidalgo y Costilla's revolt in 1810.[14]

On 16 September 1810, Father Hidalgo appealed to the masses of Mexico to discard the yoke of Spanish tyranny. The Hidalgo Revolution, which resulted from European rationalism and romanticism combined with an influx of liberal ideas from the American and French Revolutions, found a ready following among the native-born Creoles who wanted to drive Spanish *peninsulares* (those people born in Spain and who by tradition were in a special class) from the country. Father Hidalgo's preachings, however, enticed a wide audience, and within a very short time the priest found himself leading an army of peasants, mostly Indian.[15]

Hidalgo first preached loyalty to Ferdinand VII and advocated the purity of Catholicism, but the revolt soon evolved into a nationalist movement promoting Mexican independence. Although his call began in the village of Dôlores, his message spread quickly and attracted a diverse following, far beyond anything Hidalgo had envisioned. What began as a war on tyranny rapidly became a social revolution and for many an excuse to settle personal grievances. The movement ultimately attracted numerous adventurers, many of whom simply wanted to seek their fortune.[16]

Félix D. Almaráz, biographer of Texas Governor Don Manuel Salcedo, suggests that the uprising signaled Anglo-Americans at Baton Rouge to revolt against Spanish rule there. Almaráz also believes it was a sign to some in Texas who desired political change, and especially to those who sought to eliminate aristocratic control of the region.

Governor Salcedo realized that Father Hidalgo's revolution moved beyond merely arousing the passions of Mexicans and Indians. He also believed that Americans and other foreigners might use the movement as a pretext for action in Texas. Thus on 16 November 1810, Salcedo closed the frontier of Texas to all foreigners. Commandant-General Nemesio Salcedo, the governor's uncle, countermanded the attempt to isolate the revolution. The rationale for Don Nemesio's action is not only difficult to understand but also out of character. The commandant-general, usually very suspicious of foreigners, must have realized that Hidalgo's agents had actively recruited Americans and others. Even so, he revoked the order because he considered it too harsh. He probably did so to prevent angry Americans from initiating even more hostile actions.[17]

At the peak of the revolution, Hidalgo's followers captured Guanajuato, Guadalajara, New Santander, Coahuila, and eventually San Antonio, the Texas capital. Governor Salcedo tried unsuccessfully in early January 1811 to rally the loyal citizens of San Antonio. Nonetheless, sixteen days later Juan Bautista Casas led a coup, seizing the city for the revolution. Casas used the coup for his own benefit and that of his followers and gave only minimal support to Hidalgo. In its aftermath, Casas named himself governor of Texas and arrested Salcedo along with other loyal Spanish officials. He then took his prisoners in chains to the hacienda of Ignacio Elizondo in Coahuila; Casas thought the revolution was won. Elizondo, however, recanted, returned to the royalist cause, and released his prisoners. This renunciation was the movement's turning point as the royalists organized a countercoup, captured Casas, and executed him. Shortly thereafter, Hidalgo was also captured, defrocked, and then executed on 30 July 1811.[18]

Historians often consider Hidalgo's revolution the first serious attempt to establish Mexican independence. Although the revolution failed in the immediate sense, its importance should not be underestimated. This revolt set into motion events that continued to shake the foundations of the Spanish empire until its final collapse. Reasons for Hidalgo's failure merit their own study, but the movement's lack of success must not detract from the revolution's effect on the borderlands. Baton Rouge residents may very well have found inspiration for their uprising in Hidalgo's revolutionary movement. Certainly Anglo-American settlers used this as an opportunity to discard Spanish rule.[19]

A more direct effect of the revolution was the activity of José Bernardo Maximiliano Gutiérrez de Lara. Gutiérrez, a former merchant and blacksmith from the small settlement of Revilla on the Rio Grande, was commissioned a lieutenant colonel in the revolutionary forces and sent as Hidalgo's emissary to the United States. Gutiérrez reached Natchitoches, Louisiana, inside U.S.

territory, in August 1811 after only narrowly avoiding capture by Spanish soldiers.[20]

The Mexican agent's arrival became the subject of considerable communication between Captain John Overton, U.S. garrison commander at Natchitoches, and General James Wilkinson. Overton also sent letters to Governor Claiborne of Louisiana and to government officials in Washington. Gutiérrez's activities sparked great American interest, even though local officials had no idea what appropriate action should be taken. After much deliberation, the authorities at Natchitoches sent the agent to Tennessee, where he received a warm welcome from several prominent leaders, including Judge John Overton, uncle of Captain Overton. From there he proceeded to Washington, where others provided encouragement. Although Gutiérrez was not considered an official representative, he was welcomed at the State Department and had a series of conferences with Secretary of State James Monroe.[21]

When Gutiérrez presented his case to Monroe, the latter exhibited great interest in his situation. Monroe broached the subject of American support for the Mexican Revolution in exchange for an agreement to settle the border claims in Texas. Should the Mexican revolutionary government agree to this proposal, the United States would deploy an army to the Rio Grande and supply arms and money for the struggle against Spain. Monroe also suggested the possibility of extensive trade with an independent Mexico. According to Gutiérrez, the secretary of state even offered to furnish ten thousand stand of muskets and accept revolutionary bills of exchange in payment. Gutiérrez responded somewhat favorably to the offer but insisted that he be named commander of any forces in Mexico.[22]

Monroe was apparently unwilling to accept Gutiérrez's terms, since it had become clear that the agent would not bind the Mexican revolutionary government to any agreement relinquishing control of Texas to the United States. Gutiérrez declined the proposal, suggesting that he lacked the authority to make such a commitment without his government's consent. Monroe, obviously angered, suggested that Gutiérrez return to Texas and obtain such support from his revolutionary leaders. He also told the agent that in the future he must obtain proper credentials from his government if he wished to purchase arms and raise money in the United States.[23]

Monroe and other American leaders were interested in the Mexican Revolution for several reasons. They certainly wanted to settle the western boundary and gain a full claim to Texas, but American interests went far beyond this. An independent Mexico would further weaken Spain, making future expansion easier for the young republic. It would also hasten the entire Spanish empire's collapse, which in turn would allow more potential trade for U.S. citizens. Perhaps most importantly, it would follow an already established American policy of ridding the Western Hemisphere of European powers.

One should not assume that Monroe would fail to support Gutiérrez simply because the agent refused to recognize any American claim to Texas. There might be other revolutionary leaders who would accede to the wishes of the United States, and future situations might deem it desirable and even necessary for them to make concessions. Another of Monroe's concerns was that British and especially French agents were interested in the Mexican Revolution. Should the United States fail to help Gutiérrez, Napoleonic agents were poised with promises of extensive assistance; these offers continued even after Napoleon's demise. In fact, following the Bourbon restoration in France, Napoleonic agents sought a refuge in Mexico for their deposed emperor. At this point Napoleon's agents could be compared to fleas on a dog. They were always there but seldom seen unless they caused an "itch."[24]

John Graham, chief clerk of the State Department, sponsored Gutiérrez during his stay in Washington. Graham, undoubtedly at Monroe's behest, became Gutiérrez's mentor, teaching the young merchant and blacksmith proper etiquette for dealing with officials and other representatives of the government. No doubt Graham also steered him from French and English agents vying for his support for their plans. Moreover, there is good reason to believe that Graham arranged for Gutiérrez to meet and cooperate with Don José Álvarez de Toledo y Dubois, a Cuban revolutionary. Toledo, loyal to Ferdinand VII, was sent to Spain to represent Santo Domingo in the Cortes (parliament) of Cádiz from September 1810 to January 1811. While a member of the Cortes, Toledo discovered that the Spanish colonies would not be allowed any influence in the new government. He also learned that the old rules and restrictions against the colonies would be restored as well. Angered by this Eurocentricism, he withdrew from the Cortes and denounced it in a letter to the captain general of Santo Domingo. Unfortunately, Spanish authorities in Cádiz intercepted this letter and accused him of being an English agent.[25]

Toledo fled to Philadelphia, where he arrived in September 1811, hoping to gain support for a revolution against Spain. While there he requested a meeting with the secretary of state. Monroe recognized his chance to exert additional influence on the Mexican Revolution and began to cultivate Toledo. There is good reason to believe that even at this early date Monroe saw an opportunity to obtain the Texas territory through Toledo if he were unable to control Gutiérrez. In fact, this eventually became the secretary's plan.[26]

Toledo's real motives and loyalty remain a matter of speculation. While in Philadelphia he met with Don Luis de Onís, the unrecognized Spanish representative to the United States, and supposedly offered to betray the revolution to Spain. Toledo was likely more interested in personal gain than in any ideas of revolution, and Monroe probably knew this. The secretary undoubtedly realized that this man could be used to achieve American interests if the price were right.

Graham loaned Gutiérrez two hundred dollars and provided him with a letter of introduction to William C. C. Claiborne of Louisiana, requesting the governor to furnish the Spaniard with transportation to the frontier. Gutiérrez departed Washington in early January 1812 for Philadelphia, where he spent time with Toledo. Apparently the two men reached some agreement, after which Gutiérrez returned to the capital and met once more with Monroe, who apparently offered significant support. Gutiér-

William C. C. Claiborne. Engraved by J. B. Longacre from a miniature by A. Duval (Courtesy of The Historic New Orleans Collection, Museum/Research Center, accession no. 1981.206)

rez then sailed for New Orleans, arriving on 23 March, at which time he presented himself to Governor Claiborne. The governor provided him with the necessary funds to travel on to Natchitoches.[27]

Captain William Shaler, a U.S. special agent of the State Department who traveled with Gutiérrez to Natchitoches, soon became the Mexican's adviser and main liaison with the American government. The relationship between the two continued throughout Gutiérrez's career as a revolutionary leader. Shaler's mission was twofold: he observed and assisted the revolution in Mexico and Texas by raising men and money; he also worked to serve American interests through influencing the independence struggle. Whether or not Gutiérrez realized it, Shaler was the real power behind the throne.[28]

Little doubt exists about the role of the United States in the whole affair. Monroe demonstrated the American position in his request to Gutiérrez that the new Mexican government cede Texas in exchange for support of the revolution. When Gutiérrez did not comply with Monroe's petition, the secretary took a more devious course. Thus Shaler's mission became an attempt to persuade the Mexican to support Monroe's position and thereby gain American assistance for his cause in Texas and Mexico. Should Gutiérrez be unwilling to relinquish Texas, he could at least help break the Spanish hold on the area. Monroe dispensed money, leaders, and arms in order to accomplish this objective. Louisiana merchants, especially those in Natchitoches, furnished funds, supplies, and numerous volunteers. Agents implemented a propaganda campaign to convince local residents to join the revolution. Even the impending war with England did not stem the tide of American enthusiasm for this operation.[29]

About the same time Gutiérrez launched his invasion of Texas, Monroe sent Dr. John Hamilton Robinson, the surgeon attached to Zebulon Pike's expedition, on a strange mission to meet with Spanish officials in northern Mexico. Robinson, a native of Virginia, had moved to St. Louis in 1804 as a young, energetic doctor and had made friends in important places. One companion on the Pike expedition was the son of General James Wilkinson, and Pike himself recommended Robinson highly to Monroe. On the surface, Robinson's trip appeared to be a peace mission.[30] While in Mexico he met with Don Nemesio to deliver Monroe's message of peace. Robinson agreed that the United States would try to end the Gutiérrez invasion.[31]

Robinson's instructions and mission seem to be in contradiction to other American actions, and one can only speculate about the secretary's motives. It does seem that Monroe intended to create confusion and thus conceal his real objectives. Since the United States did not officially support this filibustering expedition into Texas, it would appear that Monroe used the Robinson mission to disguise the government's intention. Evidence indicates that the United States actively supported this covert invasion, whereas the Robinson mission represented the official public position. Whatever Robinson's real reasons for being there, members of the revolutionary force were very disturbed and unhappy over his presence and felt their efforts were being compromised.[32]

Spanish officials treated Robinson cordially during his visit. On his return trip, however, he stopped to visit Gutiérrez's republican army, where he received a reception less than warm. His journey through Texas nevertheless proved invaluable, as it provided him with excellent intelligence information that he could pass on to Monroe. Robinson reported that the republican army of about twenty-five hundred troops was advancing on San Antonio. People of that city, in a state of panic, even begged the doctor to carry their valuables to a safe place. He described the revolutionary army as an assortment of poorly equipped, untrained Americans, Spanish-speaking Texans, and Indians. Robinson believed Texas citizens actually supported the revolution even though they feared the army.[33]

Robinson also reported that the ever-present French agents had been offering aid to the revolution. Although they hoped to gain support for the French puppet government in Spain, they may have had designs on the area for France itself. Rumors spread that the French consul at New Orleans had promised to furnish three million francs, as well as fifteen thousand stand of arms to be landed at Matagorda Bay. No records remain to verify that the consul actually delivered the money and materials. Nonetheless, this expedition interested French agents as they worked to take control of Texas for France. The British, in the meantime, had promised to aid Spanish forces, even offering to help Spain recover New Orleans.[34]

Augustus William Magee,* a twenty-four-year-old Bostonian who had graduated from the United States Military Academy third in the class of 1808, commanded American patriot forces assembled at Natchitoches. Supposedly unhappy over his failure to secure a promotion, on 22 June 1812 Magee resigned his commission in the U.S. Army to join the rebel expedition into Texas. He had served as a trusted junior officer under General Wilkinson at Baton Rouge. Although no proof exists, his resignation likely represented one of two things: either a ploy, where he was actually encouraged to join Gutiérrez's force; or a fulfillment of his ambitions and adventurous spirit. When one considers this country's interests in Texas, it makes sense that Shaler selected an able and trusted military officer to lead the group. Since Magee died at La Bahía before the end of the campaign, it is impossible to know what his future in Texas or with the U.S. Army might otherwise have been. Magee's performance lacked some of the hoped-for luster Shaler had anticipated. This may be partly credited to his fatal illness that began in November 1812, and in addition he felt sure that Robinson's activities had worked to the detriment of the operation. He was "called on command in another world" on 6 February 1813. Gutiérrez, who had grown to dislike Magee tremendously, attributed his death to poison, which may or may not have been true.[35]

Army Captain Charles Wollestoncraft and a company of troops

---

*According to George W. Cullum's *Biographical Register of the Officers and Graduates of the U.S. Military Academy at West Point, N.Y., from Its Establishment, March 16, 1802, to the Army Reorganization of 1866–67,* Magee was not the only academy graduate to serve in the South and Southwest during this period. Samuel Noah, native of England and appointed from New York, was in the class of 1807. He resigned his commission in March 1811 to become part of the force entering Texas, fighting until the capture of San Antonio. He tried unsuccessfully to regain his commission after the United States entered the war with Britain, and ultimately fought as a volunteer in the defense of New York Harbor. Auguste Chouteau, both born in and appointed from Missouri, graduated in 1806. He served on the Southwest frontier as an aide-de-camp to General Wilkinson before resigning in 1808 to become an Indian trader in the Western Territories until his death in 1838. Samuel Champlin, an 1807 classmate of Noah from Connecticut, remained in the U.S. Army until 1816, serving, among other posts, as chief quartermaster to General Pinckney's Southern Army. He left the army to become part of MacGregor's force that captured Amelia Island.

from Baton Rouge arrived at Natchitoches to oversee the departure of the Magee-Gutiérrez expedition. This provides another interesting but inconclusive bit of evidence concerning this country's role in supporting the operation. Just days after the expeditionary force crossed the Sabine River into Texas, Wollestoncraft and his men left for Baton Rouge, returning Natchitoches to Captain Overton's command. One can only guess the true meaning of this action, but it should be noted that Wollestoncraft was another of General Wilkinson's most trusted officers. Were secret supplies and instructions to be delivered at this last minute before the expedition departed the protection of the United States? This question cannot be answered from the existing records, but if this were not some sort of special mission, the government probably would not have sent this trusted officer and men to Natchitoches for such a brief time.

An order sent by Governor Claiborne to Judge John Carr of Natchitoches instructing him to begin enforcing American neutrality laws and to stop the expedition provides still another piece of evidence illustrating the American desire to guard the record. The order, issued the day before the expedition left the country, doubtless failed to reach Carr until after the revolutionists had arrived in Texas. This document provided a clear example that the State Department could show the Spanish to demonstrate neutrality.[36] Claiborne's correspondence with Shaler in April 1812 demonstrates that he understood the real situation and also provides proof that his orders to Carr represented a mere pretense. In their exchange Claiborne acknowledged that although the United States wanted Gutiérrez to lead an expedition into Mexico, the government had not authorized him to provide any money. This correspondence proved that Claiborne fully understood the situation and that he was not the source of money.[37]

Not only did the government arrange for the expedition to be supplied with money, men, and arms, but Dr. John Sibley, the American Indian agent in western Louisiana, provided the Texas Indians with large quantities of presents and encouraged them to support the revolution. There is no doubt he had the cooperation of Samuel Davenport, former Spanish Indian agent in

Texas, who also attempted to entice the natives to aid the cause. Many Indians did in fact join the expedition under the leadership of turncoat Davenport, who apparently appropriated large quantities of Spanish supplies for this purpose. Davenport accompanied the expedition, playing a significant role in the siege of Bahía.[38]

Magee was named colonel and assumed command of the army. Although Gutiérrez was given the title of general, his primary duty was that of civil administrator and propagandist, persuading the people of Texas by whatever means to join the revolution. Using Natchitoches as their unofficial headquarters, the Magee-Gutiérrez forces called themselves the "Republican Army of the North" and persuaded Americans, Frenchmen, Mexican revolutionaries, Indians, and a collection of bandits and outlaws from the neutral ground to join their cause.[39]

After crossing the Sabine River on 12 August, the expedition quickly advanced to Nacogdoches. Bernardino Montero, the Spanish commander there, tried in vain to rally the citizens to the royalist cause; all but ten of his soldiers deserted to the revolutionary army. Magee's troops remained at Nacogdoches until September, resting and enjoying the rich plunder they had captured from Spanish forces and government stores. Ultimately Magee confiscated nearly $100,000 worth of horses, mules, wool, and cash left behind; the wool itself brought about $70,000 when exchanged at the U.S. government's trading post, commonly known as the Natchitoches Sulphur Fork Factory. Magee had promised the people his troops would not loot personal property, and he kept his pledge. It became unnecessary, since public property was plentiful enough to provide the Army of the North with an ample treasury.[40]

In September, Magee again marched his army. Governor Salcedo had withdrawn his forces from La Bahía (Goliad) and massed them on the Camino Real (the King's Highway) between Nacogdoches and San Antonio. The Camino Real, barely more than a track, ran across Texas from Natchitoches through Nacogdoches to San Antonio and beyond. One branch split off the main road toward the coastal presidio of La Bahía. Apparently

Magee's scouts informed him that Governor Salcedo had left few if any Spanish troops there. Magee turned his army toward La Bahía and captured the undefended fort without firing a shot.[41]

Three days later, royalist forces from San Antonio attacked La Bahía. Led by Lieutenant Colonel Simón de Herrera, apparently an excellent officer, the Spanish began a four-month siege of the place. Yet Herrera's efforts were greatly hindered. During the siege, a Comanche chieftain named Cordero demanded that Governor Salcedo provide a *regalo* (gift) in addition to his annual tribute payment to the tribe. When Salcedo refused, the Comanches seized five thousand sheep and ten thousand horses and mules. This greatly hindered Herrera's attempt to capture the city. Although the revolutionaries had plenty of food and never suffered, morale began to plummet after Magee's mysterious death in early February. Major Samuel Kemper assumed command of the army after Magee's death; although he was a good leader, he lacked the professional training needed to direct such a multinational force. Herrera ultimately lifted the siege on 19 February 1813, after which Kemper advanced his forces toward San Antonio.[42]

On 2 March, Kemper, with from 500 to 800 troops, including an estimated 325 Indians, again encountered Herrera's army, this time at the Salado Creek, where the ensuing battle marked a decisive defeat for the royalists. Four days later, Governor Salcedo surrendered Texas; rebel forces then occupied San Antonio, and Gutiérrez assumed control of the province. This was the high-water mark of the revolution. In the battle's aftermath, Gutiérrez declared himself governor of the state of Texas and immediately transformed it into a Mexican province. The Americans received "a gratuity of fifteen dollars, a suit of clothes and an order for two horses or mules," while the Indians were paid with two dollars' worth of vermilion for their services. Yet when the revolutionary troops beheaded Governor Salcedo and General Herrera, along with a number of loyal Spanish officers, American soldiers bitterly protested. In fact, this greatly angered the Americans, who had not been informed of the action ahead of time, and the executions prompted many to desert and return to Louisiana. This marked the beginning of the downfall of the revolution in Texas.[43]

On 6 April 1813, the new Gutiérrez government of Texas issued a declaration of independence from Spain. This document, enumerating the many grievances against Spain, resembled for the most part the American Declaration of Independence. It provided for the formation of a provisional government, of which Gutiérrez immediately became head. His first act as leader of the government was to name a president, a secretary, and five advisers who formed a junta of seven members. The junta was granted full governmental powers and the authority to write a constitution. Of the seven members, five were Spanish Texans, the other two an American and a Frenchman. The group quickly began writing a constitution that ultimately, in similar fashion to the Spanish provincial government before it, gave all real power to the governor.[44]

This new document clearly indicated to the United States that Texas planned to join the intermittent revolution then occurring in Mexico. Although Spain still for the most part controlled Mexico, Gutiérrez wanted to be part of whatever new republic was established. The constitution instituted a state religion while placing some limitations on private property and personal freedom. The government granted Anglo-Americans who had helped in the struggle for independence one league square of land for each six months of service. The new government also recognized all financial obligations to the United States and its citizens. Even with its seemingly enlightened provisions, the new constitution nonetheless dissatisfied most Americans who had fought with the army because it excluded them from power. Even Kemper left the Army of Texas and returned to Louisiana.[45]

This new revolutionary government created more problems than it solved. Americans felt they had been betrayed. Shaler and his superiors must have realized that Gutiérrez, as a Mexican nationalist, did not intend to convert Texas into a territory of the United States. They had apparently believed that with enough persuasion he could be converted into an American agent. Not only that, they had thought Magee and the other Americans could wield enough influence to allow the Texans themselves to make the "correct" choice. But Gutiérrez became the undisputed leader after Magee died and command of the army diffused. Moreover, Gutiérrez as leader exercised his choice to join Mexico.[46]

Although Americans probably viewed Gutiérrez as disloyal, he had never agreed to turn over Texas, nor had he mistreated Americans who served with him. He may have been naive in the ways of statecraft and perhaps did not comprehend what the United States expected of him. Then, too, he may have realized full well what Americans wanted but instead used whatever help he could find to realize his own dream. The United States had supported an independent Mexico, even though Monroe would have preferred the Rio Grande as the border. This had, in fact, been one objective that Monroe had stated when meeting with Gutiérrez. Knowing this, Gutiérrez may have felt that the United States should be happy with half a loaf rather than nothing at all.[47]

The Texas Declaration of Independence also stimulated great, if belated, Spanish activity. The arrogant, aggressive, but effective Spanish leader José Joaquín de Arredondo y Mioño and the bloody Ignacio Elizondo, betrayer of the Hidalgo Revolution, moved to destroy the Texas Republic. These two leaders were among the most effective and ruthless Spanish officers in Mexico.

Americans quickly reacted to Gutiérrez's government. Álvarez de Toledo, always involved in the operations in Texas, had remained in the United States and, among other things, raised troops and money for the cause. Toledo had at one point supposedly been offered command of the operations in Texas. Now with Magee's death and Gutiérrez's inevitable choices, many Americans felt that Toledo should assume command of the Army of the North. Sibley, Shaler, Governor Claiborne, and probably most of the Washington establishment supported this view, although many Texans felt otherwise.[48]

Shaler determined that Gutiérrez must be replaced to preserve American interests, and Toledo was the obvious choice. He would move the revolution toward the American objectives. Before giving him command of the Army of the North, Shaler asked Toledo in April to assume command of the disorganized outpost at Nacogdoches. The new commander quickly improved the situation, and when Shaler visited on 20 May he found it in surprisingly good order. Gutiérrez interrupted Toledo's plan to travel on to San Antonio when he sent a message requesting that Toledo return to Louisiana to continue raising volunteers and collecting equipment. Apparently Gutiérrez devised this scheme to prevent Toledo from assuming command of the army. Toledo withdrew to Natchitoches as requested, though displeased with the turn of events.[49]

In San Antonio, discord permeated the command. Mexican and American soldiers who until then had worked closely and well together began to develop a strong distrust for one another. New recruits, arriving in large numbers, found discipline and leadership lacking and American officers who sometimes refused to obey Gutiérrez's orders. Gutiérrez's inability to command the diverse force proved to be the basic problem. Although he was a good political leader, he was certainly no soldier.

The republican army—about 400 Americans, 800 Mexicans, and between 100 and 200 Indians—soon faced at least 1,500 royalists. Shaler also encountered the problem of preventing French agents from taking over the revolution. Many Frenchmen remained in the field, and Gutiérrez frequently corresponded with some of them. The French represented a serious threat, since they apparently conspired with all parties to maintain a constant state of confusion.[50]

The French unquestionably had a vital interest in Texas during the entire course of the invasion. Several French officers, all probably agents, participated in the expedition from the beginning. But Americans were not the only ones concerned with French activities during the revolution. The Spanish government also exhibited much interest in French actions, and Onís complained bitterly about this intrigue. Onís laced Spanish charges of the American relationship to the Magee-Gutiérrez expedition with references to French agents. The minister may have continued mentioning the French question merely to cause friction within American ranks. If he actually contrived to cloud the issue, he probably initiated his scheme when the expedition was first proposed. In the summer of 1813, he suggested to Monroe that Toledo, engaged in intrigue with the French, ultimately intended to overthrow Gutiérrez and seize the expedition for France. Onís even suggested that Ducoudray-Holstein and Bartholomé Lafon, who arrived in Rapides, Louisiana, in June 1813, were French agents conspiring with Toledo.[51]

Onís expressed further alarm when the well-known former French general Jean Joseph Amable Humbert and several other French officers left Philadelphia in August 1813 en route to New Orleans. In addition to having had a distinguished military career during the French Revolution, Humbert had led an attempted invasion of Ireland. Although captured by the English and later paroled, he surfaced in the United States, almost certainly as a French agent. The general had connections with the invasion of Texas, but he became best known for assisting Andrew Jackson at the Battle of New Orleans in 1814–15. No record exists proving that Humbert ever actually joined the Gutiérrez expedition, but he did participate in subsequent activities in Texas.[52]

Onís continued his protests and condemnation of the French plots concerning Toledo and Gutiérrez. Writing to Monroe, he asserted that the French had raised men in New Orleans. "I have received notice," he claimed, "that an expedition is preparing or perhaps has departed under the orders of General Humbert and of Bernardo Gutiérrez against Matagordo and Tampico, consisting of 600 (men) recruited and armed in the town of New Orleans, assisted by the pirates of Barataria." Onís was undoubtedly referring to the Laffite brothers and several other filibusters who assumed a more important role in Galveston later.[53]

Meanwhile, the Gutiérrez expedition itself continued to experience difficulties with leadership. Shaler offered the command of the army to General John Adair of Kentucky, who refused. Now with Toledo available, he turned to him. The ultimate decision as to who could name the new commander at this point is a mystery. For whatever reason, Shaler, even though the expedition was in no way an official U.S. operation, was powerful enough to select the new leader. Toledo's subsequent rejection by Gutiérrez upset Shaler. Gutiérrez had been misled as to Toledo's loyalty by Nathan Coggswell, a person of some influence but nevertheless a shadowy character. History has shed little light on Coggswell's particulars other than to cast doubt on his credibility. It is interesting to note that he died in 1813 in Rapides, Louisiana, definitely a hotbed of French loyalists. Shaler, realizing that Coggswell could not be trusted, decided to discredit him, while he tried to determine the selection of the next commander of the Army of the North. If Shaler had ever supported Coggswell's assessment of Toledo, he apparently realized his error. Convinced by others of Toledo's trustworthiness, Shaler placed him in command. Since Gutiérrez still respected Shaler, he allowed himself to be convinced that Toledo was not a traitor.[54]

At this point events probably had more impact on the situation in Texas than did personalities. The American commanders refused Gutiérrez's orders to march to the Rio Grande, clearly showing a breakdown in authority. Moreover, morale continued to worsen as the ablest American officers and their men left San Antonio to return to Louisiana. Major Reuben Ross replaced Kemper after his departure. Ross also quickly became disillusioned, as he left San Antonio on 16 June. Major Henry Perry, who succeeded Ross, almost immediately found his army facing an overwhelming royalist force. Demanding their immediate surrender, Elizondo promised the Americans a safe return to Louisiana if they would hand over Gutiérrez and his officers. Perry ignored the challenge and attacked Elizondo's camp on the morning of 20 June. As it developed, Elizondo's forces, even more poorly organized than the republican army, soon fled the field with great losses. The Battle of Alazán, as it became known, was the last victory for the republican forces.[55]

The army returned to San Antonio, arriving about the same time as Shaler's agents—Henry Bullard, Joseph B. Wilkinson, and Samuel Alden. Bullard had been a close friend and aide of Toledo; Wilkinson was the son of General James Wilkinson and also a friend of Shaler; Alden had been Toledo's aide for almost as long as the latter had been in the United States. These men began working to discredit Coggswell's report and to undermine Gutiérrez's credibility. Bullard persuaded the American officers to sign a petition requesting that command of the army be given to Toledo and calling for the junta to meet and consider their request. After a lengthy discussion and a threat by Perry to leave San Antonio with all the Americans, the junta agreed to ask Toledo to lead them.[56]

When Toledo arrived, Gutiérrez slipped out of San Antonio at night and returned to Louisiana. Unfortunately, Gutiérrez's departure and the disagreement concerning his removal left the army demoralized and badly divided. The Mexicans and Americans by this time openly opposed each other. This state of affairs existed when General Arredondo's army, along with Elizondo's revitalized forces, advanced toward San Antonio. Toledo arrived in San Antonio on the first day of August and assumed command three days later. Gutiérrez and his family departed for Natchitoches on the following day. Although he had failed as a military leader, Gutiérrez was actually fortunate to have left the city with his family at that time.[57]

Orders, schemes, and American politics were far removed from the disunity and rivalries rampant in San Antonio. The Mexicans still supported Gutiérrez and considered Toledo an outsider at best—and perhaps a traitor. Toledo had no time to rectify this opinion. When Arredondo's army approached, he had to fight with whatever forces he had. But Toledo committed an egregious error when he reorganized the army into distinct Mexican and American units. Before this time the groups had been intermixed. He apparently doubted the loyalty of the Mexican troops, an unfortunate sentiment since it deepened the growing distrust between the groups. Before Toledo could do anything else to prepare his army, scouts reported royalists advancing on San Antonio.[58]

On 18 August 1813, Toledo moved his fourteen hundred soldiers out of San Antonio to a position east of the Medina River. When he encountered the Spanish he ordered an immediate attack that forced Elizondo's forces to withdraw across the river. But the retreat, though appearing unorganized, was actually a trick; Elizondo led Toledo's army into a trap and successfully ambushed them. The Americans might have defeated Arredondo despite the surprise, had Toledo's forces not been so exhausted from the August heat and had so many of their men not already been killed. Spanish forces were also close to defeat, and many believed that the royalists would have retreated had the Americans held the field a short time longer. In any case, after three and a half hours of heated combat, Spanish drums beat out reveille as the republican army hastily retreated.[59]

The Spanish cavalry pursued the routed and scattered republican army as far as the Medina River. Panic soon reached San Antonio, whereupon many of its inhabitants set out on foot for Louisiana. Elizondo entered San Antonio with 200 cavalry, and the next day Arredondo marched through the streets of the city. The revolution was over. Arredondo sent one detachment to capture La Bahía and directed Elizondo, with 500 cavalry, to round up the fleeing rebels. By 3 September, Arredondo had executed 327 rebels and imprisoned their wives and daughters. The Spanish commander left their young children to roam the streets begging for food. After almost two months, the women were released from prison. Elizondo executed 71 rebels and captured another 100, who were returned to San Antonio only to be executed by Arredondo. The Spaniards did not treat the American prisoners as badly as they did the Mexicans. Arredondo offered land in the interior of Texas to those Americans who would take an oath of loyalty. But to those who refused, Spanish commanders gave passports, rifles, and horses for transportation to the United States.[60]

Arredondo's soldiers, in what may have been the worst atrocity committed, murdered a number of women and children who had fled San Antonio on foot. According to an angry complaint by Onís, there may have been between 200 and 300 women and children killed in this manner. Onís strongly denounced this action, even though it reflected poorly on Spanish royalists.[61]

This ended the most intensive effort ever undertaken by the United States to annex Texas. Although there were other attempts, they did not have the strong, though unofficial, support of this country. Even so, the American government made little or no attempt to stop later filibusters. The French continued their activities in Texas, and these agents made rather extensive efforts to take the region from the Spanish after the War of 1812.[62]

The Magee-Gutiérrez-Toledo expedition failed primarily because no final objectives had been agreed upon in advance. Had Gutiérrez and the Spanish Texans been willing to join with the United States, there is little doubt that the movement could have been successful. The United States would have, therefore, added Texas in 1813 or 1814, assuring Mexican independence about the same time. There are many variables that might have resulted from this action. Had Magee lived, it is doubtful whether any force in Mexico could have defeated the rebellion. There would have almost certainly been some sort of split between Magee and Gutiérrez, but the Americans would probably have dominated such a disagreement. Even Toledo could have defeated Arredondo had he won control of his men. It would certainly be interesting to speculate on the results of having added Texas in 1814 rather than in 1845.

As important as this quest for expansion was for the United States, the entire scenario becomes far more significant when one considers the actions of James Monroe and the State Department. Throughout the course of this struggle for expansion, Monroe never articulated clear-cut policy objectives, and this became even more evident a few weeks prior to the fall of San Antonio. Shaler had decided to travel to San Antonio only a few days after Toledo's departure from Louisiana, but after he had gone a short distance into Texas he was overtaken by a dispatch rider carrying a message from Secretary of State Monroe. In that contradictory message, Monroe ordered him to return to Louisiana, insisting that the United States would not support any illegal government in Texas, nor would it use its forces to overthrow the Spaniards. This message surprised Shaler, to say the least. He later answered that he had misunderstood the secretary of state in the degree of support that he was authorized to extend to the revolution. Not until he received Monroe's message did he believe that he had exceeded his instructions. Even so, the administration did not punish Shaler, as he received neither a reprimand nor a further message on this subject.[63]

In truth, Monroe probably intended this order as a subterfuge to placate Spain and other European countries should they later accuse the United States of sponsoring an invasion of Texas. Monroe also likely believed that the need to pacify Congress was even more important than the effort to appease foreign nations. These orders may very well have been intended to assuage congressional committees. There is little doubt that political candidates in the Northeast could suffer by admitting to support such aggressive policies.

Without a doubt, Monroe used the orders to Shaler, those ineffective instructions by Claiborne to enforce neutrality laws, and the mission of Dr. Robinson as a means to reinforce American interests in any further negotiations with Spain. Of course Monroe knew of Shaler's actions! Monroe, Madison, Claiborne, Graham, Wilkinson, and probably most of the people in the State Department well knew what was happening in Texas. This kind of circumvention had become a pattern for the U.S. government during this period. Later events in this expansionist policy add even more evidence to prove this blatant duplicity.

CHAPTER FOUR

The First Spanish-American War: Patriot Efforts to Annex Florida

WHEN SPAIN AND the United States finally agreed in 1795 on the thirty-first parallel as the republic's southern boundary, the American government authorized construction of Fort Stoddert at Ward's Bluff, near the headwaters of the Mobile River where the Alabama and Tombigbee Rivers converge. The fort, garrisoned with regular U.S. troops, soon became a magnet for Anglo-Americans moving into the area. The settlers, along with the army garrison, needed to use the Mobile River not only to supply the settlement and fort but also to export goods they produced. Since the Pinckney Treaty did not cover this territory, the Spanish governor of West Florida demanded a 12 percent duty on both exported and imported goods transported on the river. Although Spanish officials often neglected to tax the U.S. Army for its supplies, the settlers received no such advantage. Moreover, the high rates made it difficult if not impossible for these people to use the river to export their goods.[1]

Over the next decade, American settlers poured into the area, and most demanded removal of the Spanish duties. As early as 1804, James and John Caller, the three Kemper brothers (Nathan, Reuben, and Samuel), and others threatened to organize a force of settlers to take West Florida for the United States. (This is the same Samuel Kemper who later took command of the Magee-Gutiérrez expedition in Texas following Magee's death.) The

American government managed to keep these movements in check for a time despite continuing agitation over the fee and an ever-growing demand to seize Florida. It comes as no surprise that most settlers readily supported any movement aimed at obtaining control of West Florida.[2]

Congress's passage of the Mobile Act in February 1804 was intended to mollify the settlers but met with little success. Although the government took no direct action to secure the city at that time, nor did it until 1813, it did create a Mobile customs district with headquarters at St. Stephens, a town located just above the thirty-first parallel and slightly west of Fort Stoddert.[3]

This anger, confusion, and lawlessness on the southern frontier played directly into the hands of the expansionists. Jefferson, Madison, and even Monroe were not displeased with this situation. Each of these men philosophically supported expansion in the South and Southwest, as well as in any other area where new frontiers looked promising. Although they did not seek war with either England or Spain, they were very evidently prepared to accept as much territory as possible from the Louisiana Purchase and through any other opportunity that might present itself, but without having to do battle.[4]

Whether or not the Burr conspiracy should be considered as part of any effort to expand the United States is problematic. Certainly Burr moved at a time when popular opinion on the southern frontier advocated annexing West Florida. What he was hoping to accomplish with his expedition down the Mississippi has never been conclusively proven, but he was apparently trying to win support by telling each individual what that person wanted to hear. Burr insisted that he intended to seize West Florida for the United States.[5] As has been noted already, Wilkinson, currently in command of the New Orleans district, probably thought he could gain more for himself by thwarting Burr's activities than he could by supporting them. In any case, he enhanced his own reputation by foiling Burr's plot.[6]

Many American settlers along the Spanish border tacitly, if not openly, supported Burr and would have gladly espoused his cause, nefarious though it may have been. With such a force Burr

could have easily taken West Florida. The U.S. government, however, chose a more cautious path, not only arresting Burr but
also preventing citizens in the area from seizing West Florida.
Edmund P. Gaines, garrison commander at Fort Stoddert, and
Harry Toulmin, federal district judge of the Mississippi Territory, along with a few other officials, prevented action at this time
against Spain.[7]

Local American authorities tried to maintain a state of peace
indefinitely over the entire area, but in the summer of 1810, possibly as a result of growing unrest in Texas and word of the
Hidalgo Revolution in Mexico, a group of American settlers
seized Baton Rouge and expelled the Spanish garrison. Following a period of anarchy in that district, the citizens of Baton
Rouge declared themselves independent of Spain on 26 September 1810. They immediately requested admission to the United
States, whereupon President Madison annexed the territory,
claiming that it had been part of the Louisiana Purchase. The
United States formally took possession of the Baton Rouge district on 6 December 1810. This represented the first territory
annexed that had actually been part of West Florida.[8]

Had the United States not acted to prevent it, excited filibusters from Baton Rouge, led by Reuben Kemper and Joseph Kennedy, probably would have seized all of West Florida in November
1810. Since the Madison government appeared ready to obtain
Spanish territory either by internal revolution or by filibuster action, it is surprising that American officials stopped this attack.
The decision to discontinue the expedition may have resulted
from orders issued by local authorities and particularly Judge
Toulmin.[9]

The question remains: Why did these people care what happened to the Spanish? Local authorities wanted West Florida to
be included in the United States; Mobile could be occupied as
part of the Louisiana Purchase, since the United States had always claimed this territory as far east as the Perdido River. Spain
was entirely too weak in North America to prevent such an occupation. Who then in the United States opposed this action? Even
in 1810 an influential faction in the Northeast resisted any west-

ward expansion. In the future these same people would oppose the War of 1812 as well as the acquisition of Mobile and Florida. They also denounced efforts to annex Texas, complaining bitterly that the whole plan resembled a conspiracy to extend slavery.[10]

The presence of sectional controversy may well have influenced Madison toward a cautious course in annexing territory. Had he been forced to go before Congress in the Baton Rouge case, he might have faced an embarrassing debate. But just as in the Baton Rouge case, the United States already claimed Mobile as part of the Louisiana Purchase. Probably wanting to avoid more criticism, Madison preferred to obtain the territory without much congressional opposition. Should Spain at this point agree to cede Mobile and West Florida, most of the critics of expansionism would be silenced. Therefore, it is logical to assume that Madison deliberately employed this plan, especially when one considers that American representatives were already negotiating with West Florida Governor Vincente Folch for that territory. Folch, apparently realizing that Spain could not hold the area, indicated that he might consider an honorable negotiation in order to save face for his country. Yet once the filibusters returned home and the threat of immediate action subsided, he stopped negotiating with U.S. officials.[11]

Spain's hold on Florida or any other borderland territory could not withstand a concerted American attack, a situation its officials recognized full well. Since France dominated Iberia, Spain had no reinforcements to spare for far-flung military outposts, least of all unimportant ones in North America. South America, Mexico, and the Caribbean, where Spain's most valuable assets lay, merited a greater share of any available military or monetary resources. Therefore, diplomacy and occasional alliances with the Indians became the only weapons Spain held in this hemisphere. As long as peace was maintained, the Indians remained a potential force. Since Spain had only diplomacy and allies, Folch's actions demonstrated a superb example of defensive tact. His negotiations effectively stalled an invasion that surely would have led to Spain's loss of West Florida. Unrecognized Spanish minister Don Luis de Onís proceeded with yet an-

other version of this defensive action. Onís and probably a number of other Spanish officials argued that Spain's best recourse in the event Americans seized the territory would be to work for the return of lost lands with the settlement of the European war.[12] Remarkably, the Spanish succeeded in maintaining control over most of their North American territory until the European war ended. Had Spain's allies been victorious in the American version of the war, those lost lands probably would have been returned. Even territory included in the Louisiana Purchase, in Spain's eyes an illegal bargain, might have been retroceded.

Governor Folch was the first Spanish official to initiate negotiations regarding West Florida lands. In a letter to President Madison in December 1810, he wrote, "I have decided on delivering this province to the United States under an equitable capitulation, provided I do not receive succor from the ports of Havana or Vera Cruz during the present month."[13] The U.S. authorities at St. Stephens apparently received overtures about Folch's intentions even before the letter arrived in Washington.[14]

On 15 January 1811, Congress granted Madison's request to accept the governor's offer. That body also authorized the president to occupy the Floridas east of the Perdido River with the agreement of local Spanish authorities or if the area was threatened by another power. Moreover, Congress empowered Madison not only to use the army and navy but also to spend up to $100,000 to secure the area should a third power threaten an invasion.[15]

In late January 1811, Madison instructed General George Mathews, former governor of Georgia, and John McKee, Choctaw Indian agent, to arrange secretly the surrender of the Floridas. Mathews, given the authority to negotiate with any Florida official, could withdraw funds from banks in New Orleans and Savannah to pay passage for a Spanish garrison's evacuation from West or East Florida.[16] Soon after Madison appointed Mathews to this post, however, Folch withdrew his offer to negotiate. Not to be outdone, Mathews traveled to St. Mary's, Georgia, apparently hoping to negotiate with the governor of East Florida.[17] He was familiar with the situation in East Florida because many of the area's settlers were Georgians whom he already knew. No doubt he felt comfortable in dealing with these people.

When the British evacuated East Florida in 1784, large numbers of English residents moved to the Bahamas, leaving the area seriously underpopulated. In an effort to reestablish the colony, Spanish officials not only invited settlers to the region but also removed many of their usual trade restrictions to encourage immigration. As a result, Georgians and others from neighboring areas quickly settled in East Florida. In fact, so many Americans moved into East Florida that they became a majority in that province and established close relations with Savannah and Charleston. By 1804 the Spanish realized they had created a monster in their own colony and closed East Florida to additional American immigration.[18]

It is doubtful that Anglo-Americans in East Florida displayed any more loyalty to Spain than their fellow settlers living in the Baton Rouge district. A sizable number of Englishmen who had remained in East Florida after 1783, some of whom continued their illicit trade business with the Lower Creek and Seminole Indians, further exacerbated the situation. None of these groups felt loyalty to Spain. Since Spain's hold on the area was tenuous at best, East Florida, like the Gulf Coast, became a haven for outlaws, smugglers, and privateers. These groups often acted against Spanish commerce or smuggled goods into the United States and operated entirely beyond Spanish control. Thus, East Florida became a continuing source of trouble for both the United States and Spain.[19]

This turmoil in East Florida convinced Mathews to seize the colony. He still had authority to negotiate with the Spanish, and he also claimed to have secret orders from the president and the secretary of state. He apparently interpreted the president's orders as carte blanche to invade and capture East Florida. Although there might be some question as to whether or not the orders—assuming they really existed—actually invested Mathews with that much authority, he probably believed that he was doing exactly what President Madison wanted. Mathews maintained that he had orders authorizing his support of these American settlers in their efforts to overthrow Spanish rule and join the United States. Several people declared that they, too, had seen the orders, but officials in Washington later denied the existence of such documents. Mathews asserted that his instructions permitted him to occupy any part of Florida, providing that local authorities invited him to do so or that the territory was being invaded by a hostile power. Since the instructions did not define the meaning of "local authorities," he assumed, rightly or not, that these officials could be a revolutionary government. Should there be an uprising in East Florida, he interpreted this to mean that he could then accept the territory from the "new" gov-

ernment. This explains his motives for organizing and supporting the "Patriot Revolution."[20]

Mathews probably interpreted President Madison's wishes accurately and very likely had oral instructions from the government assuring him that his understanding of the orders was absolutely correct. There remains, of course, no written record to
substantiate this, although actions of the army, navy, and other
official branches of the government at both local and national
levels offer much circumstantial evidence supporting this conclusion. Madison probably knew—and completely approved—exactly what Mathews had planned. This provided an opportunity
for Madison to annex more land to the United States without
running the risk of war. If Mathews succeeded, the territory
could be quietly annexed; should there be complications or a
threat of war, the president could insist that Mathews had acted
without orders. In any case, Madison ventured nothing.[21]

Before setting out for St. Mary's, Georgia, in August 1811,
Mathews again attempted to persuade Spanish officials in Mobile
to relinquish their claim to the Floridas. Their refusal provided
Mathews the opportunity he was seeking to organize a frontier
group of Georgia-born settlers into a revolutionary army and furnish them with arms. These people, calling themselves patriots,
were to become the local authority in Florida. According to the
plan, as Mathews conceived it, this group of patriots would revolt
and seize East Florida. They could then represent the local
authority and ask to be annexed to the United States. This action
set no precedent because it practically duplicated what had happened in the Baton Rouge district when local residents revolted,
threw out the Spanish officials, and requested annexation. The
only difference was that the United States did not claim East Florida as part of the Louisiana Purchase.[22]

Mathews initially encountered major obstacles that delayed his
campaign for months. Major Jacint Laval, U.S. Army commander
at Point Peter, disagreed that the governor's orders authorized
him either to request assistance from the army or to invade Florida. Insisting that Mathews had exceeded his orders, Laval refused to cooperate in the venture.[23] Part of the difficulty between

the two men stemmed from the governor's refusal to show Laval a copy of his orders. Mathews did not trust Laval, so he proclaimed that his orders were secret.

When Secretary Monroe later removed Mathews and gave control of the operation to another Georgia governor, David B. Mitchell, he instructed army and navy forces to follow Mitchell's orders, seemingly in the exact same manner as those originally given to Mathews.[24] Despite Laval's objections, the patriots continued their invasion of Florida, and Laval was soon transferred, indicating once again that Mathews did have the full support of Washington. Laval's successor, Lieutenant Colonel Thomas A. Smith, not only permitted Mathews to invade Florida but eventually came to the aid of the invaders with American troops. Navy Captain Hugh Campbell, as commander of a squadron of gunboats on Cumberland Sound, also provided considerable aid in the capture of Fernandina and Amelia Island.[25]

Under Mathews's direction, East Florida inhabitants organized themselves into the "Republic of Florida," with General John H. McIntosh as their leader. McIntosh planned to take Amelia Island first and then move into all of East Florida.[26] The initial action began on 14 March 1812, when the patriots assembled on Rose's Bluff, about four miles from St. Mary's and directly across the sound from Fernandina. When such a large group gathered at the bluff, the alarmed islanders armed themselves to defend their town and homes. The following morning Captain Campbell anchored five gunboats off Fernandina. These boats, carrying 24- and 32-pounders, the largest guns in contemporary naval use, were obviously ready for action. Members of the rebel force, claiming not to be under Mathews's command, demanded the surrender of Fernandina. When town officials visited the American fort at Point Peter, they asked Colonel Smith whether the United States supported the invasion force. Smith refused to answer that question. As the islanders prepared to defend themselves on the morning of 16 March, gunboats anchored in the Fernandina harbor. They took aim at the town's defenders while crews stood ready with lighted matches.[27]

Mathews refused the town's offer to surrender, insisting that he was not in charge of the attack. As the invaders embarked on large boats obviously intending an amphibious assault, the islanders again tried to surrender, this time to Captain Campbell. He too refused to deal with the islanders, although he did inform Captain José López, commander of the small Spanish garrison at Fernandina, that the naval force's presence was "but to aid in support of a large proportion of your countrymen in arms, who have thought proper to declare themselves independent and are now in the act of calling on you to join in their undertaking."[28] It became apparent by this time that the U.S. government armed the attackers and that Captain Campbell's flagship determined the barges' sailing orders. Having exhausted all options, the islanders surrendered to the rebels, who immediately raised their flag over the fort. López quickly took stock of his inadequate force and realized his fort was too weak to withstand an attack by Campbell's gunboats. As a result, the captain surrendered and withdrew with his troops to St. Augustine.[29]

Campbell later claimed that his support for the action resulted from orders issued by President Madison. Although Mathews refused to share his instructions with Laval, he had shown them to Campbell. The captain not only felt compelled to obey the orders, since they originated from the president, but also interpreted them as directing him to support Mathews. Campbell's later correspondence with Secretary of the Navy Paul Hamilton indicated his concern about the situation. Even so, he did limit his support of the expedition when he ordered his gunboats not to fire on Fernandina unless fired upon first. In the event that the Spanish did fire, he instructed his officers to give a good account of themselves. Hamilton alleviated Campbell's situation on 8 April when he ordered the captain to withdraw from the action. Hamilton apparently issued the command because President Madison wished to avoid a confrontation with Spain at that time. The secretary, in direct contradiction to what Campbell believed, stated that Mathews's actions did not have the president's authorization, and, therefore, the captain should withdraw. The new orders did not condemn Campbell's action, nor did the tone of the letter indicate any displeasure on Hamilton's part. It is likely that the government fully authorized Mathews's actions but that the growing probability of war with Britain convinced Madison and his advisers to retreat from a possible conflict with Spain at that time.[30]

Soon after the capture, Mathews received assistance from Colonel Thomas Smith with a detachment of regular troops and a company of marines commanded by Captain John Williams. Supported by the availability of these forces, the patriot army advanced on St. Augustine. Leaving Amelia Island on 22 March, the army encamped near St. Augustine four days later. But even with these reinforcements, the patriots, now commanded by John H. McIntosh, had no more than two hundred men, a force greatly outnumbered by the Spanish garrison. McIntosh, not one to be intimidated by the enemy's greater strength, demanded that Governor Juan de Estrada surrender the city. Estrada's refusal to surrender initiated a siege that continued for more than a year.[31]

Mathews wrote Captain Campbell on 2 April that his patriot forces had gained control of all of East Florida as far as the walls of St. Augustine and had requested annexation to the United States. He also asked Campbell to blockade the Spanish city. Without a doubt Mathews sincerely believed that he had executed the president's orders and that East Florida would now be part of the United States.[32]

At this point, Secretary James Monroe removed Mathews's commission, claiming that the Georgia governor had exceeded his orders. According to Monroe, Mathews had not been authorized to take the territory of Florida unless that land had been voluntarily offered by the Spanish or threatened by invasion. Since neither situation existed, Mathews had acted without orders. It should be noted that in similar fashion to the orders from Secretary of the Navy Hamilton to Captain Campbell, Monroe's recall of Mathews expressed an extremely mild tone seemingly not intended as a reprimand. Yet when Madison wrote to Jefferson he insisted that Mathews completely ignored his orders, thus placing the United States in a "distressing dilemma."[33]

Probably Monroe's orders represented a real but perhaps tem-

James Monroe. Portrait by Asher B. Durand after Gilbert Stuart (Courtesy of the National Archives)

porary change in plans. With the shifting European situation and the course of events rapidly moving toward war with England, Monroe perhaps believed it advisable to terminate the operations in Florida for the immediate future. Certainly the United States did not want a serious conflict with Spain at the same time it might be entering a war with Britain.

An impending war with Britain, however, was not the only reason for the removal of Mathews. Opposition to such a conflict loomed large in the Northeast, as did the invasion of Florida. Madison undoubtedly felt compelled to maintain his own party's loyalty. Although Republicans held a majority in Congress, many of them opposed these expansionist overtones in Florida. Even

many southern and western representatives who normally supported expansion along the Gulf Coast did not approve of the
patriot revolution. Within Georgia, Governor Mitchell favored
the invasion, whereas General John Floyd opposed it. The latter,
along with a number of other southern leaders, wanted to seize
Florida openly with regular military forces. There were also numerous Republicans who felt that the United States should obtain Florida through diplomacy, not by an improper use of force
against Spain.[34]

This division among Republicans, as well as Federalist opposition, undoubtedly prevented Madison from seeking the necessary congressional support to annex Florida. The act Mathews
used as his authority for the invasion itself represented a compromise. The restriction that Florida could be occupied only if
local officials requested it or if Florida was threatened by an invasion resembled a diluted version of an earlier Florida occupation bill. The occupations of Baton Rouge and Mobile had been
justified because the United States insisted that these areas were
part of the Louisiana Purchase. The only claim the U.S. government could develop against East Florida was that the territory
could be payment for spoliation claims against Spain, a weak legal argument at best.[35]

In his book *Florida Fiasco*, Rembert Patrick argues that Monroe
removed Mathews because of the so-called John Henry letters.
John Henry was supposedly a British agent employed by Governor-
General James Craig of Canada to report on disaffection among
the New England states and to encourage that area to separate
from the United States and join Canada. The letters, obtained
by Republicans and published in the American press, resulted
in unfavorable Federalist publicity. If Republicans attacked Federalist activities and loyalties on the one hand and supported
Mathews's invasion of Florida on the other, they stood to look
even worse. Therefore, political necessity forced Madison to re-
pudiate Mathews.[36]

The action of the patriots could not be so easily dismissed. In
his public explanation, Campbell insisted that he had taken no
part in the invasion of Amelia Island, despite his letter to Hamil-

ton to the contrary. His gunboats, he claimed, were simply taking gunnery practice in the sound. When he saw the patriots' invasion in progress, he moved his gunboats closer to Fernandina simply to watch the landings. He never explained the unsuccessful blockade of St. Augustine. Monroe's dismissal letter reached Mathews only two days after the governor ordered Campbell to increase his blockade. As a result, the whole action might have been delayed and then called off.[37] Campbell's real situation is probably more accurately explained in his correspondence with Secretary of the Navy Hamilton, who denied that the captain had been given any order to support the patriots.[38]

The role of Mathews's associate Choctaw agent John McKee cannot be clearly defined. McKee apparently disapproved of Mathews's actions, as his name was never mentioned in the activities in East Florida. Although there is no evidence that McKee was a Spanish spy, he did carry on a continuous correspondence with the Innerarity brothers, partners in the John Forbes Company of Pensacola and Mobile. McKee expressed his disapproval of the invasion in a letter to James Innerarity written in April 1812. He wrote that the United States intended to take East Florida by force and that Spain could not prevent it so long as it was preoccupied in Europe. McKee regretted that he did not control the situation because he believed that he could settle the matter peacefully.[39]

The patriot victory completely disrupted any semblance of law and order in northeast Florida and left a state of anarchy in its wake. The Spanish concentrated their troops in the town of St. Augustine, thereby withdrawing any protection or authority for the outlying areas. The presence of bandits, undisciplined soldiers, and deserters, along with numerous belligerent Creeks and Seminoles roaming the vicinity, created a dangerous environment.[40]

When Secretary of State Monroe removed Mathews, East Florida was left in a state of chaos. Monroe, in an effort to restore order, appointed Governor Mitchell to assume command of the operation. Monroe's instructions to Mitchell—unlike those he issued to Mathews—are part of the public record, and they autho-

David Mitchell (Courtesy of the Georgia Department of Archives and History)

rized him to obtain assistance from the U.S. military forces. Monroe's actions regarding the orders represent a complete about-face. The secretary of state also instructed the governor to arrange a peaceful settlement with the Spanish, but he was not to withdraw U.S. troops from the region. The decision about troop removal was, however, left to Mitchell's discretion. Monroe did inform the governor that "it is not expected, if you find it proper to withdraw the troops, that you should not interfere with the Patriots."[41]

It soon became obvious that Madison and Monroe wanted neither to evacuate Florida nor to end the patriot war. Their strategy apparently was to mediate with Spanish Governor Kindelan and allow these negotiations to continue for a long period of time. Meanwhile, Monroe undoubtedly hoped the patriots would capture St. Augustine or that Congress would authorize U.S. forces to seize Florida officially. Failing all else, patriot pressure on Spanish forces might eventually compel them to surrender East Florida by diplomacy. The most immediate objective was to gain the territory, either by capture or, with a valid excuse, by invasion. Even though aided by navy gunboats and regular army troops, the patriots had not captured St. Augustine. Colonel Smith had no artillery, and Captain Campbell's gunboats could not effectively blockade the town. As a result, American forces lacked enough power to capture the position.[42]

Since Mitchell also had authority to use the army and navy, it is fairly evident that he was instructed to continue Mathews's work. His orders, nearly identical to those purportedly issued to Mathews, were vague enough to leave much to Mitchell's own judgment. Mathews's recall had two purposes: first, it was an act of political expediency; second, it would permit Mitchell to continue the existing operations as soon as the furor over the John Henry letters had subsided. Madison and Monroe, interested as ever in annexing East Florida, needed an overzealous expansionist to blame. Mathews became their scapegoat.

The government in Washington required a new list of grievances to continue its pursuit of territory in East Florida. There were always the spoliation claims against Spain, but the government had already realized its full potential from these demands. Thus, new grievances were needed. After the removal of Mathews, the best case entailed the need to protect the lives and property of the patriots, making sure that they were not punished by the Spanish officials once they restored Florida to its owners.[43]

Mitchell began negotiations with Governor Kindelan in an effort to convince the Spanish to pardon the patriots and not seize their property. Although Kindelan seemed to have been willing to do this from the beginning, he constantly delayed his communications. Meanwhile, Mitchell added new demands and insisted on guarantees, in fact so much so that Mitchell's real intent appeared to be to delay a settlement. The prolonging of these talks for many months was undoubtedly sanctioned by the Madison administration as it sought new excuses to seize Florida.[44]

East Florida, for years a haven for runaway slaves, had become home to numerous African-American settlements that either allied themselves with or even joined the Seminoles. When the patriots first invaded Florida, both blacks and Seminoles remained neutral, but as a result of Spanish persuasion and ill treatment afforded them by some patriots, they became hostile, especially those followers of Seminole chief Billy Bowlegs.[45] This enmity resulted in an increasing number of raids on farms and plantations in northern Florida. Their activities became such a serious threat that they were endangering settlers not only in Florida but in Georgia too. The marauders made no distinction between the farms and property of patriots and those loyal to the Spanish government. American citizens, blaming this animosity on Florida officials, viewed the situation as yet another grievance against Spanish rule, and correctly so, for Indian alliances had always been crucial to Spain's defense of Florida. Moreover, Spanish officials had encouraged the Indians to attack.[46]

Another American grievance regarded Spain's use of black troops recruited from runaway slaves and from regular Spanish forces from Cuba. The seizure of Baton Rouge and then the invasion of East Florida and the Mobile district outraged Spanish authorities. Although it commanded only a few military resources, especially in North America, Spain was nevertheless proud and its leaders wanted to defend the Spanish colonies. Thus the Spanish used all the troops they could muster, regardless of color. These forces not only caused great alarm in neighboring Georgia but produced fear and anger in much of the United States. Georgians and other southerners feared that the example of Florida's soldiers would incite a slave rebellion. Blacks were not encouraged to think of themselves as successful soldiers, since that would almost guarantee a slave revolt, or so southerners thought. Mitchell, other Georgia leaders, and those in neighboring southern states protested vehemently to Spanish authorities about using these troops. Southerners considered this uncivilized action, and violent rumors of atrocities against women and children spread throughout Georgia.[47]

Excuses needed to justify reinforcing the Americans and patriots were not long in coming. The Seminoles and blacks, never friendly to border whites, commenced hostilities. Although Mitchell continued negotiating with the Spaniards, it soon became apparent that he too was in no hurry to settle matters, especially since the Florida authorities were supplying Americans with enough complaints for Smith to keep his forces in Florida. At one point during the negotiations, Spanish troops even fired on Smith's camp. In retaliation, Americans tried to seize a position on Moosa Creek in an effort to prevent supplies from reaching St. Augustine. During the melee the Spanish sent soldiers and an armed schooner that fired its guns and landed men, forcing the Americans to evacuate the place. Mitchell used this attack as an additional excuse to break off negotiations.[48]

Mitchell delayed a settlement because he anticipated that the government would legalize the seizure of Florida. Legislation introduced in Congress would have, if passed, annexed all of Florida. When the bill eventually failed, Monroe advised the governor to make the best possible arrangements with the Spanish authorities to protect the patriots and evacuate American troops. Instead, Mitchell protested the orders and sent reinforcements to Florida. Monroe took no additional action to force Mitchell's withdrawal. No doubt the secretary decided not to press Mitchell further because he had once again entered into negotiations with Onís. Moreover, Georgia Senator William Crawford, a man of considerable influence in Washington, also pressured the administration to intervene in Florida. Monroe, therefore, chose to be deliberately slow and vague.[49]

When the Seminoles and their black allies undertook action against the patriots, they only occasionally raided farms and plantations of white settlers in northern Florida. It was, however, not long before this irregular force threatened American supply lines. A band of some fifty to seventy blacks and Seminoles

attacked Captain Williams and a wagon train with a detachment of twenty men on 12 September 1812. During the ensuing
battle the renegades killed Williams and a sergeant, wounded six
others, and captured the wagons; the remaining soldiers escaped.
Although many accounts of this action described the attackers
as untrained maroons, other reports offered considerable evidence that these men belonged to the regular Spanish militia, trained by black Haitian General Jorge Biassou. Biassou, his
family, and his staff had been evacuated to St. Augustine when
the Spanish withdrew from Santo Domingo. The general later
trained a number of East Florida free blacks as light infantry.
After his death, Jorge Jacobo, Biassou's brother-in-law and former staff member, undertook this task. Jacobo and his father-in-
law, Prince Witen, the leader of runaway slaves from the United
States, became commanders of the Spanish black militia in East
Florida, as well as the men who planned and led the attack on
Williams's wagon train. The loss of this wagon train and the obvious threat to the patriot supply line precipitated the withdrawal
of U.S. forces from the siege of St. Augustine.[50]

In the meantime, Mitchell sent Colonel Daniel Newnan with a
force of two hundred Georgia volunteers to assist Smith and the
patriots. Although Mitchell, like nearly all other southern gover-
nors, wanted to drive the Spanish from Florida, his more immediate concern was the news that they had landed a large force of
Cuban troops at St. Augustine. The presence of such a large force
threatening nearby Georgia triggered Mitchell's apprehension.
Soon after he arrived there, Newnan conducted unsuccessful
raids on several Seminole villages. Following the elusive Indians
into the swamps, the Americans, hungry and near defeat, stag-
gered out of the wilderness with no more than a fruitless search
to show for their trouble. Even though many of his men became
sick and almost half were unfit for duty, Newnan still attempted
to punish the Seminoles for their attacks. Not only did his actions
fail to accomplish the objective, but Newnan ran out of supplies
and nearly lost his entire force.[51]

Newnan's failure and the illness of so many troops created a
crisis in Florida. Nearby Georgians feared a slave revolt in their

own state to such an extent that in November the state legislature authorized the governor to muster the militia should it be necessary to protect the state's border. Moreover, citizens in the area were assured that this group could be used in Florida if needed. A similar force was activated in East Tennessee, and these troops, along with some from Georgia, began moving into Florida.[52]

Although there were undoubtedly legal questions concerning these militia troops, the government in Washington raised no protest. President Madison and Secretary of State Monroe failed to control the forces because they deemed it inevitable that the United States would eventually occupy all of Florida. By the end of February, General Wilkinson organized a force to capture Mobile and West Florida while General Andrew Jackson and two thousand West Tennessee volunteers marched south in support. Apparently the president and his advisers had by this time decided to take Florida by force. Madison had at last persuaded Republicans to introduce a bill in Congress authorizing the seizure of Florida. With all indications that the bill would pass, Madison and Monroe made preparations. No doubt this was the action they had long anticipated, as it makes plausible their failure to force Mitchell to evacuate East Florida.[53]

The plan to seize Florida was not new. The bill authorizing Mathews's occupation of the area resembled the diluted annexation bill, and the current action was nothing more than a revival of the old one. Madison believed the new bill would pass, since Republicans controlled a majority of Congress. He naturally assumed they would all vote for the bill. Surprisingly, a number of northern Republicans, dissatisfied with America's failure to take Canada, saw no reason why the South should benefit from annexing Florida. In fact, Albert Gallatin wrote Monroe that a conflict in order to obtain East Florida would "disgust every man north of Washington." Enough Republicans ignored party loyalty and voted with Federalists to defeat the bill.[54]

Since Congress derailed Madison's attempt to annex Florida, the government could only withdraw U.S. troops; however, Mobile, West Florida, would remain in American control. The administration instructed the patriots to terminate operations in

Florida. General Thomas Flournoy, later replaced by General Thomas Pinckney, continued to negotiate with Governor Kindelan to settle the patriot affair. Pinckney, as commander of the Sixth Military District, an area including Georgia, reached an agreement with Kindelan: the patriots, misled and "seduced" by Mathews, would be protected from Spanish punishment. Additionally, U.S. forces would be withdrawn from East Florida.[55]

Kindelan's decisions were obviously influenced by the patriot siege of St. Augustine, because the action had been conducted not only with the cooperation of American forces but also with their active support. When Pinckney offered to withdraw U.S. troops in exchange for a promise not to punish the rebels, Kindelan quickly agreed. This provided the governor with a way to save East Florida with honor. The troops finally withdrew from the Florida mainland and Amelia Island on 16 April.[56]

Spain's inability to restore order to Florida again left the area in a state of anarchy. As a result, authorities gladly accepted almost any help to maintain at least official Spanish sovereignty over the region. Adventurers controlled most of East Florida, and although the patriots may have withdrawn their headquarters to Georgia, they continued to instigate trouble in the area. Many of the bandits were probably "patriot" raiders.

It appears that the United States chose to terminate the patriot war only because the war with England made it desirable to avoid simultaneous conflict with Spain. Although Spanish Florida posed no threat to the United States, its territory would make an excellent base for a British attack on the lower South. This situation, already obvious to many Americans, soon became apparent to the British. The War of 1812 with England brought no peace to East Florida. Instead, it fanned the flames of Indian hostilities, intensifying an already strained situation. After the war, a revitalized group of patriots with new leadership and an international flavor added to the region's uncertainty. Their objectives, however, remained much the same, and next time they would succeed.[57]

CHAPTER FIVE

"Pacified by Paternal Solitude": Indian Wars as an Expansionist Movement

PENNSYLVANIA REPUBLICAN Charles Jared Ingersoll, speaking to a Philadelphia audience on 4 July 1812, predicted tremendous geographic and commercial expansion for the country. Mesmerizing his listeners, he described a United States that was industrially vibrant, stretched to the Pacific Ocean, and where "the Indians were pacified by 'paternal solitude.'" Ingersoll, however, was addressing a group that was more concerned with industrial development than with Jefferson's agrarian ideals. Nonetheless, expansion and conquest of the Indians would have to occur if the country was to grow as Ingersoll predicted. In fact, a major part of the country's development during the Jeffersonian period resulted from territorial expansion at the expense of Native Americans.[1]

The appropriation of Indian lands remained as much a policy of the Jefferson, Madison, and Monroe governments as the seizure of the borderlands. Actually, it represented a much older policy that had begun with European contact during the earliest colonial times and has continued well into the twentieth century. Although Indian lands were considered to lie within the boundaries of the United States, they were of little use and could not be taken until the native inhabitants were either removed, killed, or assimilated into the white nation.

The South and Northwest supported territorial expansion into

82

Indian lands. These areas not only included the main agricultural lands, but they were also the regions that had the most direct contact with the native inhabitants. Although these leaders wanted to appropriate Indian lands for their own security, they also had economic and political motives. Furthermore, the groups and regions who protested the unfair treatment afforded the Indians and the seizure of their lands remained much the same as those who opposed territorial expansion in general. Just as the South and Northwest could envision economic and political gain from expansion, the Northeast anticipated a decline in its political influence.[2]

The War of 1812 is usually described as a conflict between Britain and the United States over issues of impressment of seamen and the seizure of American ships and cargoes. Although impressment and violations of American neutrality certainly created controversy along the Atlantic seaboard, territorial expansion and the pacification of Indians antagonistic to those goals seemed more pressing concerns for southern and western frontiersmen and farmers. They became the emotional issues that historians such as Julius Pratt consider of secondary importance. Yet, if these were in fact secondary issues, why then did the South and Northwest strongly support that war and the Northeast bitterly oppose it? Ships belonging to residents of the Northeast and the seamen on those vessels were, after all, the victims of violations of the neutrality laws.[3]

The probable answer is really not that complex. The seized ships were usually released, and, although the cargoes were often sold at Halifax, Nova Scotia, for a poor price, the money was frequently returned to the shippers. Shipowners lost money and the use of their vessels for an extended period; yet they still made a handsome profit from the war in Europe. In reality, southern and western farmers became the true losers because they received low prices for their products as a result of the seizures.[4]

The impressed seamen were frequently foreigners or Americans, both African Americans and Caucasians, of the poorest social classes. Their losses, though inconvenient for northeastern businessmen, hardly provided a reason to go to war and lose a large profit. To southerners and northwesterners who knew little about seamen or sea culture, these men were still Americans, and impressment greatly offended their sense of honor.[5]

Although national honor was certainly important in the South and West, where duels and feuds were still fought over minor points of personal and family honor, there were also other motives for supporting a war with England. Many throughout the region believed that the recent Indian hostilities resulted from foreign intrigues and that eliminating British influence in Canada and Spanish control over Florida was the only way to obtain peace with the natives. Actually, later history clearly demonstrated that an American occupation of Florida and/or Canada would not have brought lasting peace with these Native Americans; it would, however, have made them less dangerous and, therefore, easier to control.[6]

It is not certain whether the Northeast's fear of losing political power and influence or its concern over declining profits represented the main reason for opposing the War of 1812. Despite the motives, many of the region's leaders had come to realize the growing power of the South and West. Perhaps they also understood that Indian removal would allow expansion into the borderlands, thereby opening more territory for settlement. If that occurred, the Northeast's political influence would continue to erode. This rationale surely provided motivation for opposing expansion and demanding better treatment for Native Americans.[7]

It is impossible to determine if Indian control and removal encouraged southern and western support of the war. Regardless, the war isolated the Indians from foreign support and allowed the defeat of the Creeks, the Shawnees, and their allies. The destruction of Spanish power in Florida between 1812 and 1821 and the subsequent cession of that province soon thereafter eliminated nearly all European support for the southern Indians.[8]

Spain had used the southern Indians prior to the War of 1812 as an intricate part of its Florida defenses. Yet that country's inability to offer any serious help to the Creeks and Seminoles during the War of 1812 virtually destroyed Spanish credibility with these groups. Article Nine of the Treaty of Ghent supposedly restored the lands of all of England's Indian allies to their antebellum status quo. Instead, this provision was not enforced, and afterward the British government completely abandoned its former Indian friends. In fact, unofficial support to the Creeks in their dispute with the United States concerning Article Nine resulted in the execution of the British trader Alexander Arbuthnot. Ultimately, the loss of foreign support weakened Indian power in the South to the point that removal or death became the only options.[9]

The Napoleonic Wars had preoccupied Europeans and allowed the United States to acquire Louisiana and use its undefined boundaries as an excuse to expand into Spanish Florida and Texas. That conflict also permitted Americans to continue pressuring the Indians to cede more land. U.S. policy since the days of Washington's administration had attempted to force Indians to sell their lands for money or worthless trade goods. It was in the face of such aggression and loss of tribal hunting grounds that a growing Indian resistance emerged to confront the white man's endless land hunger. The government responded by trying to assimilate Native Americans into white culture: teach the Indians agriculture and they would need less land. Although this policy had some success, it also stirred considerable resentment among Indians who saw their culture and religion being destroyed.[10]

This assimilation policy, along with the intrusions of Christian missionaries active among the various tribes and the opening of the Federal Road in 1810, soon became points of contention between Native Americans and the U.S. government. These also produced tremendous internal Indian conflict because, although many Native Americans were quite willing to accept the path of the white man, others were adamant about retaining their own style of life. Some months before the beginning of the War of 1812, these factors had so divided the Indian community, especially the southern tribes, that they were already embroiled in hostilities.[11]

One major character in this bitter division was Tecumseh, a Native American with enormous powers of persuasion. Tecumseh himself was an interesting person. He and his brother, Tenskwatawa (also known as the Prophet), were sons of a Shawnee father and a Creek mother. Although they lived with their father's people in present-day Indiana and Michigan, they carried a strong Creek heritage, especially since Creek lineage followed their mother's lines. In the Northwest, Tecumseh and his followers were responsible for revitalizing Indian nativism and culture among the Shawnees and a number of their neighboring tribes. Tecumseh created a pan-Indian confederation to resist both assimilation and encroachments on their native lands. The northwestern Indians had been forced by provisions of the Treaties of Greenville (1795) and of Fort Wayne (1803 and 1809) to cede much of their land. In 1810 and 1811 there were new attempts to force them to relinquish additional territory. These attacks helped popularize Tecumseh's preachings, messages calling for nothing less than the rejection of the white man's way. Tecumseh instructed his people to spurn the plow and loom and return to the hunt. They should discard the gun for their native bow and arrow. These ideas, although nativistic, never gained widespread support among his followers. Usually the only Indians who fought with bows and arrows were either out of ammunition or had no usable firearm.[12]

William Henry Harrison advanced on Prophetstown and was attacked by Tenskwatawa's followers in November 1811, at the Battle of Tippecanoe. Although this conflict broke Tecumseh's hope of a great confederation, it did not end Indian belligerence in the North. If anything, the Battle of Tippecanoe drove Tecumseh and his followers closer to Great Britain. The War of 1812 gave the Indians yet another chance to defeat the Americans, but probably at the expense of becoming English pawns.[13]

British policy toward the natives changed in the war's aftermath. Before the conflict, Britain had supported the northern Indians as part of its Canadian defenses. Additionally, both legal and illegal English traders had been active in the South, especially in Spanish Florida. Following the war, Britain's policy toward the United States became more conciliatory as the British decided to rely on diplomacy rather than force to protect Canada. This change indicated that Indian alliances were useless and even harmful because they aroused American suspicion and enmity. Afterward the British abandoned their former Indian allies, leaving them at the tender mercies of white settlers on the American frontier.[14]

The defeat of the Creek Indians during the War of 1812 and the weakening of the other southern tribes consequently led to their removal. It also allowed American expansion into the borderlands of the South and Southwest. In 1811 Tecumseh visited the Creek Nation with his message of hostility against the white man. Although he did persuade many Creeks to abandon the white man's culture and return to their traditional ways, others did not choose this path. Those who did not heed the Shawnee leader's message were soon engaged in a civil war with the rest of their Nation.[15]

The main issue dividing the Creeks was that a number of them had accepted the leadership of U.S. Indian agent Benjamin Hawkins. The agent's orders, signed by President Jefferson, instructed him to persuade the Indians to forgo hunting and accept farming and cattle raising as a means of livelihood. Hawkins, whose main base of operation was near present-day Macon, Georgia, strongly supported these orders because those vocations required less land. He also believed—like Jefferson, his immediate successors, and probably most of official Washington—that assimilation provided the only humane solution to the Indian problem. Furthermore, it would benefit the Indians by bringing "civilization" and an improvement over their "savage" way of life.[16]

Although some Americans had sincere, humane reasons for supporting assimilation, no doubt others in the movement harbored very specific political motives. Jefferson himself wrote that "when they . . . cultivate small spots of earth, and see how useless their extensive forests are, they will sell" their lands. Frontiersmen, too, seemed generally pleased with the prospect of assimilating the Indians because it would open additional lands for settlement. Integrating Native Americans into white society allowed an obvious continuation of the expansion movement that had become so important to the South and Southwest. Besides, it would not provide northeastern enemies of expansion with a moral reason for opposing the confiscation of Indian lands or for blocking westward growth. Unfortunately for these people, many Indians such as Tecumseh and his followers believed in fighting to the death to prevent the movement from destroying their culture.[17]

Those Creeks loyal to Tecumseh's nativism attempted to force their views on the entire Nation. This conflict resulted in a bloody Creek civil war that eventually merged with the larger War of 1812. The conflict among the Creeks, however, had more than just cultural causes. British and Spanish influences, resulting from American efforts to expand into the borderlands, played a major role in producing and perpetuating the conflict.[18]

The belligerent Creeks, or Red Sticks as they became known, came to dominate the majority of Upper Creeks, or those who lived on the Alabama River system. Although Tecumseh's message prompted the Red Sticks to join his pan-Indian confederation, it had less effect on the Lower Creeks, who lived on the Flint and Chattahoochee Rivers in Georgia. Though not swayed by Tecumseh's message, the Lower Creeks did have genuine grievances against American settlers in Georgia. Moreover, they were also influenced by several foreign groups, including a number of British merchants. Even though British predominance played a role, Lower Creek malevolence was more likely encouraged from Pensacola. When Spanish officials in that isolated city believed the United States was about to invade Florida, the southern Indians became the first line of defense.[19]

Although foreign intrigues and Tecumseh's message certainly influenced Creeks, perhaps equally important was the completion in 1810 of the Federal Road, which crossed directly through their territory. This road extended from Georgia across the Creek Nation to new white settlements in the western part of present-day Alabama. Its completion permitted a constant stream of white settlers to move into territory west of the

Nation. The Creeks felt great alarm because they were now sur-rounded by the whites and feared additional encroachments upon their lands.[20]

Lower Creeks and their Seminole brethren in Florida un-doubtedly felt more concerned about relations with Great Brit-ain than with Tecumseh. The Shawnee leader's belligerent words fostered a split so intense between the Upper and Lower Creeks that the lower tribe remained at peace when the upper tribe be-came embroiled in civil war in 1811. Although this peace was largely an illusion, it led Americans to believe all Lower Creeks were friendly. In reality nothing could have been further from the truth. The Lower Creeks were not influenced by Tecumseh but rather by the British; thus, when their English friends en-tered the war against the United States, the Lower Creeks joined the redcoats as they arrived on the Gulf Coast.[21]

The Spanish role in this conflict is more significantly related to territorial expansion. When the United States seized Mobile from Spanish forces in 1813, the governor of West Florida called on the Creeks to help repel the Americans. Although the seizure of Mobile represented another encroachment against Spanish territory, it became even more important as the Spanish encour-aged Indian hostility, causing explosive American reaction.[22]

On 14 April 1812, four days after Louisiana's entrance into the Union, Congress incorporated Mobile and its surrounding area into the Mississippi Territory. It is probable that the U.S. Con-gress did not really intend to change the status of Mobile at that time, because war with England appeared a distinct possibility. More likely, however, the government believed that the admission of Louisiana would strengthen the U.S. along the Gulf Coast. Congress did not want to relinquish its title to Mobile, a claim that could be traced to the Louisiana Purchase. But at the same time, any attempt to include the territory in the state of Louisi-ana would force the government to take a stand on its assertion. Perhaps those interested in the Gulf Coast believed that assign-ing Mobile to another territory, such as the Mississippi Territory, would not necessarily change the status quo. At this point, Con-gress's thinking as a body is unclear. It is likely, however, that

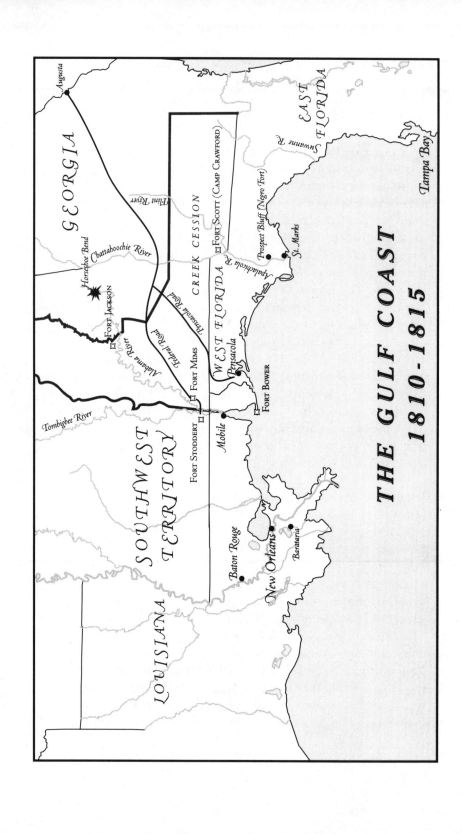

THE GULF COAST
1810-1815

indecision about Mobile may have resulted from sectional divisions within its own ranks.[23]

Governor David Holmes of the Mississippi Territory was not officially informed of the change in Mobile's status, nor was he given any information concerning the district at this time. In fact, he did not discover that the Mobile district had been added to his Mississippi Territory until he read a newspaper account reporting the congressional action. He was not given any official notification of Mobile's changed status or any official instructions concerning his relationship to the territory until it was finally occupied by the United States. Holmes, an aggressive frontier governor, began organizing the Mobile district once it became part of his domain. He appointed officials, including a sheriff for Mobile County, to control the territory. He also divided the region into militia districts and established a city government for Mobile. Although he took these steps on his own authority, he did not try to enforce his jurisdiction.[24]

By the end of the summer of 1812, Holmes's actions had created a dangerous and unusual situation. The United States and England were at war, and Holmes was risking a conflict with Spain as well. Fort Charlotte in the city of Mobile contained a Spanish garrison of 130 men. Although this force was not strong enough to expel the Americans from the territory, its presence provided a source of danger and potential trouble. The United States made no official effort to seize the Spanish fort, nor did the Spaniards interfere with the Americans. This strange situation lasted until April 1813, when Secretary of War John Armstrong ordered General James Wilkinson to oust the Spanish garrison. The original orders issued in February to Wilkinson instructed him to occupy both Mobile and Pensacola and may have resulted from an American's killing of a cow owned by the Spanish. The second part of the order was canceled soon after the general arrived at Mobile; U.S. forces occupied only the territory west of the Perdido River.[25]

Wilkinson arrived in Mobile on 11 April 1813 with eight hundred men and five gunboats. The gunboats cut communication with Pensacola from the sea while the troops surrounded the fort from the landward side. Wilkinson's force, strengthened by four hundred additional men from nearby Fort Stoddert, completely surrounded the Spanish position, isolating it from any hope of assistance. In the face of such limited options, Captain Cayetano Pérez, who commanded the Spanish garrison, surrendered on 13 April 1813. Pérez and his troops were evacuated to Pensacola with their personal weapons and equipment; Spanish cannon and munitions remained within the fort.[26]

The seizure of the Mobile district was the most flagrant U.S. attack on Spanish territory up to that time. With the exception of the action in the patriot war when U.S. regulars temporarily intervened, ostensibly to protect the lives and property of American citizens, all attacks on Spanish territory had been perpetrated by filibusters or rebels. But the seizure of Mobile was executed by regular U.S. forces. This could have resulted in a full-scale conflict had Spain not been so weakened by the war in Europe and preoccupied by revolt in its more important colonies to the south.

Luis de Onís believed that his country could hope to retain Florida only through diplomacy. He bitterly opposed any effort to defend Florida with military forces because he considered that such a defense would be hopeless. Spanish resistance, he argued, might cause a needless and futile loss of life. He concluded that diplomacy could accomplish what military force could not. Therefore, his country should, at all costs, maintain good relations with the United States. Using such logic, Onís made only a mild protest to the U.S. government when its forces occupied Mobile.[27]

Onís also opposed any alliance with either the Indians or Great Britain. The Indians were not strong enough to assist Spain. An Indian war would also draw the full wrath of the United States upon the poorly defended Florida territory. British assistance would be equally dangerous. Should Spain allow Great Britain to occupy Florida, the Spanish would become embroiled in a full-scale war with the United States. Onís saw no advantages in either situation. His only realistic recourse was diplomacy. He believed that if Britain won the war, then Florida and Louisiana

Juan Ruíz Apodaca. Reproduced from Vicente Riva Palacio's *México a través de los siglos* (Barcelona, 1889)

would be returned to Spain. If the United States won, all would be lost, especially if Spain were a British ally. In short, Onís believed Spain had nothing to gain and everything to lose should it use any force to defend Florida.[28]

Juan Ruíz Apodaca, the captain general of Cuba, whose province included East and West Florida, did not agree with Onís. Apodaca, a military man, believed that Spanish honor required defending Florida. Although he had no illusions that Florida could be held against the United States with the limited forces available, he did not want to give up without a fight. He seems to have believed, like Onís, that if Britain won the war, all of Spain's Florida and Louisiana lands would be returned. The captain general apparently believed that a military defense or even an honorably fought defeat would not lessen Spain's chances of getting its territory returned through diplomacy. It would also, he concluded, improve Spain's reputation and win for it respect.[29]

Like Onís, Apodaca did not want British help in defending Florida. He completely opposed such an idea. The captain general seemed to believe, and probably with good reason, that if British troops were landed in Florida they would never leave. If the United States won the war and British troops had been based in Florida, Americans could use this as an excuse to seize the region. Apodaca realized that he did not have the forces to prevent the British from landing in Florida if they chose to do so, but if they landed against Spanish will, they might be persuaded to relinquish the territory after the war. He also believed that an uninvited landing would not produce a hostile reaction by the United States. Given these beliefs, an Indian alliance was the only possible assistance Spain could expect, but Spain lacked war materials with which to arm the Indians. The Spanish were actually critically short of all types of stores, and their own Florida garrison was nearly out of supplies and without pay or uniforms.[30]

Governor Mauricio Zúñiga called the Indians to a meeting at Pensacola soon after the Americans seized Mobile. He wanted to plan for future actions against the United States. But the Spanish call for aid was misunderstood by Indians who believed the meeting would be a plea to commence hostilities. The Lower Creeks eventually received the correct message and waited for their British friends to come to their aid. Upper Creeks used this as an excuse to begin attacking whites.[31]

Not only were the Spanish unable to aid their allies, but when Indian delegations arrived at Pensacola, Zúñiga had been replaced by Governor Don Mateo González Manrique. The new governor had no knowledge of the invitation or any instructions concerning the Indians. Although Manrique soon concurred with Zúñiga's ideas, the communication lapse hurt both the Indians' feelings and the success of the Spanish cause. They left

Pensacola angry and without any quantity of supplies. Worst of all, they had already started hostilities and thus alerted Americans to the impending danger. The Indians had begun a war with little or nothing with which to fight.[32]

In the late summer of 1813, Creeks attacked the American settlement at Fort Mims, destroying the place and killing at least 250 friendly Indians and whites who had taken refuge there. This massacre began the Creek Indian War, a conflict that lasted until the following spring, when Andrew Jackson administered a resounding defeat at Horseshoe Bend.[33]

Spanish aid to the Creeks ultimately resulted in a disaster. Spain's feeble efforts provided just enough success to convince the United States that Spain had instigated the Creek War. Many Americans blamed that country for the Fort Mims massacre. Moreover, U.S. forces captured from the Creeks documents signed by Governor González Manrique praising the Indians for their success at Fort Mims and indicating Spanish backing for the war.[34] These records, combined with later official Indian support, convinced Americans that Spain and Britain had allied and that in Florida, at least, Spain had actually participated in the war. There is no doubt that General Andrew Jackson considered Spain to be at war with the United States, and this provided one reason for capturing Pensacola in 1814.[35]

Although Jackson and most American historians considered that the Battle of Horseshoe Bend ended the Creek War, in reality it did not. Jackson thought, or perhaps hoped, that by forcing the friendly Creeks and a few captured Red Sticks to sign the Treaty of Fort Jackson, an agreement that ceded most Creek lands to the United States, the war would cease.[36] Horseshoe Bend, however, only concluded the first part of the Creek conflict. About a thousand of the most antagonistic Red Stick followers of Tecumseh, under the direct leadership of Peter McQueen and Josiah Francis, fled into Florida and camped around Pensacola.[37]

In June 1814, British Major Edward Nicolls, commander of a small detachment of Royal Marines, established an operational base at Prospect Bluff near the mouth of the Apalachicola River.

Nicolls began arming and training the Lower Creeks, who had patiently waited for their ally. After Nicolls arrived he learned of a large number of Red Sticks encamped around Pensacola. Along with this news he also received a request from Governor Manrique to provide British forces with help in defending Pensacola against an expected American attack.[38] This plea, issued by Manrique on his own authority, apparently was counter to those he received from his superior, the captain general of Cuba. Even though Manrique violated orders, Apodaca took no action against the governor at this time or made any comment concerning this violation.[39]

Nicolls, acting on this invitation, took most of his troops to Pensacola and reorganized the Red Sticks there. He also raised a substantial detachment of troops from among the town's Spanish slave population. Soon thereafter, he led an unsuccessful attack on the American position at Fort Bowyer at Mobile Point. Following this assault, Nicolls and his force of Indians and marines retreated to Pensacola.[40] Manrique, after much consideration, decided against asking Nicolls and the British navy to defend the town. With the Spanish decision, Nicolls withdrew to his base at Prospect Bluff.

Jackson considered Spain responsible for the attack on Fort Bowyer and retaliated by attacking Pensacola on 7 November 1814. Although the general did not believe Spanish forces in Pensacola to be strong, he was unsure what action would be taken by the British warships still in the city's harbor. Wishing to avoid casualties, Jackson used a ruse. He established his camp in the woods west of Pensacola, causing Governor Manrique to place his troops in a position to defend that side of the city. The general then moved most of his troops through the woods at night to the east side of the town, where he arrived at sunrise. He attacked immediately, catching the Spanish out of position and the British fleet out of firing range. The Spanish offered only token resistance, as they were out of position and very short of supplies. The resultant battle lasted only a short time.[41]

Governor Manrique reported to his superiors that he had only 268 men at Pensacola and that his supply situation was unmanageable. He insisted that with such a limited force he had no choice other than to surrender. Actually, the governor possessed at least 200 additional men in nearby Fort Barrancas and countless men at other smaller forts around the harbor. Manrique did not want to admit that he had more men and supplies in these forts—enough strength to offer more than token resistance. Spanish authorities always blamed local commanders for defeat, even when they lacked adequate means of defending themselves. Manrique was certainly aware of the court-martial of Cayetano Peréz, the commander who surrendered Mobile to the United States in April 1813. Thus, his report was probably intended to show his superiors just how hopeless resistance might have been. Furthermore, his own reputation would be protected were it absolutely clear no other options existed.[42]

There is little doubt that Jackson, well known as a supporter of expansion, wanted to hold Pensacola. The general and certainly the Madison administration surely wanted to keep the city. Nonetheless, other considerations preempted a permanent occupation and possession of the town. General John Coffee, Jackson's second-in-command, believed that the general would have held Pensacola had the British not destroyed the forts guarding the harbor, thereby making the town nearly indefensible. A more likely explanation for evacuating was that Jackson received a report of an impending British assault on the Gulf. From the information available, he had good reason to believe that the British planned to attack New Orleans through Lake Pontchartrain. Jackson already knew of a proposed British assault on New Orleans via Mobile and the Mississippi Sound, so this report probably did not surprise him. The information did, however, convince him that the invasion was imminent. He therefore needed all the men he could muster in Mobile and New Orleans. This information probably persuaded him to evacuate Pensacola and march with most of his force for Mobile.[43]

Governor Manrique gave no additional support to the British afterward and apparently had no choice but to cooperate with the United States. Jackson would almost certainly return if the place were again used as an English base. Because Spanish forces at Pensacola were well treated by Jackson's army after the surrender, their hurried evacuation left no lasting anger among the townspeople. But perhaps the most significant part of the attack was that it demonstrated that the British could not protect Florida, and therefore they were an unwelcome force to have based in Pensacola. While stationed in the town, the British governed the place according to their own wishes. They mistreated the civilian population and acted more like an occupying force than an ally. Furthermore, when the British evacuated they demolished some of the Spanish forts and carried off many of the slaves belonging to the people of Pensacola. This slave stealing, part of a British plan to raise regiments of black troops to occupy New Orleans after the conquest, caused great anger among the people of Pensacola. Even though the majority of Pensacola's inhabitants were former British loyalists who settled there during the American Revolution, the army's actions apparently produced an anti-British sentiment so strong that these people apparently welcomed annexation to the United States a few years later.[44]

After Nicolls returned to his base at Prospect Bluff, he organized a large force of blacks and Indians for the purpose of overrunning the interior of Georgia and the Mississippi Territory. Fortunately for Americans, the signing of the Treaty of Ghent soon interrupted this plan.[45] According to Article Nine, all British Indian allies with whom the United States might be at war at the time of the signing of the peace treaty would have their rights and lands restored as they had existed in 1811. This provision depended on the Indians' agreement to cease hostilities and also assumed that the Creek lands taken under auspices of the Treaty of Fort Jackson would be restored. This apparently represented the English view, and it was completely logical considering that only one or two of the hostile Red Stick chiefs had signed the Treaty of Fort Jackson. Also, more than a thousand Creeks had joined the British at Prospect Bluff, where Nicolls assured them that their lands would be returned.[46]

When Vice Admiral Alexander Inglis Cochrane received news of the Treaty of Ghent, he decided to leave Nicolls, the marines, and a detachment of West Indian troops at Prospect Bluff until some final settlement occurred. As commander of British forces in North America, Cochrane planned the operations along the Gulf Coast near New Orleans, supplied the Indians with arms, and recruited numerous black troops from the runaway slave population. He also strengthened Prospect Bluff by landing substantial supplies of food and equipment.[47] Cochrane ordered Nicolls to remain at Prospect Bluff until peace was concluded and Indian lands were returned, but he did not expect this occupation to continue for a long time. The admiral never considered that the U.S. government would ignore the provisions of Article Nine unless it rejected the entire treaty. Therefore, his orders only considered that the entire treaty would be accepted or that a full-scale war would resume.[48]

Cochrane's orders made it clear that Nicolls should remain at Apalachicola until the United States restored Creek lands. In addition to the marines and a detachment of West Indian troops, the admiral deployed several warships under Admiral Pultney Malcolm's command to protect the Indian position. Cochrane instructed Malcolm to leave cannon and military supplies at Prospect Bluff for the Indians.[49] In late March 1815, Malcolm learned that the Treaty of Ghent had been ratified. Like Cochrane, he assumed Article Nine would be implemented, and he instructed Nicolls to withdraw his troops and embark with them for Bermuda. The major faced conflicting orders, having first been instructed to stay at Prospect Bluff until Indian lands were restored, then directed to embark his troops immediately. Nicolls chose to delay his evacuation as long as possible, but nonetheless he departed Prospect Bluff by mid-June 1815.[50]

Apparently, most officials of the Madison government agreed that Article Nine covered the Creeks. Jackson argued, however, that the Treaty of Fort Jackson had ended the Creek War and that the Indians at Prospect Bluff consisted mainly of Seminoles and Creeks who lived in Florida. Therefore, Article Nine did not apply to the Creeks who signed the Treaty of Fort Jackson. The Madison administration did reach some agreement, although it may only have been a pretense. In June 1815, Secretary of War

Alexander J. Dallas* reminded Jackson of the provisions of Article Nine and instructed him to implement them. Instead, Jackson ignored these orders and continued enforcing the Treaty of Fort Jackson.[51]

The Madison administration's real intention is unclear in this case, but given the government's extreme interest in obtaining land, it is probable that it unofficially supported Jackson's "land grabbing." Probably Jackson, on his own authority, expelled the Indians from their land and devised his argument that the terms of the Treaty of Fort Jackson superseded those of the Treaty of Ghent. Once the land cession occurred, Jackson's superiors in Washington decided to concur with his views, especially since these were popular in the South and West. Britain seemed unwilling to resume war simply to enforce Article Nine.

By ordering Jackson to enforce Article Nine and then ignoring his actions, the Madison government had a perfectly safe means of obtaining Indian lands. Should Britain decide to use force to restore Creek lands, U.S. government officials could at that point produce the order to Jackson and insist that the general acted in an insubordinate manner and violated his instructions as well. At that time they could evacuate the lands, reprimand Jackson, and be no worse off than if they had originally enforced the Treaty of Ghent. If, on the other hand, the British did nothing, which seemed likely, the United States would have gained most of the Creek lands. In short, there was no risk. The situation fit perfectly into the Jeffersonian policy of acquiring all possible lands short of waging a war for them. Once the administration decided to support Jackson's position, the government insisted that all of the Indians had relinquished their lands, except for a small number of renegade Creeks and Seminoles whose lands had not yet been taken.[52]

Whether or not those Indians assembled at Prospect Bluff by Nicolls really represented the Creek Nation, they were cer-

*The office of the secretary of war was held by many people during this time. Individuals who served in the post between 1812 and 1817 included William Eustis, John Armstrong, Alexander J. Dallas, William H. Crawford, James Monroe, George Graham, and John C. Calhoun.

tainly more representative than those who signed the infamous Treaty of Fort Jackson. Nicolls strongly disagreed with the U.S. interpretation that there were only a few renegade Creeks at Prospect Bluff. He insisted that more than four thousand were encamped at the fort and that at least a thousand Red Stick warriors had joined him late in the war. He even maintained that many Tuckabatchee and Coweta Indians who had been fighting for the United States, as well as several entire towns previously neutral, joined him by the end of the war.[53]

Because of this impasse and a continuing argument with U.S. Creek agent Benjamin Hawkins concerning terms for the Indians, Nicolls refused to evacuate his forces until June 1815. Once it became apparent that the United States would not accept the British interpretation of the Treaty of Ghent, he drafted a formal treaty with the Creeks and Seminoles at Apalachicola and established a regular government for them. According to this agreement, the Indians would be treated as an independent nation allied with Great Britain.* The British agreed to furnish them with arms and trade goods; the Indians, in return, would have no relations with either the Americans or the Spaniards.[54]

Americans viewed Nicolls's activities with considerable alarm. They were rightly worried that the British officer's actions might renew Indian enmity. Many within the United States became concerned lest the formerly friendly Indians join the Red Sticks in another war.[55]

Despite Indian threats and constant rumors of impending attack, the new Creek boundary line was surveyed and the land

---

*Prior to the Treaty of Paris in 1783, which gave Florida to Spain, the Creeks and the Seminoles belonged to the same loose confederation. U.S. agents organized a quasi-government for the Creek confederation. The United States considered all remaining Indians living south of the boundary with Spanish Florida (usually the thirty-first parallel) to be Seminoles. During this period, groups of Creeks hostile to the Americans took refuge in Spanish Florida, whereupon the government took the official position that these Creeks became Seminoles when they entered Florida. Following this precedent, therefore, the United States treated as Seminoles the thousands of Creeks who fled to Florida following their defeat by Jackson in 1814. Unfortunately for the Indians, many of these refugees as well as the British failed to comprehend this U.S. position and still considered themselves Creeks.

cession made. Although many incidents of violence and several deaths occurred, the overwhelming power of the U.S. Army cleared the ceded Creek lands in Alabama and Georgia. The settlement of the boundary line, however, did not end the difficulties, and the Indians in Florida prevented any real peace on the Georgia-Florida border until after Jackson's invasion of the Spanish territory in 1818.[56]

The defeat of the Creeks finally broke the organized power of the southern Indians. Thereafter, "no Indians, not even the determined Seminoles imperiled the republic." Although a token resistance from Spanish Florida emerged and operated after the war, it too would soon be destroyed. Shortly thereafter, the U.S. government moved all significant southern Indian settlements west of the Mississippi River.[57]

The southern Indian wars had two distinct effects on American relations with the Spanish Gulf borderlands. First, the Indian buffer state that had protected the sparsely settled Spanish colony of Florida soon disappeared. The clearing of so much new land brought a flood of American settlers into the area. This only served to accentuate the basic problem for Native Americans: a declining population relative to that of expansionist Americans. A second result was the extreme fear that these new settlers experienced about the Indian menace operating from Spanish Florida. Many Creeks had fled to Florida, where they joined renegade Seminoles and runaway slaves. These groups, armed and trained by the British, began raiding the American frontier. They no doubt believed the raids to be proper retaliation, since Americans stole their land. The Spanish could not control these contentious groups, and American frontiersmen soon realized that peace could be obtained only by vigorous military action and/or by annexing Florida to the United States.[58]

CHAPTER SIX

A Leftover of War: Negro Fort

THE CONCLUSION OF the War of 1812 and the Napoleonic Wars in Europe had a tremendous impact on North America because it uprooted individuals and left events unsettled. Peace disoriented many who had for a whole generation known nothing but war and its excitement. This became especially true as many displaced soldiers and sailors became pirates, mercenaries, filibusters, and patriots in a New World conflict for independence; still others searched for adventure in an untamed, ungoverned land. With peace in Europe and the United States, the crumbling Spanish empire in the Western Hemisphere, including Florida, acted as a magnet for restless souls searching for adventure. One graphic description of these unemployed soldiers/sailors and their efforts to find new adventures is recounted in the anonymous *Narrative of a Voyage to the Spanish Main, in the Ship "Two Friends."* This account tells the story of a group of British officers who, being unable to adjust to peace, looked to join the independence movements in Latin America.[1]

Florida, with its weakened government and state of near anarchy, appeared to be a natural port of entry for those who had lived for so long by the sword. Not only did Spain exercise little control after 1815, but the area of East Florida included belligerent Creeks and Seminoles. The region also had many runaway slaves who had been recruited, armed, and trained by the British

103

at Prospect Bluff on the Apalachicola River during the recent conflict. In 1815 after the British evacuation, this group took possession of the post that was later known as Negro Fort. In short, the lack of order combined with the presence of armed marauders transformed Florida into a perfect base from which adventurers could seek their fortunes.[2]

The Treaty of Ghent, negotiated under the tutelage of Secretary of State James Monroe, attempted to end the disarray within and ambiguity surrounding Florida. Article Nine of that treaty promised the Creeks restoration of the lands they had lost to the United States under the terms of the 1814 Treaty of Fort Jackson. In 1815, when the English evacuated their fort at Prospect Bluff, twenty-five miles inland from the Gulf of Mexico on the east side of the Apalachicola River, Major Edward Nicolls negotiated an unauthorized treaty that pledged British support for lost Indian lands. Should they not get their land back, Nicolls assured the Creeks, Britain would recognize and support an Indian state carved from part of East and West Florida. The government in London later repudiated this agreement and, consequently, the Creeks never received from Britain, Spain, or the United States compensation for or restoration of their lost lands.[3]

The presence of numerous runaway slaves who had taken refuge near the British position on the Apalachicola further complicated the problem. During the war Major Nicolls had raised a fighting force of four hundred to five hundred soldiers, both runaways and free blacks, who had settled with their families near Prospect Bluff. This old community included large numbers of maroons, some there for several generations. Intended to be agricultural, the settlement surrounded the fort and had pastures and fields extending for more than fifty miles north and south along the river. Once the war ended, many runaways chose to evacuate Florida and settle in the British West Indies, while many others elected to remain at Prospect Bluff.[4]

When British forces departed, Nicolls left behind not only a well-defended bastion but also at least three thousand stands of muskets, a tremendous quantity of ammunition, and an assortment of other weapons. He had also provided the fort with several cannon, thus leaving it a strong, secure position that commanded transportation and communication routes into southern Georgia and the Mississippi Territory. Additionally, the British had either stored or distributed to their Indian allies in the area at least six thousand stands of muskets, rifles, and carbines.[5]

This equipment allowed the renegades to become a dangerous menace along the frontier. An armed black settlement so near the border of the United States also gave rise to the threat of grave trouble. Americans were well aware of the bloody uprising on Santo Domingo in which several thousand slaves, in an effort to emulate the French Revolution, revolted against their French masters between 1791 and the end of 1803. The whites who were lucky enough to escape with their lives, as well as some blacks who had supported the French, moved first to Cuba, then some to the British West Indies, and even more to Louisiana and Florida. Much closer to home had been the Louisiana insurrection in January 1811 on what was called the German Coast, some forty miles upriver from New Orleans. A free mulatto, originally from Santo Domingo, led this sizable slave revolt and marched toward New Orleans. The Louisiana militia and the U.S. Army and Navy were all needed to stop the carnage. Therefore, a general slave uprising remained a legitimate concern to plantation owners along the Florida border.[6]

Government officials in Florida had expressed interest in eliminating Negro Fort because many of those former slaves were located in and near the fort. Although officials in Madrid had tried to convince the English to destroy the entire settlement and return the slaves to Spanish control, the British had conveniently ignored those pleas. Spain's weakness during the recent war had forced the Spanish, in an attempt to avoid conflict with either Britain or the United States, to claim that the region around Apalachicola belonged to the Creek Nation. But once the war ended, the Spanish government quickly reversed its position and again asserted its right to the territory under provisions of the 1783 Treaty of Paris. Spain also belatedly protested the presence of British forts and supply depots in Florida, demanding that Britain destroy the strongholds, withdraw troops still in Florida, pun-

ish the officers responsible for establishing the base at Apalachicola, and pay indemnities for losses sustained by the Spanish government and people.[7]

The citizens of Florida also had tried to persuade British commanders to return the slaves to their former masters. The British
had responded that they would allow any person to go back un-
molested to a master but would not force any to return against
his or her will.[8] They refused to modify this position despite a
barrage of Spanish protests. Although the British did not require
slaves to return to positions of servility, the ministry did agree to
pay claims for damages, including $20,000 to the Forbes Com-
pany, probably the largest single claim.[9]

The former slaves who remained in Florida took complete control of the bastion at Prospect Bluff after British forces evacuated
in June 1815.[10] Most of the Indians who had sought refuge there
during the war returned to their villages and renewed their intermittent raids on the Georgia frontier, again causing considerable discomfort and annoyance. They renewed their conflict because they almost certainly believed Britain planned to provide
them support. Many Georgians were also convinced that the British intended to honor their commitment to the Indians, and the
very presence of Negro Fort only assured them of the inevitable.[11]

The fort was built under the supervision of George Woodbine,
an Indian trader used by the British. It had an earthen parapet
120 feet in diameter, 15 feet high, and 18 feet thick, and sat on
a cliff commanding the Apalachicola River. A moat, 14 feet wide
and 4 feet deep, and a double row of pine logs serving as a pali-
sade surrounded the position. In the middle of the structure
stood a 30-foot octagon-shaped powder magazine constructed of
earth and logs. With the river in front, a swamp to the rear, a
large stream to the north, and a small creek to the south, the
stronghold was well protected from artillery. The fort also had
one 32-pound, three 24-pound, two 9-pound, and two 6-pound
cannon, in addition to an "elegant five and a half inch howitzer."
These weapons rendered the position virtually invincible to a
landward approach.[12]

The fort and arms depot offered not only tokens of rebellion

Edmund P. Gaines as a lieutenant in 1808. Engraving by Charles Saint-Memin
(Courtesy of the U.S. Naval Historical Center)

for Indians, but also a visible symbol of slave insurrection for
blacks. After the war, Brigadier General Edmund P. Gaines, commander of the southern sector of the Southern Military District,
planned an expedition against the fort. No immediate action occurred, however, since most available troops were needed to
guard the commission surveying lands acquired by the Treaty of
Fort Jackson. By December 1815, the commission had mapped
the new Creek boundary, thereby releasing eight hundred men
to concentrate on other problems. General Jackson also assigned
to Gaines an additional thousand men to help control the frontier. Certainly a force of this size could anticipate positive results.[13]

In September 1815, before Jackson and Gaines had the opportunity to take action, U.S. Indian agent Benjamin Hawkins dispatched the friendly Creek chief William McIntosh and a band of
about two hundred loyal Indians against Negro Fort. Hawkins was
acting without any official military orders, but as Indian agent.
Though he was acting only on his own authority, his decisions
were not questioned in Washington. This assault, though unsuc-

cessful, provided the defenders with a false sense of superiority, and in its aftermath they began recklessly attacking any vessel on the river not flying the Union Jack.[14]

The U.S. government, though still unprepared to launch an assault on the fort, had tried to persuade Spanish officials to do so. In the spring of 1815, Georgia Governor Peter Early had protested to East Florida Governor Sebastian Kindelan, demanding that Spanish authorities not only destroy the bastion but also stop Indian incursions into Georgia. From the tone of Kindelan's reply, Early concluded that even if Spain did stop the raids, neither the governor nor other Spanish officials would protest American retaliation against the lawlessness.[15]

Kindelan's replacement, Juan José de Estrada, did not continue the conciliatory correspondence but instead belligerently reminded Early of American-sponsored filibustering missions into Spanish Florida. In June 1815, Estrada informed the governor that although he had no control over the matter, he had referred the issue of Negro Fort to his superiors.[16] Later that September, Estrada, again complaining of American border violations at Amelia Island and other places, reported that British forces had evacuated Apalachicola.[17] Meanwhile in Washington, protests to Don Luis de Onís resulted in countercharges against filibustering in Texas and Florida, as well as objections to Latin American privateers using U.S. ports as bases of operation.[18]

During the spring of 1816, a more forceful and direct effort to eliminate Negro Fort occurred when Secretary of War William Crawford instructed Jackson to send a military representative to Pensacola to request that Spain take action against the position. Another new governor, Mauricio de Zúñiga, though unwilling to act against the fort without instructions from Madrid, freely admitted that the Spanish government considered the runaways and Indians at Apalachicola to be rebels. Zúñiga even confessed that while he could not authorize a unilateral attack by the United States, he would willingly join Jackson on such an expedition.[19]

With this tacit Spanish approval, Jackson ordered General Gaines in April 1816 to reduce the fort; Gaines instructed Colonel Duncan Clinch to establish a base (Camp Crawford, later re-named Fort Scott) at the confluence of the Flint and Chatta-hoochee Rivers, about 120 miles north of Prospect Bluff. Camp Crawford, constructed in early June 1816, served as the opera-tional base for the joint army-navy expedition against Negro Fort.[20] Clinch advanced to a position near Prospect Bluff to await supplies coming by navy gunboats from New Orleans. The first shipment of provisions arrived at the mouth of the Apalachicola River on 10 July aboard the schooners *Semilante* and *General Pike,* convoyed by gunboats *Nos. 149* and *154,* commanded by Sailing Master Jairus Loomis.[21]

Because the Apalachicola River flowed through Spanish terri-tory, Gaines needed to secure permission from Governor Zúñiga to transport supplies north to Camp Crawford. The governor agreed but informed Gaines that Negro Fort physically con-trolled the river; a safe passage therefore might not be possible. After receiving this news, Clinch sent John Blount, a friendly In-dian leader also called Lafarka, south to meet the vessels. Clinch instructed Lafarka that Loomis should wait at the river's mouth until army forces could escort the convoy north. During the interim the gunboats should anchor in a defensive position to blockade the river.[22]

While awaiting further information from Clinch, the U.S. na-val force encountered a boat trying to exit the river. Loomis sent a small dispatch vessel to intercept the craft and determine its intentions. As the two boats approached, the native craft harm-lessly fired on the dispatch vessel, gunboats, and transports. The gunboats returned fire, compelling the craft to turn back.[23]

On the following day, 16 July 1816, Loomis ordered Midship-man Luffborough, "a young Gentleman of fair promise" who had recently resigned but volunteered for this mission, to lead a de-tachment of men to replenish the vessels' freshwater supply. Dur-ing this search Luffborough encountered a black maroon, prob-ably a decoy, standing along the riverbank. The midshipman ordered his crew to proceed cautiously, hoping that a captured fugitive could provide much-needed information about the for-tress upstream. But as the U.S. vessel landed, a volley of musket

fire blazed from the undergrowth, instantly killing Luffborough
and two seamen. John Lopez, knocked overboard by the body of
a fallen comrade, swam desperately for safety. Edward Daniels,
dazed by the onslaught, surrendered in the confusion, only to be
scurried into the woods by the renegades. The Indians stripped
the clothing from the dead sailors and scalped them. Ultimately,
only Lopez survived the mission and was later rescued from a
sandbar at the river's mouth. This latest action heightened the
sailors' awareness as they waited aboard their vessels for army
forces to arrive.[24]

On 17 July, the same day the renegades attacked the water
party, Clinch and 116 "chosen men" departed Camp Crawford
to unite with the naval force at Apalachicola. During the same
evening, William McIntosh and 150 friendly Creeks joined the
American group. The following morning another 150 mostly un-
armed braves led by the old chief Captain Isaacs and Kotchahaijo (Mad Tiger) agreed to assist in the attack. Clinch wanted
to establish communications with the supply vessels, to use his
Indian allies as an advance party to harass the fort, and to sur-
round the position with his own men.[25] The first objective, con-
tacting the gunboats and supply vessels, proved to be more difficult than he had anticipated. Loomis, fearing a trap, refused to
move his craft upstream until Clinch dispatched a party of white
soldiers to protect the vessels, thus delaying the mission until
25 July. By this time Clinch had encamped about four miles below
Negro Fort.[26]

The joint army-Indian force had done little more than harass
the fort before the naval craft and its much-needed artillery
pieces arrived. Clinch reported, however, that his "irregular fire"
had the "desired effect, as it induced the enemy to amuse us with
the incessant roar of artillery." On the evening of 23 July, Clinch's
Indian leaders entered the fort under a flag of truce to demand
its surrender. Once they were inside, black chief Garson treated
the Creeks contemptuously. He refused to surrender, instead pro-
claiming that he would "sink any American vessel that should
attempt to pass, and would blow up the fort if he could not defend it." As the Indians departed, they noticed that the blacks

had hoisted the red flag of "no surrender" above the Union Jack, an ominous sign indeed.[27]

Clinch's initial plan of attack called for landing artillery to the rear of the fort, but upon reconnoitering he located an almost inaccessible spot for the guns. Clinch and Loomis agreed to bring the gunboats up under cover of darkness during the night of 26 July; Loomis would assault the fort without land support the next morning.[28] At 6:00 A.M. on the twenty-seventh, the renegades inside the fort harmlessly fired their 32-pound cannon while the gunboats moved into position near the west shore of the river. Gunboat *No. 154,* commanded by Sailing Master James Bassett, returned four volleys to determine the range of the fort. The fifth discharge, a hot-shot heated in the gunboat's galley, struck the fort's largest powder magazine, causing an explosion that instantly destroyed Negro Fort and killed 270 of the 334 defenders inside. After only five shots, "the largest and most heavily armed Maroon community ever to appear in the Southeast," as well as the threat it represented, had been eliminated.[29]

Most accounts describe the hot-shot that obliterated the fort's magazine as a lucky discharge, but this maneuver included far more than luck. William Hambly, who had once served under Nicolls at the fort and who knew the exact layout of the compound, including the location of its magazine, directed the U.S. fire. When Nicolls departed, he left Hambly in command, but the Indians questioned his loyalty and refused to accept his authority. Apparently the natives had judged Hambly correctly, because he quickly deserted Negro Fort to join the Americans.[30]

The hot-shot ended in a few minutes what otherwise might have been a prolonged siege. In his report Clinch described the damage from the explosion as "awful, and the scene horrible beyond description." "The fort," he continued, "contained about one hundred effective men (including twenty-five Choctaws), and about two hundred women and children, not more than one-sixth . . . saved." The "war yells of the Indians, the cries and lamentations of the wounded, compelled" even the most experienced soldiers to grimace at the sight. Clinch reported arrogantly that the victors realized the "great Ruler of the Universe must have used [them] as his instrument in chastising the blood-thirsty and murderous wretches that defended the fort."

Only three Indians within the fort escaped without serious injury; U.S. troops took twenty-five runaway slaves as prisoners. Surprisingly, despite the relatively small number of survivors, the Americans captured alive both Garson and the chief of the Choctaws. After Clinch and his Indian allies learned that captured seaman Edward Daniels had been tarred and burned alive, the Creeks immediately and brutally executed both captives. Hambly, acting as an agent for Forbes and Company, assumed custody of most of the surviving blacks, since they had once belonged to Spanish residents. The army transferred the American blacks to Camp Crawford, where they remained for a time before being returned to their owners. Not surprisingly, most of them had already fled long before the attack, escaping into the woods either to move south out of harm's way or to join the Seminoles.[31]

Clinch soon found that the fort's remaining magazines contained 2,500 stands of muskets with accoutrements, 500 carbines, 500 swords, 300 quarter casks of rifle powder, and 162 barrels of cannon powder. The village outside the fort had an additional 500 kegs of powder. Considering the amount of powder needed to produce such an "awful" explosion and reduce the fort, the position must have been extremely well supplied. Additionally, U.S. soldiers found many other stores—including a considerable amount of clothing—that Clinch valued at more than $200,000.[32] This large amount of military stores would seem to confirm the suspicion that the fort's inhabitants were abundantly prepared as well as eager to wage war on anyone, settlers and all others, who might come to the area.

Prior to the attack, Clinch had agreed during meetings with McIntosh and the other chiefs to reward the Indians with all the captured property except the cannon and shot. This pledge was made without knowing the vast contents of the fort, and after the capture Clinch likely did not give all the weapons to the Indians, though he undoubtedly supplied them well with arms, powder, and clothing.[33] No record exists of exactly what materials Clinch gave to the friendly Creeks, but he probably allowed them to take whatever they could carry, truly an insignificant portion of the rifle powder, cannon powder, weapons, or probably much of the large store of clothing. Ultimately, the artillery pieces, cannon powder, seven carriages, 502 guns, 1,200 bayonets, and the fort's two battle flags were transported to New Orleans. U.S. troops took most of the remaining supplies upstream to Camp Crawford.[34]

After the attack, Clinch ordered most of his force, including McIntosh and about two hundred Indians, to confront a large Seminole force advancing downriver. These hostiles, called "cowardly wretches" by Clinch, no doubt knew about Negro Fort and took to the woods before the American forces could attack them. Apparently Clinch made no attempt to pursue them but rather withdrew north to Camp Crawford, thereby bringing an end to the Negro Fort saga.[35]

Before departing for the Gulf, Loomis burned the remainder of the fort and the settlement. On its descent downriver the convoy encountered the armed Spanish schooner *Maria,* whose commander, Don Benigno García Calderón, demanded the surrender of the captured artillery and ammunition. Loomis wisely used an old Spanish evasive tactic by responding that he would have to pass the demand on to his superiors because he could do nothing without their orders.[36] Since the Americans had already destroyed the fort, the Spanish commander simply returned with Loomis to Pensacola, where he remained; Loomis and the gunboats proceeded with their spoils to New Orleans.[37]

Though not overjoyed with the American intervention, the Spanish were nonetheless pleased with the results of the expedition. Officially, they complained that their troops should have reduced the fort; unofficially, they were relieved that the Americans had removed the menace. Eliminating Negro Fort became significant in itself, but the main U.S. objective was likely to expel any powerful obstacle to future expansion. It may have also discouraged any hostile action by the remaining renegades in Florida.[38]

What happened to British aid that the Indians had so desperately hoped to receive? Nicolls had promised trade and protection as well as a restoration of Indian lands, in return for which the Creeks and Seminoles had agreed to keep peace. The Creeks even sent Josiah Francis, under the name Hidlis Hadjo, to England along with Nicolls to represent their interests during ratification of the treaty.[39] In mid-August 1815 Francis requested that the Earl of Bathurst, British minister of war and colonies, arrange an interview with the Prince Regent. British officials, apparently embarrassed by the entire episode, had no desire to meet with Francis.[40] In fact, the Prince Regent wanted the Indians to make peace with the United States. Moreover, neither the War Office nor the Foreign Office knew of the arrangements between Nicolls and the Creeks; both offices had seemingly accepted the U.S. statement that Article Nine of the Treaty of Ghent did not include the Creeks because they had made peace before the war ended. Thus, the arrival of Nicolls and Francis created an uproar and caught the British ministry unprepared.[41]

Bathurst eventually met with Francis and clearly indicated to the chief that the English did not intend to ratify Nicolls's treaty or use military force to support Indian claims.[42] The British, perhaps wishing to pacify the Creeks or to salve a guilty conscience, bestowed on Francis more than £325 sterling in gifts and arranged for his return passage to Florida.[43] On 30 December 1816, after spending more than a year in England, representative Hidlis Hadjo departed for Nassau. Upon arriving in the Bahamas, Francis received another £100 as additional evidence of British friendship.[44]

Once Francis had left, the British government demonstrated no further interest in the Creeks. Lord Bathurst and the Foreign Office even refused to accept from Nicolls further messages regarding the Indians. Nicolls collected his pay and expenses and apparently had no further dealings with either the Creeks or the Seminoles.[45] Francis returned to Florida via New Providence, where he left the gifts for safekeeping with George Woodbine, who, according to Alexander Arbuthnot, plundered them.[46] Upon returning to Florida in June 1817, after a two-year absence, Francis immediately called a council of all the Creek chiefs to relay the information given him in England. The message urged his brethren to make peace with the United States—wise advice considering that the Americans had already shown tremendous force at Negro Fort.[47]

Apparently, the British government by 1817 had become very anxious for the Indians to make peace. Charles Bagot, British minister to the United States, reinforced this view when he reported to his superiors that he did not wish to discuss American violations of Article Nine. Bagot willingly sacrificed those concerns because he hoped for better long-term relations between the two countries. To introduce the problem of the Creeks would have undoubtedly delayed or even prevented any agreement with the Americans. It was clearly in the best interest of Great Britain to avoid the Indian issue altogether. As a result of Bagot's advice, plus many other misgivings in London, the British government abandoned the Creeks to their inevitable fate at the hands of the Americans.[48]

The Francis episode did not represent the last Creek attempt to protest the treatment afforded them by the United States. In September 1818, George Perryman, who had been an interpreter for Nicolls, arrived in England aboard the HMS *Leariramis*. Perryman, representing the Lower Creeks from Apalachicola, argued that his people had faithfully served England and should now be allowed to settle in a British colony. John Bidwell interviewed Perryman aboard the British warship and instructed him to make peace with the Americans. Subsequently Bidwell put Perryman, who never set foot in England, aboard the first ship bound for North America.[49] As an aftermath, the government instructed naval commanders not to bring any more Indians to England, especially those with grievances against the United States. Those same orders also indicated that Perryman should never have been brought to England and that the government would no longer support the Creeks.[50]

The Perryman case demonstrated bluntly the British position. The government would provide no additional help for Indians in the United States, even if they lived in Spanish territory when attacked by Americans. This reflected a changing relationship with the United States. It was apparent that the young country would not return to the British empire, and moreover, the United States, now growing in strength, could threaten Canada. Once the British recognized this they abandoned their aggressive policy toward the United States in favor of conciliation. The Rush-Bagot Agreement and the Convention of 1818 illustrated improving Anglo-American relations and reinforced this changing policy. As it happened, by the time Perryman arrived in England the British government had just settled the Ambrister and Arbuthnot cases and was probably especially sensitive to anything that might upset this developing relationship.[51]

The new British attitude toward the Indians represented an important change in Anglo-American relations and played a significant role in future expansion. Until this time, Britain had supported the Indians as a potential ally against the United States and American aggression. Although most British support had come via Canada, a substantial amount of aid had filtered to the southern Indians from the West Indies and the Bahamas. This support, whether official or not, provided the Indians with encouragement and a degree of independence, influencing them to offer considerable resistance to American land hunger. The defeat of the Creeks and the subsequent Treaty of Fort Jackson broke the power of the southern Indians, and the destruction of Negro Fort demonstrated that the United States would no longer tolerate any resistance to American expansion. It also forecast the inevitable, that even with British aid the Indians would fall victim to American expansion. In real terms, the attack reopened the Apalachicola River and its tributaries and did so without arousing complaint from any European power. Even Spanish comments concerning the engagement do not appear to be a protest.[52]

The destruction of Negro Fort certainly demonstrated to the remaining hostiles in the area that, even if they had British arms, they were no match for the Americans. It also illustrated that promises of aid and support were nothing more than just that. Lastly, this attack represented a dress rehearsal for Jackson's invasion of Florida, a maneuver that occurred slightly more than a year later.

The operation against Negro Fort fits well within the parameters of Jeffersonian expansion. The stronghold threatened the security of American citizens and served as a visible symbol of opposition. The elimination of that obstacle, although tacitly authorized by Secretary of War Crawford, occurred without Madison's prior knowledge or approval. Although the U.S. government may not have had prior knowledge, the operation vividly demonstrated the inherent weaknesses of Spain's North American empire. Furthermore, once Negro Fort had been destroyed, Spain could no longer deny this weakness.[53]

CHAPTER SEVEN

"A Set of Desperate and Bloody Dogs": The Acquisition of Amelia Island

To ALL APPEARANCES, the U.S. government's interest in expanding into foreign lands lessened greatly after 1815. Not only was there little immediate need for more land, but the major opponents of expansion had lost ground in Congress, thus making the political conflict less explosive. The country had just completed a war involving the British and Indians that broke the power of the Native Americans. It also ended any future British support for the Indians, who by this time had neither the energy to fight the Americans nor the strength to hold their lands. This loss of power meant that within the next two decades all significant landholdings of the southern Indians and most of those belonging to the northern tribes would be confiscated by the United States. The government systematically relocated the Native Americans to the West. In 1813 the Madison administration had added the Mobile district to land owned by the United States. By the end of the war the country had also secured tacit recognition from Britain for its title to the Louisiana Purchase.

For once the United States had enough available land to accommodate even a rush of new immigrants from Europe. At last the government could sit in its nest like a spider waiting for prizes to fall into its web. Although interest in expansion was still as great as ever, no longer was there a sense of urgency to add more acreage or a need to devise elaborate plots to seize neighboring lands, as in the past. Only the danger of a European power's moving into the borderlands would distress Americans. Spain no longer posed any threat whatsoever, with its empire crumbling and the country itself exhausted. The United States could assist in the decline of Spanish power, and if in the process more territory was gained, that was beneficial. Time, as Jefferson had prophesied, was on the side of an expanding America. There was no hurry. Spanish authorities, realizing that they could not hold Florida, had entered into promising negotiations with the United States with the eventual object of giving up the area in exchange for other concessions.[1]

The election of James Monroe as president and his appointment of John Quincy Adams as secretary of state exerted considerable influence on the policy of U.S. expansion. Though Adams was not opposed to expansion, as many other New England leaders continued to be, he nonetheless represented that section, and as such he was certainly not the active expansionist Monroe had been. Although the election of 1816 did signal the end of the Federalist party, its political leaders joined the Republicans to continue promoting the interests of the Northeast.

Monroe and Adams differed greatly not only in philosophy but also in style. Adams, far more methodical than his predecessor, actually began the process of logging in and out all official correspondence and directives. At the same time, he appeared to be more overt and not as likely to engage in the clandestine behavior that characterized Monroe's term as secretary of state. Although negotiations for Florida actually began during Monroe's tenure, they became the main thrust of the Adams State Department; Adams was much more of a diplomat than Monroe.[2]

The absence of war did not bring peace to those people living in Spanish possessions, and the residents of East Florida were no exception. During the War of 1812, Spain had not been able to prevent either the British from using the area to recruit slaves for their black regiments or the refugee Creeks from joining their Seminole brothers. In short, East Florida—with the exception of the towns of St. Marks and St. Augustine—resembled a state of anarchy. Most of the Spanish garrison—a small cadre of

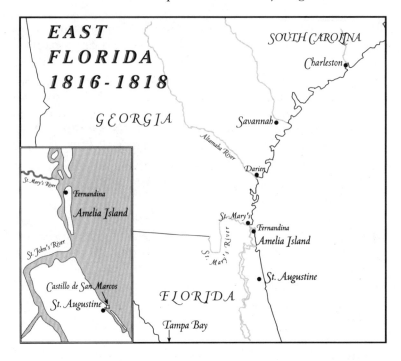

exhausted troops, many of whom had served thirty or more years in the army—and its government officials lived inside the walls at St. Augustine. Spanish retirees were typically assigned to this frontier outpost.[3]

Finally, in the summer of 1816, a group of influential men decided to bring law and order to the area. George I. F. Clarke, surveyor-general of East Florida, Henry Younge, and Zephania Kingsley, representing Spanish Governor José Coppinger, met with a number of citizens on the Spanish side of the St. Marys River near St. Marys, Georgia. The location's proximity to Georgia made this a choice spot because many East Florida residents had taken refuge in Georgia to escape the region's rampant anarchy. Although some of these inhabitants may have been part of the "patriot" forces before 1813, the group seemed to represent all factions of the East Florida population.[4]

The citizens' council agreed that East Florida north of St. Augustine, but excluding Amelia Island, would be designated the

120

Northern Division of East Florida. Amelia Island had a small Spanish garrison and, therefore, was not included in the Northern Division. The assembled group divided the territory into three districts and established a magistrate court and militia company for each. Next they drafted a constitution modeled after the one in Georgia, and after its acceptance they elected three magistrates and nine militia officers. The council of the Northern District appointed Clarke, a Floridian of English ancestry, to serve as executive. This republic really appeared independent as created, but it maintained a tacit allegiance to Spain. Spanish authorities made no attempt to collect taxes and, with the exception of a cooperative view of defense, left the Northern Division to its own affairs.[5]

Governor Coppinger, realizing that he and his meager forces could neither control nor protect the area, agreed to all of these arrangements. Although this "republic," or whatever else it might be termed, represented a unique experiment in the Spanish empire, its formation offered the only way northern Florida could be controlled without many more Spanish troops, a resource unavailable at the time. Most of the people living in East Florida were former citizens of the United States, some loyalists left over from the Revolution, and a few Germans; virtually all spoke English. This system worked fairly well, and for the first time in years East Florida had a degree of law and order. There is no evidence that American agents or the U.S. government were involved in this activity, but certainly the idea of East Florida's relative independence from Spain pleased expansionists.[6]

Unfortunately, peace could not last. Amelia Island in particular provided a tempting target for adventurers, filibusters, and privateers, who appeared throughout the Gulf of Mexico/Caribbean region. The state of affairs in this area, with all its capacity for instability and violence, should not have come as a surprise to anyone. The war in Europe had ended, and with its conclusion came thousands of unattached men, some young, some older, who in their entire lives had known only war and now sought adventure and more employment as soldiers and sailors. The decaying Spanish empire attracted this large group of renegades searching for power, adventure, plunder, and excitement. Amelia Island, so close to the main shipping routes of the area, offered an ideal base for privateering. On the land side of the island were numerous entries into Georgia where plunder could be smuggled into the United States with little or no risk. Here, too, East Florida had a non-Spanish population with no loyalty to the government in Madrid. These people might be easily persuaded to join a revolution or some other adventure.

In the summer of 1817, one of the most interesting adventurers appeared on the scene. Gregor MacGregor, grandson of the Lord of Inverardine, yielded to the temptation to seize Amelia Island and use it as a base against the Spanish. MacGregor, born into Scottish nobility in 1786, served in the British army before leaving in 1811 to join General Francisco de Miranda in Caracas, Venezuela. He had a fairly distinguished record with Miranda, serving as a colonel of mounted troops. While in Caracas, he married a cousin of Simón Bolívar, Doña Josefa Antonia Xeres Aristequienta y Lovera Bolívar. MacGregor must have had a good marriage or a very determined wife, since Doña Lovera accompanied him on all his adventures after that time.[7]

In 1812 a devastating earthquake destroyed Caracas and so damaged the resources of the revolution that Miranda believed he had no choice but to surrender the city. MacGregor, like most others, lost virtually all his property in this disaster. Nonetheless, he joined Bolívar's army, where he received considerable distinction and won promotion in 1816 to general of the division. When MacGregor eventually believed himself a victim of discrimination because of his non-Spanish background, he left Bolívar and set out to find his own piece of Spanish America to free from the tyranny of Ferdinand VII.[8]

Native Spanish-speaking adventurers often wanted to employ Anglo-Americans and other foreigners in an effort to gain independence, but once they felt secure they usually either greatly diminished or eliminated altogether any power held by outsiders. MacGregor's treatment in Venezuela, even though he had a Spanish wife and was Catholic, almost mirrored that accorded the American followers of Bernardo Gutiérrez in Texas. Though

Gregor MacGregor. Engraving by Lizars of Edinburgh. Reproduced from Thomas Strangeway's *Sketch of the Mosquito Coast* (London, 1822)

Gutiérrez knew full well that his American supporters wanted to annex Texas to the United States, and therefore did represent a real threat to Mexican sovereignty there, MacGregor did not threaten Venezuelan sovereignty. He may have maintained some loyalty to Britain, but it was unlikely that he had any notion of trying to make Venezuela into a British colony. The apparent problem was almost certainly nationalistic fervor beginning to develop among the leaders of Venezuela, Mexico, and other emerging Latin American states. In addition to this cultural chauvinism, there were likely numerous young Spanish officers jealous of MacGregor's success.

MacGregor's plans took shape in March 1817 when he traveled

to Philadelphia to meet with merchants and other potential financial backers. He proposed that they support his cause, an effort he promised would be both worthy and profitable. His search for money met with little success for one very good reason—he would not share his plans with prospective backers, and as a result, they would not fund a blind adventure. Although he felt compelled to keep secret the exact destination of his proposed expedition for the obvious reason that the Spanish might be waiting for him, he could not gain the trust of the group, probably for equally obvious reasons.[9]

One positive result of his stay in Philadelphia was that he received a commission from a group calling itself "The Deputies of Free America, Resident in the United States of the North," who authorized him to take possession of East and West Florida.[10] The commission, allowing him to grant rank and establish a government, was signed in Philadelphia on 31 March 1817 by deputy for Venezuela Don Lino de Clemente, deputy for New Grenada Pedro Gaul, proxy for F. Zarate, deputy from Mexico, and deputy from Río de la Plata Martin Thompson. Although it is not clear just how many nations recognized the commission, it did give MacGregor's actions the cloak of legality rather than the appearance of piracy. Spain would have undoubtedly hanged MacGregor had its authorities been able to apprehend him, regardless of what type of commission he carried.[11]

MacGregor apparently placed considerable value on this document. Once he had his commission in hand, he doubled his efforts to raise money and recruit men. He found little more in Philadelphia, however, and moved on to Baltimore and then to New York and eventually to Washington. He encountered the same old problem as he sought financial aid—people unwilling to support his expedition unless they were made aware of its goals. He did receive some support in Baltimore, and he ultimately acquired considerable reinforcements from New York and other areas in the Northeast once he revealed his objectives.[12]

MacGregor, in an effort to avoid difficulty with the United States, attempted to apprise the government of his plans through John Skinner, the Baltimore postmaster. MacGregor described

his plan to Skinner, who in turn informed the appropriate government authorities. He told Skinner that he intended to free
Amelia Island and that, at a more favorable time, he would surrender the island to the United States. The government generally
avoided interfering in any official way with activities concerning
Amelia Island and East Florida, but at the same time it certainly
made no effort to halt these actions. Private U.S. citizens provided substantial backing, and most of MacGregor's officers and
men were American. No doubt the government's position was
that if the situation presented itself, the area would be annexed.
In any event, the Spanish hold on Florida would be weakened,
and eventually, like a ripe plum, it would all fall into the American lap.[13]

Having received what amounted to an unofficial blessing from
the government of the United States, MacGregor chose to di-
vulge his efforts to the British because he feared that they might
think he was preparing a refuge for the Bonapartes. He had been
approached in Philadelphia on several occasions by a M. Regnault, probably Regnault St. Jean d'Angey, who promised him
substantial funds if he would assist the Bonapartes in establishing
a refuge in the Western Hemisphere. They claimed to have several million dollars to support such an effort and were planning
an attempted rescue of Napoleon himself. Wanting nothing to
do with this group of exiled Frenchmen, MacGregor suspected
that British agents were watching and might interpret his actions
against Amelia Island as part of a Bonapartist plan. This could
bring some sort of British intervention, a situation he certainly
wished to avoid. MacGregor was also concerned about Britain's
relationship with Spain, as the two had been allies during the
recent war, and he very much wanted to know whether or not
Britain would help Spain hold Florida against his forces.[14]

To clarify his position, MacGregor visited the British minister
to Washington, Charles Bagot, on 15 April 1817. Bagot, after lis-
tening to the objectives of the expedition, informed him that the
British had no intention of interfering in the affairs of Florida
or Spain. In fact, he indicated that he believed the territory of
Florida would soon be signed over to the United States by Spain

in exchange for a more secure western boundary. According to Bagot, Don Luis de Onís had asked Britain to act as a mediator in this discussion. He obviously did not know or would not say whether this mediation role by the British would be offered or accepted by the Americans, but he did not doubt that Florida would soon belong to the United States. MacGregor seemed to understand this and expected eventually to turn Amelia Island over to American authorities.[15]

Bagot exhibited an interest in MacGregor's reports on French efforts to secure a refuge in the hemisphere. He apparently already knew about the plans to rescue Napoleon, calling them "daydreams" of former French officers. He was even more interested in MacGregor's information that the French exiles, recruiting men for an expedition against Texas or Mexico, had considerable money to spend in this manner. Bagot seemed to think that there was some danger of Joseph Bonaparte's raising a French force and either conquering Mexico or establishing a strong base in Texas. He knew of numerous French officers in a settlement on the Tombigbee River in the Mississippi Territory, and probably others in Philadelphia and New Orleans. Bagot likely feared that the French exiles could recruit men similar to MacGregor and other Spanish colonial dissidents.[16]

MacGregor left the Northeast with a few men and some funds and sailed to Charleston in early June 1817. At last he began to be successful, raising a great deal more money and men than he had previously. A number of respectable young men recently discharged from U.S. military service in the War of 1812 joined his cause. MacGregor had demonstrated his lack of knowledge about American politics in his efforts to seek out funding for his expedition. The expansionists were located mainly in the South and West, and it would have been advantageous to him to recruit sooner and more heavily in the lower South.[17]

At Charleston, MacGregor purchased a schooner large enough for him to take aboard men and supplies for his expedition. He established a base at the mouth of the Altama River near Darien, Georgia, where he collected and trained his forces. Still without enough manpower to suit his plans, he sailed back to Savannah and succeeded in raising more men and considerably more financial backing from local merchants. One merchant even went to Amelia Island as an advanced agent and told the local people that resisting MacGregor would be useless since his force numbered over a thousand, an exaggeration at best if not an outright lie.[18]

Amelia Island had a Spanish garrison of fifty-four officers and soldiers and an additional militia of about fifty men. The town had a fort, two blockhouses, and a fairly substantial battery of guns ranging from 4- to 16-pounders. Like most of those in Florida, the Spanish troops were old regulars, and it is likely that none of their equipment was in good condition. Even so, they should have been able to offer a suitable defense of Fernandina, especially since the area was protected by marshes and bluffs.

MacGregor actually used trickery and propaganda rather than force to capture Fernandina. He had fifty-five men and would have been evenly matched with the regular Spanish troops. He advanced all of his men out of the woods and over an open marsh where they would have been easy targets. He scattered them like pickets in front of a supposedly larger force that presumably remained in the woods. Spanish Commander Francisco Morales, believing the advanced agent's story that MacGregor had a thousand men, ordered his troops not to fire on the "advance" party. When MacGregor's men reached the fort, Morales surrendered his garrison; only one shot was fired by the Spanish, and that one violated Morales's orders. The Americans disarmed the Spanish force and allowed them to march back to St. Augustine, where Governor Coppinger court-martialed Morales for cowardice. Although Morales was sentenced to death, it is likely that his execution never took place.[19]

MacGregor's flag, a green St. George's cross on a white background called the Green Cross of Florida, was raised over Fernandina on 28 June 1817. In a proclamation, MacGregor promised to protect the citizens and property of Amelia Island, but it is doubtful if many people believed him. What MacGregor captured at Fernandina were buildings left empty by residents who took every means available to flee the island. Many, thinking that their property would be confiscated, had moved everything to a safe place.[20]

After a show of flamboyant proclamations, MacGregor organized a regular government for Amelia Island. He ordered a printing press for a newspaper and established both a post office and an admiralty court. Creating the admiralty court was probably his single most important action in this port town. Now he had a court that could condemn prizes taken by privateers of the West Indies who flew the flags of Venezuela, Mexico, and Grenada. This court, placed under control of the Charleston lawyer John D. Heath, became significant to MacGregor's operation because it provided a means of raising money. With Heath as admiralty judge, the court charged a fee, 16.5 percent against the gross value of the prizes, as a source of revenue to operate the government of Amelia Island. The judiciary also levied regular court costs.[21]

Upon landing, MacGregor quickly dispatched parties to the mainland, one of which advanced to a point near St. Augustine before returning to Amelia Island. This group so upset the garrison at the blockhouse of Fort San Nicholas that on 4 July the Spanish burned the place and retreated to St. Augustine.[22]

MacGregor's master plan called for seizing control of East Florida and eventually driving out the Spanish. His scheme for the territory failed, however, because he had mistakenly expected the citizens of East Florida to join his cause en masse. Most had been satisfied with their government since the midsummer of 1816. In that one year they had finally regained enough control to establish a degree of law and order. Then they unhappily fell victim to MacGregor's foraging parties in search of food and supplies for the garrison at Fernandina. These undisciplined groups resembled the banditti who had roamed Florida before the establishment of the Northern Division. As a result, MacGregor received little or no support and even some opposition from the veterans of the patriot forces. Even the smugglers on Amelia Island were probably unhappy with MacGregor. The prizes condemned in the admiralty court did provide them a ready supply

128

of merchandise to smuggle into Georgia, but the new government's tax policy made it little more popular than the old Spanish regime.[23]

MacGregor ultimately wanted to take all of East Florida, but to accomplish this he needed to capture St. Augustine. He had planned to attack the city at the point where he considered his force strong enough for such an operation, but he erred in judgment when he did not attack quickly. If he had made his assault only a few days after landing, his chance of success would have been greatly improved. Had MacGregor been able to invade East Florida before the establishment of the Northern Division, his cause would have had much greater appeal to the population. But now the leaders of the new government had solved enough of their problems that they had no need for MacGregor's brand of control. Another, equally important, advantage that MacGregor might have gained from an earlier attack on St. Augustine would have been that such an action might have thrown the Spanish into a panic. Morales had fled Amelia Island thinking he faced an overwhelming force, and his counterpart at Fort San Nicholas had also evacuated in a total state of disarray. If the attitudes exhibited by these two officers were at all typical, a sudden attack on St. Augustine would likely have had the same result. Earlier aggressive action by MacGregor would probably have benefited his own forces. Certainly they were better organized and disciplined before he sent them all over East Florida on foraging parties.[24]

The most vexing problem MacGregor faced at Amelia Island proved to be maintaining an effective garrison. As with almost all such expeditions, he constantly faced money and supply shortages. Moreover, his men began to desert to the point where this presented an increasing problem. They had come seeking adventure and plunder and generally lacked discipline. When the action they craved did not follow, they lost faith in the operation. Then, too, MacGregor had no real national authority to force the men to behave or obey his orders. Not only was this the nature of this particular force, but it was also the general reason why many privateers and filibusters failed. These same factors had played a significant role in the failure of the Magee-Gutiérrez expedition into Texas.[25]

MacGregor's lack of an effective ground force put Amelia Island in danger of a counterattack by the Spanish garrison, especially if reinforcements arrived at St. Augustine. Indeed, as time passed, the situation worsened on the island, particularly after Governor Coppinger received additional men from Cuba. When MacGregor's reinforcements and supplies did not arrive in sufficient quantities or in a timely manner, affairs on the island continued to decline.[26]

Although the situation on land worsened, maritime strength at Amelia Island increased. Unfortunately for the filibusters, however, profits from the admiralty court still did not meet the island's expenses. Moreover, the condemnation of prizes, though often a source of money for MacGregor, also resulted in serious points of dispute because most countries did not recognize the authority of the Amelia Island admiralty court. The case of the schooner *Camella* and its cargo provides a good example. The Spanish ship *Camella* was captured and condemned at Amelia Island. When *Camella*'s new owners brought the ship into the harbor at Savannah, they were met by the Spanish consul, who promptly laid claim to the ship and denied the legality of MacGregor's proceedings. This incident probably typified issues facing MacGregor when he attempted to raise funds by selling captured ships. Cargoes of the questioned ships were easier to dispose of because most goods captured by the privateers could be smuggled into the United States through Georgia and never be traced to their original owners. Colonel Jared Irwin, treasurer of Amelia Island, tried to raise funds by issuing paper money on land warrants. This plan enjoyed limited success, but not nearly enough to solve the critical money shortage.[27]

MacGregor and his followers, trying to establish themselves in this territory during this immediate time period, faced other troubling dilemmas as well. The U.S. Navy brig *Saranac* seized the *Iris,* a private ship loaded with munitions and supplies sailing from New Orleans to Amelia Island. Officials released the ship, charging its owners with making an illegal cruise against Spanish commerce. Although the expedition to claim East Florida may have had tacit approval in Washington, this case provides evidence that the United States did not always support the adventurers at Amelia Island. Even MacGregor's own privateers faced seizure. MacGregor, however, did not find his tribulations limited to the sea or foreign recognition. Judge Heath resigned in a dispute over a French vessel, supposedly carrying Spanish cargo. Jared Irwin, already there as treasurer, became head of a commission to determine the legality of the ship's seizure. MacGregor's letters of marque allowed him to take Spanish ships but not those of French origin. Irwin, a former Pennsylvania congressman and militia officer, thereafter became increasingly powerful in island affairs.[28]

MacGregor's position weakened considerably when his troops declined in number to only twenty-five. Although he still had crews on several ships, he desperately needed ground forces. His situation improved somewhat with the arrival of the privateer *Patriota* from Chesapeake Bay with a few reinforcements. What MacGregor anticipated, however, was the arrival of Ruggles Hubbard, former high sheriff of New York City, who reportedly was bringing three more ships. Hubbard landed on 28 August with the three ships and their crews, but without the men and supplies promised by MacGregor's backers. Another ship, the *Two Friends,* also arrived about the same time Hubbard landed. This vessel carried a company of Scottish and English adventurers, mostly officers—again unsuitable replacements for MacGregor's dwindling force. This group literally had too many officers and not enough men; finding few troops to command, they soon left to seek their fortunes elsewhere.[29]

MacGregor's resolve to remain at Amelia Island faltered as a result of these disappointments, and he departed from Amelia Island with his ship and crew on 9 September. A few days earlier, the British schooner *Venus*, rumored to belong to the well-known filibuster and adventurer George Woodbine, had arrived at Amelia Island. MacGregor visited Woodbine aboard ship and agreed to meet the adventurer several days later at New Providence in the Bahamas.[30]

Though MacGregor appeared to be severing ties with the Amelia Island expedition, he seemingly maintained his idea to take over East Florida. Woodbine apparently convinced him that he could find men and money in the Bahamas, where there would be a plentiful supply of potential recruits in the West Indies, especially among the blacks who had served in the British West Indian regiments during the War of 1812. Woodbine's plan was that MacGregor could first recruit as many as fifteen hundred men in the West Indies and then land his army at Tampa Bay, march overland, and capture St. Augustine. This would give him control of the entire peninsula of East Florida.[31]

The MacGregor-Woodbine efforts in the Bahamas did meet with a measure of success, and they were able to recruit about two dozen men for the anticipated invasion. MacGregor sailed for England on 27 December 1817, apparently intending to settle some personal business and to raise more money for the expedition. Woodbine remained in the West Indies in charge of recruiting efforts for the project. His best-known recruit by far was his former lieutenant, Robert Christie Ambrister, who took a small detachment of blacks to Florida. Ambrister was to lead the advanced party to announce the coming of MacGregor to Tampa Bay, but MacGregor never arrived and Jackson captured Ambrister before he could do more. Woodbine, in the meantime, sailed to Jamaica, where he continued to seek recruits from the former West Indian troops. Unfortunately for his mission, British authorities put a stop to his efforts in Jamaica, and this apparently was the last time either MacGregor or Woodbine recruited in the West Indies. Woodbine continued to assist MacGregor for some time afterward, but the capture and execution of Ambrister, combined with the British government's curtailment of any further recruiting, effectively paralyzed the possibility of any invasion of Florida. In fact, these actions stopped any new attack on the territory of North America. Although these events will be discussed at length in the next chapter, it is worth noting here that a direct connection existed between the occupation of Amelia Island and the Ambrister-Arbuthnot incident.[32]

Near the time MacGregor left the island, the brig *Saranac* arrived at St. Marys to watch Amelia Island and to send to Washington reports concerning any activity there. This ship and an accompanying gunboat anchored there not only to monitor events but also to maintain an American presence in the area. This naval party would assure the United States that its territory was not violated. It is likely that the navy was trying to suppress smuggling from Amelia Island, especially the illegal slave trade.[33]

Following MacGregor's departure,* Jared Irwin commanded Amelia Island. Although Irwin's land forces had diminished, he had three fairly formidable ships—two privateers, *Morgiana* of eighteen guns and *St. Joseph* of ten guns, and the armed schooner *Jupiter*. With these vessels, Irwin and his men felt secure because if advancing Spanish forces proved too strong, they could always evacuate by sea. This resolve increased even more with the arrival of the *Margaret* from New York with a load of arms and ammunition.[34]

The island's remaining civilian population departed quickly once they learned of the decision to defend the place against the Spanish. Governor Coppinger had tried desperately for months to strengthen his forces, but he received only a few companies of Spanish blacks from Cuba to add to his small garrison at St. Augustine. Coppinger's only alternative was to call out the East Florida militia, a risky action indeed since many of the inhabi-

---

*MacGregor, after his return from England, first went to a small island, St. Andrews, off the coast of Nicaragua where he and Woodbine intended to capture Portobelo. Next he went to the Mosquito Coast on the eastern shore of Honduras, hoping to establish a colony. While he was in England, the colony failed. Hoping in vain for better times, MacGregor went to France, only to land in jail for seven months. Around 1839 he applied to Venezuela for citizenship and the renewal of his military rank. The Venezuelan government restored his rights and even gave him money. In 1845 MacGregor died in Caracas. Woodbine, when he saw that MacGregor's failure was imminent, left and moved to Campeche, Mexico, where he and his family were murdered in 1837. Davis, *MacGregor's Invasion*, 67–68.

tants had participated in the patriot action and had questionable loyalties at best.[35]

The governor ultimately collected a force of some 350 militia and Cuban black troops supported by two Spanish gunboats for an attack on the island. They gathered at a point across the inlet from Fernandina, and during the night of 9 September they landed on the island about one mile south of the town. The next morning they advanced and drove Irwin's men back into Fernandina. Although more fighting ensued later that day, the outcome of the conflict was indecisive. On 11 September Irwin's men took the *St. Joseph* up the Amelia River to raid and plunder several plantations that the Spanish had been using as bases of operations. Though the Americans had hoped to force a troop withdrawal from the area, their action did not have the desired effect. One hundred additional Spanish black troops arrived on 12 September.[36]

The following day, the Spanish, supported by the two gunboats, attacked Fernandina. The *St. Joseph* and the fort at Fernandina both returned fire. Irwin's gunfire hit the enemy's camp, throwing its commander into a panic and prompting him to withdraw, an action that prevented another Spanish assault. This failure to attack, together with the arrival of a small group of American reinforcements almost every day, brought improved morale and confidence to Irwin's men. Not only did the Spanish not muster another attack, but Governor Coppinger removed from duty and court-martialed the officer in charge of this force for his incompetence. The end result was that Irwin maintained control of the island when the Spanish withdrew.[37]

All of this action occurred about the same time that MacGregor had planned for his blockade to become effective. On 21 August he ordered a blockade for all of Florida from Amelia Island to the Perdido River, insisting that any merchant ship trading with Spanish Florida would be subject to seizure. MacGregor had originally announced that his intended blockade would become effective on 15 September, but he had left the area himself around 9 or 10 September, and the available records do not indicate whether it was ever enforced. MacGregor and Irwin both

134

Daniel Todd Patterson, circa 1810. Artist unknown (Courtesy of the U.S. Naval Historical Center)

recognized the need for superior seapower to enforce the blockade, and Irwin's success probably owed more to his ships than his ground troops. Irwin's actions caused the Spanish to retreat to St. Augustine, a victory of sorts that left Irwin and Hubbard in control of Amelia Island.[38] Afterward they called this area the "Northern Company for South American Emancipation," with Irwin as military leader and Hubbard in charge of civil affairs.[39]

This arrangement with Irwin and Hubbard was short-lived, ending on 17 September when Luis-Michel Aury and his force of "about one hundred and thirty brigand negroes—a set of desperate and bloody dogs" arrived on the island. This unflattering description of Aury and his men came from New Orleans and reflected the sentiment of many throughout the lower South. Aury had originally established himself at Galveston with the support of the New Orleans Association, an organization that included several prominent Americans such as Abner Duncan, former federal district attorney at Natchez, Edward Livingston of New York, and Daniel Patterson, U.S. naval commander at New Orleans. This group had already planned, among other things, to capture Florida and sell it to the United States. Because these men had extremely close ties to the government, one can assume that they probably had the administration's approval for their actions. The association had initially chosen Galveston as the port from which to carry out its operation but willingly looked toward Florida as another profitable option. More important to Aury than this operation was his long-term relationship with the other Latin American revolutions, particularly that of Mexico.[40]

Aury's background was not unusual for a man in his position, and he was, above all else, an adventurer.* At the time he claimed to represent the Republic of Mexico, and, like MacGregor, he had served with revolutionary governments in Latin America. There were, however, tremendous differences between the two men, and Aury suffers somewhat in comparison. As a product of the French Revolution, he was far more ambitious and arrogant. Historian Frederick Davis has charged: "In all his [Aury's] proclamations—and like MacGregor, he was fond of issuing them, but with the difference that Aury's were camouflage, while MacGregor's were sincere—the words 'patriotic cause,' 'republicanism,' and 'independence' were shrewdly played-up for the benefit of the outside world." He had supported the Mina expe-

---

*Luis Aury, whose name was originally Luis-Michel Aury, was born in 1786 or 1787 in the Parisian neighborhood of Montrouge, where his widowed mother and sister remained long after he joined the French navy. Much of the personal information about Aury comes from his correspondence to his relatives. He first came to the West Indies in 1803 on a naval ship and likely deserted to become a corsair soon after. In New Orleans in 1810 Aury became part owner of a French colonial privateer and joined the ranks of the best-known Caribbean adventurers. He increased his power base in Galveston, and the changing revolutionary government of Mexico made him military and civil governor of Texas. His stay in Texas was short, however, and he next appeared in the Atlantic and subsequently at Amelia Island.

dition against Spain in Mexico, even allowing Mina to organize and collect his men at his base in Galveston. Aury had, in fact, following some disagreements with Mina over command, used his ships to transport part of the expedition to Mexico. Once the two settled their disputes, Aury became commander of Mina's naval forces.[41] After landing Mina's expedition on 21 April 1817, he proceeded to raid Spanish commerce; he eventually landed his forces at Amelia Island. Aury's commission from the Mexican government had been given to him by José Manuel de Herrera, the unrecognized Mexican minister to the United States. On this authority, Aury raised the Mexican flag over Amelia Island. Even though he issued some of his proclamations to cover both Amelia and Galveston Islands, he personally took charge of the East Florida expedition. The Galveston holdings, described later, would be controlled by Aury's lieutenants, with Jean Laffite as primary leader and supposed governor.[42]

The records are unclear as to why Aury established bases at both Amelia Island and Galveston, except that both were very profitable. He ultimately used the two bases for privateering raids on Spanish commerce, and they obviously afforded him positions at both the eastern and western ends of Florida and the Gulf of Mexico. A privateer could cruise from Amelia Island to Galveston and back in such a way as to cross all the major Spanish trade routes. Another great advantage of having two bases was that they offered excellent places to dispose of cargoes. It was nearly impossible to prevent the smuggling of goods from Amelia Island into Georgia because the U.S. government could not adequately patrol the many inlets and the St. Marys River. Galveston offered much the same advantage, since there were numerous ways of moving captured goods into New Orleans. Without a doubt, plunder and profit provided strong motives for Aury.[43]

Aury's use of the Mexican flag was very likely a matter of convenience, since he had no desire to be classed as a pirate. There is some evidence that he cooperated with the French exiles who had planted settlements in Alabama and eventually in Texas. But there does not appear to be any hard proof that Aury was a French agent. Nevertheless, he operated with the French and may have been involved in their plans to rescue Napoleon and perhaps find a new empire for him in Texas or even in Florida.

Irwin and Hubbard soon realized that they could gain little if anything by opposing Aury. Since they did not have enough troops to hold Amelia Island for very long, they made the necessary alliance. Aury's men became essential to the defense of the place, and Aury himself refused to remain on the island unless he had command. Eventually Aury and Hubbard reached a compromise whereby Aury became military commander and Hubbard civil governor.[44] When the Mexican flag was raised over Fernandina on 17 September, a proclamation signed by Aury as commander and Hubbard as governor announced the Mexican claim to the island.[45] This arrangement lasted only briefly because a conflict quickly arose between Aury and Hubbard. The strain of this situation soon proved too much for Hubbard, and he died on 19 October, leaving the American faction without a leader. The group of English officers who had come to join MacGregor some two months earlier also complicated the struggle for a time. Eventually Aury gained full control of the island.[46] His motives for wanting Amelia Island differed very little from those of Irwin and Hubbard; all three wanted to capture Spanish commerce, take Florida, and make a huge profit.[47]

Aury had considerably more success in his administration of Amelia Island than his predecessors, perhaps because his West Indian–Haitian troops were better disciplined. He had been assisted at Galveston by Major Joseph Savary, formerly a member of the French army in Haiti. Savary was best known as the commander of one of Jackson's two battalions of "free men of color" at the Battle of New Orleans. He had rescued Aury from a mutinous situation in Galveston, and was very adept at bringing order to untrained troops.[48] This was the force that Aury had brought with him. His use of these men did, however, lead to serious trouble for the island and ultimately proved a major factor in American intervention. Aury tried in vain to persuade the civilian population to return to Fernandina, but the residents, closely related to Georgia slave owners, were fearful. The idea of armed blacks prompted most former inhabitants to resist his encouragement to return. Another problem Aury encountered was the loyalty that supporters of Irwin and Hubbard felt toward the United States. Aury claimed Amelia Island for Mexico, but these people wanted it to belong to the United States. Actually, this division into Mexican and U.S. factions probably hastened the annexation process. In a sense, the followers of Hubbard and Irwin probably won their objective by losing their fight. Aury's blacks and his claim of the territory for Mexico apparently caused American authorities to view his operation there as a threat to the safety of the United States.[49]

Another factor in Aury's greater success was that he had more experience at sea than did MacGregor. He assembled a fairly large fleet of armed ships with crews. Their experience and their willingness to follow orders enabled Aury to enjoy a measure of success MacGregor never attained. All of this helped Aury reach his desired level of profitability. He decided that life would be more fruitful as a privateer than by annexing more land. He had engaged in smuggling slaves into the United States while based at Galveston, and he found this to be equally lucrative at Amelia Island. According to Lloyd's of London, Aury's privateers captured more than $500,000 worth of Spanish goods in two months, most of which they smuggled into Georgia through Amelia Island in the form of slaves.[50] Aury's ships apparently made a special effort to capture Spanish vessels carrying slaves in order to accommodate the ready market in Georgia. The opening of new lands in that state had greatly increased the demand for slaves at that time. Clearly Aury was a shrewd businessman, though a poor revolutionary. He suffered numerous disappointments before he finally captured Old Providence Island, off the eastern coast of Honduras, from the Spanish on 4 July 1818. Working from the island base, Aury continued to aid the republican cause until his death at Old Providence on 30 August 1821.[51]

One thing MacGregor, Aury, Hubbard, and Irwin all had was support from numerous American businessmen and at least some government officials. While Adams was secretary of state, the operation at Amelia Island was not as clearly identifiable as a planned expansion attempt. Nonetheless, the silent hands of the government seemed to have touched all of these adventurers and their operations in trying to cover all possible bases. It would appear that the government had some influence with all of these groups, even with Aury.

The United States adopted a "wait and see" attitude as long as the administration thought the filibusters at Amelia Island had a chance to disrupt Spanish control or to capture, by whatever means, all of Florida. They saw a distinct advantage to doing nothing, so long as there was no danger to the country. Should the Spanish be driven out of Florida, the United States could then annex it without having any direct confrontation with Spain. Not only would the seizure of Florida from a group of filibusters, called bandits by many people, be far more acceptable than taking the territory from Spain, but it would also be justified on the grounds of protecting law and order. When the filibusters turned their attention to privateering operations and it seemed unlikely that they would ever take East Florida, the American government saw no benefit in allowing the activities at Amelia Island to continue.[52] The administration, therefore, decided at that time to take control of the place for the United States by using the secret law that had in 1811 authorized Mathews to take over Florida if the local authorities requested it or if it were about to be occupied by a foreign power. In this case Mexico claimed Amelia Island.[53]

It was probably the illegal slave trade more than the raising of the Mexican flag that attracted serious attention by the U.S. government. In any event, the Monroe administration soon came to consider the privateers and smugglers on Amelia Island as a nuisance and determined to be rid of them. In 1818 Secretary of War John C. Calhoun ordered General Edmund P. Gaines to take possession of Amelia Island for the United States. Gaines immediately dispatched Colonel James Bankhead to conduct this operation, and Bankhead soon occupied the island without firing a shot. He allowed Aury to evacuate peacefully, and Amelia Island had fallen to the Stars and Stripes.[54]

CHAPTER EIGHT

Destiny Becomes Manifest: Andrew Jackson Invades Florida

ONCE THE WAR of 1812 had ended, "a new episode in American history began," one in which U.S. citizens viewed themselves as a single people and nation, with a destiny they alone could fulfill. It was a fresh beginning for the country; it was, according to historian George Dangerfield, the awakening of American nationalism. Before the conflict the nation had conducted its affairs in a diffident fashion, always leery of European reactions. Afterward, Americans became more self-confident, more aggressive, and more determined to plot their own course.[1]

But troubled times in the Gulf region did not change just because Americans had reformed their attitudes. Nor did the destruction of Negro Fort or the capture of Amelia Island bring any measure of settlement. Instead, all this vividly illustrated Spain's tenuous hold over Florida. In fact, after the War of 1812, Spain, weaker than ever, was unable to prevent incursions across the international border. This lawlessness provided an opportunistic motive for U.S. territorial expansion at the expense of those Native Americans inhabiting the region.[2]

Many believed that Spain's inability to prevent American encroachments would bring about Britain's support of the Indians as a means to limit the growth and development of the United States. But following the Treaty of Ghent the British government did the opposite, abdicating any responsibility for the fate of the

141

Creeks. This action was not supported by all English officials, and was bitterly opposed by many British subjects still in Florida. Although the important John Forbes Company, owned by the Innerarity brothers, had made its peace with the United States by 1815, there were still other merchants, filibusters, and numerous citizens unwilling to abandon their Indian friends.

Alexander Arbuthnot, a prominent Scottish trader, and other residents of the island of New Providence in the Bahamas, unaware of the new hands-off policy, expected the British government to honor its commitment to protect its former Creek and Seminole allies. Moreover, many Englishmen anticipated that their government would force the United States to honor the terms of Article Nine of the Treaty of Ghent, which had, in effect, promised to restore Indian lands. Since Arbuthnot operated under this assumption, he and other merchants encouraged the Creeks and runaway slaves in Florida to expect a retrocession of their lost lands. These assurances prompted Creeks and Seminoles to threaten the surveying party mapping the new Creek boundary because it appeared that support from English officials would be forthcoming.[3]

Unlike earlier actions in the Florida borderlands, this time the U.S. government was unwilling to offer semi-covert aid to adventurers and filibusters. The administration felt that any unfriendly action on its part might have a detrimental effect and endanger the attempt to secure Florida through diplomatic negotiations. But there were local leaders and military commanders, such as Andrew Jackson and other southern and western state officials, who may have been unaware of the negotiations taking place, who believed they would be unsuccessful, or who were unwilling to allow diplomacy to run its course. This uncertainty about the government's intentions was probably the most important reason for immediate action, as well as the main source of trouble along the border.

There was a great drama being played out in Florida during this time; few, if any, inhabitants were happy with the turmoil. Certainly there were altruists like Arbuthnot who seemingly had the best interests of the Indians at heart. At the same time, the

Andrew Jackson. Portrait by Samuel Lovett Waldo (Courtesy of The Historical New Orleans Collection, Museum/Research Center, accession no. 1979.112)

area abounded with adventurers, many of whom were British subjects, out to make a fortune and ready to stir the boiling pot. One almost needs a scorecard to keep track of these people. George Woodbine and Robert Christie Ambrister were two men always ready to light a fire. Others, such as Peter Cook, William Hambly, and even Gregor MacGregor from Amelia Island, appeared to change sides. All in all, there was a considerable contingent of people in Florida who caused turmoil.

British officials were of a divided mind as to what should be done about Florida and the Indians. Although many within the region, such as Arbuthnot, ardently supported the Indians' claims, there was a substantial number of others who did not.

Before the Americans reduced Negro Fort, William Hambly, who had been left in command by Major Edward Nicolls, and Edmund Doyle, agent for the Forbes Company at Apalachicola, had furnished the Innerarity brothers with information regarding British movements at Negro Fort. Though it was unclear whether Doyle and Hambly knew that the Inneraritys were passing these reports on to the U.S. government, those dispatches nonetheless found their way into official American records. Whatever doubts the Americans might have had regarding Doyle's and Hambly's loyalty were quickly dispelled once the British withdrew from the bastion. Afterward, Hambly established direct contact with the Americans, providing them with pertinent information that led to the demolition of Negro Fort.[4]

Even though the destruction of Negro Fort did not have the desired effect of quieting Indian hostility, it did eliminate the best source of weapons within the region. With the most important threat to stability eradicated, U.S. troops felt free to leave Camp Crawford (later renamed Fort Scott), a post located at the confluence of the Flint and Chattahoochee Rivers. The Creeks and Seminoles, however, interpreted this as a sign of weakness, and the withdrawal probably stimulated more hostile action rather than less.[5]

As early as December 1815, rumors circulated among the Indians that the British were promising aid in the immediate future.[6] Arbuthnot, who had for years traded extensively with the Indians from his base in the Bahamas, was undoubtedly one source for these stories. After the War of 1812 the elderly merchant moved to Florida, where he established two trading posts. Although the exact date of his arrival on the mainland is uncertain, he was identified as a resident on 13 November 1816, when his name appeared as a witness to a list of slaves belonging to the Seminole chief Bowlegs.[7]

According to Forbes agent Edmund Doyle, Arbuthnot was one of several smugglers who illegally opened stores in early 1817 near the Forbes trading establishment at Apalachicola. Doyle vehemently resented Arbuthnot's having located a store on Ocklockoney Bay because he considered it unfair competition.[8] Doyle firmly believed that Arbuthnot was an illegal trader even though the *Royal Gazette* reported that the merchant did, in fact, have a legal Spanish license to trade in Florida.[9] The Forbes agent apparently regarded his competitor as illegal because the Spanish government had in 1783 granted Forbes an exclusive right to control the Indian trade in Florida. As that company became increasingly friendly to the United States, the Spanish government responded by issuing additional permits, although still validating the Forbes Company's licenses. The fact that Jackson captured Arbuthnot at St. Marks, inside the governor's residence, suggests that the merchant did indeed have a proper trading license.[10]

Soon after Arbuthnot arrived, he reminded the Indians that the British had promised to restore their lands. He even accepted a power of attorney from the displaced Creeks. Arbuthnot felt strongly about acting as the Indians' representative because they were, as he wrote, "children of nature . . . [who] till their fields, and hunt the stag, and graze the cattle, [and whose] ideas will extend no farther." As a people, he angrily contended, "they have been ill treated by the English and robbed by the Americans." The English left them after the war "without a pilot to be robbed and ill treated by their natural and sworn enemies the Americans." Instead of complying with the Treaty of Ghent, Americans continued "to extend their encroachments and aggression" against the natives. This disturbed the trader and obviously motivated him to serve as the Creeks' legal agent.[11]

As the legal spokesman for the displaced Indians, Arbuthnot entered into correspondence with the Americans, the British governor of Nassau, the British minister to the United States, and Spanish officials, calling for the return of Creek lands. In August 1817 he addressed a letter to Major Nicolls reminding him of the British promise to restore Indian lands and complaining that Captain George Woodbine had stolen the British gifts presented to the Indian leader Josiah Francis.[12]

Woodbine and his assistant Robert Christie Ambrister represented the real outside source of belligerence in Florida. It was Woodbine whom Jackson wanted to hang. During the War of 1812 Woodbine had served as Major Nicolls's Indian agent and chief recruiter in Pensacola and later Apalachicola. He was well known to Spanish and Americans and disliked by both groups. Woodbine had been tried in Nassau in October 1815 on charges of slave stealing, stemming from his recruiting of blacks at Pensacola and other parts of West Florida. Though he was not convicted, the trial received widespread interest.[13]

Following his exoneration, Woodbine made several trips to Florida to encourage the Indians and runaway slaves. Although no specific record of his promises exists, he apparently persuaded those groups to resist the United States. He also convinced them that he was the advance agent of a British force coming to help them regain their lost lands. The Indians found this easy to believe, since only two years earlier he had been exactly what he was now claiming to be, a British military agent. Moreover, Woodbine was an adventurer, and his own interests appear to have been a more important motive for his actions than any ideals he may have espoused. The Indians had supposedly given him considerable acreage in Florida, which he surely hoped to keep. He also thought that he could gain title to the Forbes Purchase, a large tract of land between the Apalachicola and Wakulla Rivers, given to the Forbes Company in 1804 and later confirmed by Spanish authorities. Apparently, Woodbine had convinced the Indians to cede this land to him once the Spanish were expelled.[14]

Clearly, Woodbine planned to take advantage of the unrest in East Florida, now filled with militant Indians and blacks and agitated by a disorganized band of white border raiders. In this situation it would have been an easy matter for any organized force to seize control of the region. As part of his plan, he had joined the filibuster-privateer Gregor MacGregor at Amelia Island.[15] Woodbine and MacGregor had traveled to the Bahamas and recruited from recently disbanded West Indies regiments in nearby New Providence and Jamaica. In MacGregor's absence, Commodore Luis Aury, a filibuster commanding about fifty men, had claimed Amelia Island for the Republic of Mexico. Soon afterward, Woodbine left New Providence for his native Jamaica to recruit for the Florida expedition.[16]

Later, Woodbine believed he could organize the renegade Creek Indians and blacks of Florida who served with him during the recent war. These latest efforts were too radical for conservative Bahamian Governor Charles Cameron, who had previously offered support to the Indians in Florida. Now opposed to Woodbine's actions, Cameron issued a memorandum to Jamaican officials instructing them to stop Woodbine's attempt to obtain arms. According to Cameron, Woodbine's intentions were no less than the conquest of Spanish Florida. Considering the force available to him, there is little doubt that Woodbine would have succeeded had he not been stopped by British officials.[17]

Robert C. Ambrister, one of the best-known men Woodbine recruited at New Providence, had first enlisted with Nicolls in the summer of 1814 and then served with Woodbine as a lieutenant of Colonial Marines at Pensacola and later at Apalachicola. He served with Nicolls and Woodbine until the evacuation of Apalachicola, sometime after March 1815, at which point he returned to New Providence.[18]

Ambrister was directed to establish a base on Tampa Bay where the expedition could be landed and supplies collected. The Woodbine plan, apparently with MacGregor's approval, instructed Ambrister and twenty armed blacks to proceed to Chief Bowlegs's village to recruit the leader and organize his Seminole followers. This part of the expedition was quickly doomed to failure when Ambrister arrived in Bowlegs's camp without realizing that it had already been captured by Jackson. Ambrister was immediately taken prisoner.

Woodbine's efforts were curtailed by British authorities, and this was apparently the last time either he or MacGregor was able to recruit in the West Indies.[19] The two continued to work together for some time after this, but the capture and execution of Ambrister and the active intervention by the British government to halt Woodbine's expedition against Florida seem to have prevented any new attacks on North America.[20]

According to Ambrister's father, an old South Carolina Tory who had become the secretary of the Bahamian legislature, the younger Ambrister held no commission of any kind after the War

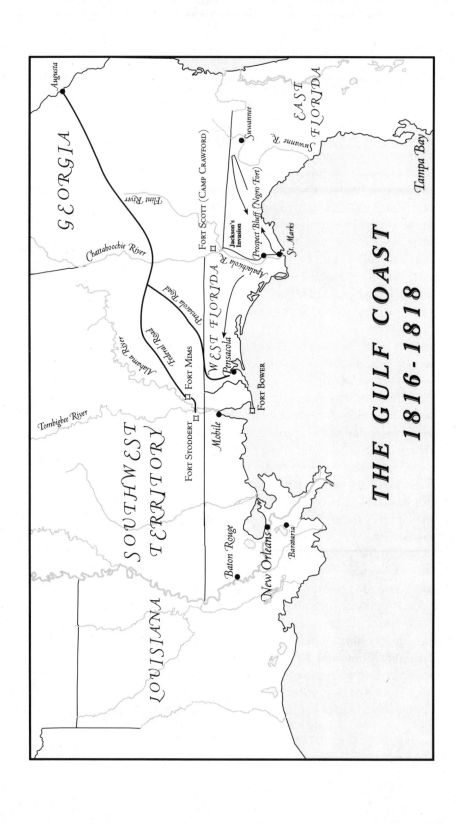

of 1812. The elder Ambrister insisted that his son's visit to Florida in 1818 was a trading mission.[21] This story is certainly interesting when contrasted with the account young Ambrister provided during his capture and trial by the United States. In these statements, he claimed that he had been wounded at Waterloo and had guarded Napoleon at St. Helena. Following this service he was sent to the Orient, where he was suspended from rank for one year for dueling. He then traveled to New Providence to serve his suspension. It was during this year that he claimed he met and was recruited by Woodbine. Moreover, he maintained that a young woman was waiting to marry him in England. Yet from the dates of the above statements and the information contained within, he could not have possibly performed all of the services, and very likely the entire tale was a lie.[22]

What Ambrister expected to accomplish by the false statements concerning his background can only be surmised, but it seems most probable that he hoped the Americans would not know of his part in Nicolls's mission to the Creek Nation in 1814. This expedition was so unpopular in the United States that he doubtless believed he would have no chance of avoiding a death penalty if it were known that he had been at Apalachicola. Whether his account was believed or not is unclear, but certainly some American officers knew the truth. William Hambly had served with Ambrister at Apalachicola, and Hambly was the main prosecution witness at the trial. In any case, Ambrister's elaborate story did him little good, because he was shot for his more immediate transgressions. In the overall view of what happened during this period, the terror, both real and imagined, incited by these men and their Indian and black followers probably did more to precipitate Jackson's invasion than any other factor.

American reaction to increased hostility and lawlessness in the area was not long in coming. General Edmund P. Gaines gradually began to concentrate troops in the area of the Escambia River before rebuilding Fort Scott above the Apalachicola.[23] This position had been evacuated by the United States in the fall of 1816 after the successful reduction of Negro Fort. Once abandoned, the stronghold was looted and occupied by Indians and

149

blacks who forced the evacuation of the few settlers who had taken up land around the bastion. Early in 1817, some six hundred armed blacks, commanded by Bowlegs's chief slave, Nero, began plans to punish the Americans for the bloodshed at Prospect Bluff. Later that fall, Ambrister arrived in the region and commenced the training of this force. Reprisals for the destruction of Negro Fort continued along the Georgia-Florida border until the spring of 1818.[24]

Gaines's efforts to bolster the American presence in the region were frustrated in part by José Masot, the governor of West Florida. Masot, heretofore seemingly a friend to the United States, suddenly refused in early 1817 to allow supplies to be transported through Pensacola and Spanish territory. This change of attitude was probably in retaliation for American incursions into Florida. Whatever the reason, it made Gaines's position somewhat difficult, since supplies had to be brought up-river through Spanish territory.

Once Gaines had amassed what he believed to be an adequate number of troops, he began to sweep through the Gulf frontier in search of belligerent runaway slaves and Indians. He also demanded that the various Seminole chiefs surrender those fugitives who had been responsible for the violence along the frontier. The Indian chiefs responded that there were no murderers among the Seminoles and that the blacks involved had already moved elsewhere. Moreover, King Hatchy asserted that he would resist if any Americans tried to pass through the territory.

Conflict between the Americans and the Indians began at Fowltown, an Indian community about fifteen miles east of Fort Scott near the Georgia-Florida border, on 21 November 1817. When American troops concentrated on the west bank of the Flint River, Chief Inihamathla of the Fowltown Indians warned that he would attack if the Americans crossed the river. Facing this threat, Gaines ordered Major David Twiggs and his force of 250 men to proceed to Fowltown and capture the chief of the village. Even though the general seemingly only wanted a conference with the chief, he ordered Twiggs to fight should the group be attacked. The U.S. force arrived at Fowltown early on the morning of 21 November, only to face a group of belligerents. Twiggs ordered his men to return fire, and within a short time the Indians had dispersed. In an immediate search of the town, the Americans found a British uniform and a certificate signed by Nicolls stating that the chief was a friend of Great Britain. With the strong evidence that Fowltown had supported the British in the recent war, and since the Indians of the settlement appeared to still be hostile, Gaines ordered the town burned.

Indian retaliation for the destruction of Fowltown was quick in coming. On 29 November, Lieutenant Richard W. Scott attempted to sail up the Apalachicola River with a small detachment, including several women and children. About a mile below the confluence of the Flint and Chattahoochee Rivers, Indians ambushed Scott's party. Although most of the whites were killed in the fight, the remainder were later massacred in a feast of torture in which the survivors were scalped and the children taken by the feet and their heads smashed on the side of the boat. Seemingly there were three survivors: two men escaped by swimming the river, eventually reaching Fort Scott; a woman who was taken prisoner was later recaptured. Five other boats were attacked for a period of four days in midstream before a detachment of troops from Fort Scott could relieve the vessels. At about the same time, a party of Indians from Fowltown attacked and looted the Forbes store at Apalachicola, driving away Hambly and Doyle. During this time there were continued reports that Arbuthnot and Woodbine were arousing the Indians.[25]

Gaines began preparations for what would doubtless become another major Indian campaign. But these plans were interrupted by a directive from Secretary of War John C. Calhoun that ordered Gaines to proceed immediately to Amelia Island and take possession of the place for the United States. President Monroe believed that an armed expedition against the island would demonstrate American resolve and pressure Spain to cede Florida. Though Monroe was considering national objectives, neither he nor Calhoun had knowledge of the violence on the Apalachicola River; Gaines had no choice but to comply.[26]

Meanwhile, as Gaines marched toward Amelia Island, Jackson

moved against the Indians who were raiding the Georgia border. Jackson had also received a copy of the directive sending Gaines into Florida. A second order, not yet received by Gaines, forbade the capture of Spanish towns but otherwise gave the general a free hand.[27] Less than two weeks later, Jackson received similar instructions. Gaines had been cautioned not to attack Spanish towns, but Jackson was instructed to "adopt the necessary measure to terminate a conflict."[28]

Although Jackson's orders were issued by Secretary of War Calhoun, they no doubt reflected President Monroe's feelings on the subject. In a letter to Alabama Territorial Governor William W. Bibb, Calhoun repeated the orders and claimed that Jackson was "authorized to conduct the war as he thought best." With these instructions, the general believed he could act as he saw fit, and he suggested that if President Monroe wished, he would take all of Florida. Knowing that the president could not make a public statement approving the acquisition of this area in such a manner, Jackson suggested that he express his wishes through Congressman John Rhea of Tennessee. The general later maintained that he had received a letter from Rhea in which the president authorized him to seize Florida; Jackson claimed that he subsequently burned the letter. It has never been established whether such a letter truly existed.

In a comment written by Monroe on Jackson's letter, the president explained that he did not read the correspondence until much later. He was being deliberately vague as to whether he had authorized the Rhea letter. Monroe did admit that the congressman might have thought he was giving presidential approval to a plan to capture Florida. The president must certainly have known what Jackson intended. Historian Robert Remini asserts that Monroe knew exactly what Jackson would do in Florida and that that was the reason the general was sent.[29]

Monroe and his cabinet preferred to obtain Florida through diplomacy, but an invasion by Jackson was certainly a means of pressuring Spain on the Florida question. There is too much evidence that the government was well aware of the situation to believe that the president did not know what Jackson was doing or that he did not want this kind of action. This was the vague type of authorization that was so characteristic of Monroe, both as secretary of state and as president. There are remarkable similarities between Jackson's authorization to invade Florida, the orders Monroe gave Governor Mathews in 1812, and the planned support of Bernardo Gutiérrez in his invasion of Texas.

When Jackson was ordered to Fort Scott to assume command in Gaines's absence, he was authorized to raise the militia units needed for the expedition from adjacent states. Because Georgia was the only bordering state and its militia was already engaged, Jackson interpreted his orders to mean that he could raise troops in Tennessee, which he promptly did. By calling on his old volunteer officers he was able to enlist more than a thousand men, most of whom had served with him before. This army was to march overland to Fort Jackson, located at the confluence of the Coosa and Tallapoosa Rivers, for supplies and then proceed south to Fort Scott.

Jackson himself departed Nashville on 22 January 1818 with two companies and arrived at Fort Hawkins in Hartford, Georgia, eighteen days later. While at Hartford, the general learned that American forces at Fort Scott were starving because supplies could not be ferried through Spanish territory. Taking what he could muster, including eleven hundred hogs previously purchased by Gaines, Jackson started out for Fort Scott. Soon after leaving Fort Hawkins, Jackson met General Gaines, who was returning from Amelia Island. This force, when combined with nearly two thousand friendly Creeks under William McIntosh, increased Jackson's army to almost five thousand. Upon arriving at Fort Scott on 9 March, the general found that his troops had only one day's rations, with none expected from Georgia. Moreover, having swept the country behind him, he knew there was no chance of resupply should he retreat. Though critically short of supplies, Jackson divided his food and proceeded south into Florida. Fortunately, he encountered a boatload of flour destined for his troops. With this modicum of supplies, Jackson marched on to Prospect Bluff, the former site of Negro Fort, where he rebuilt the bastion, naming it Fort Gadsden. Additional supplies arrived before the end of March.[30]

General Gaines, who had been sent ahead to Fort Scott with a small force, had not arrived when Jackson's main army reached the place, leading many to believe he had succumbed to the Indians. Days later, Gaines and a few of his men arrived at the fort. It seems that the boat Gaines and his troops were using had hit a snag and sunk, causing the general to lose several men and all his equipment. Afterward, Gaines had spent six days stumbling through the woods before reaching the fort.

Once Gaines arrived, Jackson took stock of his situation and decided to advance on the hostile Indian towns. The first action occurred when Jackson's troops advanced on the Miccosukee towns, where they met little opposition. Once the Indians fled, American troops found about fifty fresh scalps believed to have come from Lieutenant Scott's party. The additional discovery of some equipment and about three hundred old scalps substantiated the general's belief that this group was one of the principal raiding parties.[31] Jackson's reaction to the grim findings at the Miccosukee towns was to order those places burned. The work of torching some three hundred Indian houses proceeded without incident, but only after the Americans removed the considerable quantities of corn they found—these stores would replenish Jackson's dwindling supplies.

After Jackson determined that the inhabitants from the Miccosukee settlements had fled toward St. Marks, he marched quickly in pursuit. He reported that the Indians and their black allies had demanded the surrender of St. Marks and that the Spanish garrison was too weak to defend the place. Thus, Jackson claimed that Spain's weakened state and its inability to offer any defense were his overriding reasons for occupying the town and sending a garrison to Pensacola. Though there is little doubt that some hostiles did enter St. Marks, they probably did not offer the primary cause for Jackson's action. From the tone of Jackson's report, one would have to assume that his main objective was simply to occupy the settlement, thereby preventing the Spanish from furnishing any more arms and encouragement to his enemies.

Although Jackson encountered only a few Indians at St. Marks, he did find someone far more important. He captured Alexander Arbuthnot, whom he believed to be the principal instigator of Indian hostilities. Jackson also learned from Master-Commandant Isaac McKeever of the U.S. Navy that he had disguised his gunboat as a British vessel and tricked Hidlis Hadjo (Josiah Francis), a Red Stick menace since the beginning of the Creek War, and Himollemice into coming aboard. Once they were on board, McKeever took the two Indians prisoner. Later on, Jackson happily hanged both men as examples. The fact that these Indians were using St. Marks as a refuge to escape Jackson's army greatly reinforced the belief that Spain was assisting the Indians.[32]

Jackson remained at St. Marks for only two days. On 9 April, after leaving a strong garrison in the town, he took his main army, including William McIntosh and a band of friendly Indians, on a forced march to Bowlegs's town on the Suwanee. En route the friendly Creeks fought one minor battle with the Seminoles in which they killed thirty-seven of the enemy and captured ninety-seven women and children and six hundred head of cattle before the survivors escaped into the swamp. This proved to be the only significant action, because Bowlegs's town had been abandoned by the time the troops reached it. Even so, the deserted village yielded about thirty-seven hundred bushels of corn and a number of horses and cattle.

As a result of his sudden move to the town, Jackson was able to capture Robert Ambrister and Peter Cook, two British citizens. On the evening of 18 April, the two men, accompanied by several armed blacks, rode into Bowlegs's village before realizing the place was occupied by Americans. Soon after his capture, Cook admitted to Jackson that Ambrister had arrived on Arbuthnot's schooner, by now anchored at the mouth of the Suwanee River. The general immediately dispatched a party to seize the ship and return it to St. Marks.[33] Jackson's speed in returning to St. Marks was even greater than his advance, covering the entire 107 miles in only five days. Once there, he issued orders to set in motion trials for Ambrister and Arbuthnot.

There is little evidence that Arbuthnot encouraged the Indians to resume hostilities against the United States, but when he was captured he did have a memorandum for arms for King Hatchy written on the back of one of his letters. Although the letter was in his possession, Jackson never proved that Arbuthnot was the author. On the contrary, most evidence indicates that he indeed encouraged the Indians to retreat during Jackson's invasion, believing they could not withstand the Americans.[34]

Only Hambly testified that Arbuthnot had encouraged violence. Hambly, suffering from the mercantile competition offered by Arbuthnot, was eager to believe the worst about the Scotsman. History did not record whether or not he consciously lied in his testimony, but his correspondence to his superiors in the Forbes Company indicated that he honestly believed Arbuthnot was inciting continued conflict. Whatever Hambly's motives, much of his testimony about Arbuthnot did not accurately reflect the merchant's character and is, therefore, suspect. Not only was Hambly eager to believe the worst, but so was Jackson. Since most of the case against Arbuthnot was based on Hambly's testimony, it is highly probable that the Americans unjustly convicted and executed the Scotsman.[35]

Hambly's testimony is doubly questionable when examined in the light of the documents that seem to prove the truth of Arbuthnot's statements at his trial. The Scotsman believed that the British government should, if necessary, force the United States to restore the Indian lands, as guaranteed by Article Nine. He was a very active letter writer who corresponded with virtually every official, both British and American, even remotely concerned with the Indian situation. So much did Arbuthnot use the pen as a weapon that any encouragement of Indian violence would be completely out of character. Had Arbuthnot been the real British agent Jackson thought, then why was the merchant so critical of Britain's failure to aid the Indians? The British government was trying to disassociate itself from the Indian alliances and make peace. The last thing Britain would have wanted was for an agent to start a new war.[36]

Jackson's determination to hang Arbuthnot probably rested on his trust of Hambly and his frustration at not being able to catch Bowlegs and Woodbine, rather than on any real desire for justice. His treatment of Arbuthnot was extreme and unjust considering the trader's actions. The Scotsman became a martyr in the cause of fair treatment for the Indians. Since the natives had killed many whites, fair treatment for them was perhaps too much to expect. Jackson viewed Arbuthnot as the instigator of increased hostilities because of the trader's association with persons known to be encouraging new Indian uprisings. At least on one occasion, he had brought the "notorious" George Woodbine to Florida to consult with Indians. Even so, Arbuthnot did not trust Woodbine because of his grandiose promises that he obviously could never deliver.[37] Public opinion in many parts of the country indicated that most Americans believed Arbuthnot was a former army officer and an agent of the British government. None of this takes into consideration the questionable legality of the proceedings, which took place on Spanish soil rather than in the United States.[38]

The case against Ambrister was considerably better. Ambrister had been a part of the old Nicolls and Woodbine force during the War of 1812, and despite his efforts to conceal his past, the young American ex-patriot's actions were no doubt familiar to Jackson. Ambrister was leading a group of armed blacks at the time of his capture, leaving no doubt that he was engaged in filibustering activities with Woodbine. Although Jackson believed that Ambrister's expedition was aimed at the United States, it was in fact directed at Spanish Florida. In any case, the general refused the court-martial officers' recommendation of clemency for Ambrister and thereby demonstrated rather clearly his intention from the start to execute the young man.[39]

Because Ambrister and Arbuthnot were tried and executed at the same time and on similar charges, many people have assumed that the two were partners. Nothing could have been further from the truth. Ambrister had come to Florida from Nassau with a group of armed men and had seized Arbuthnot's store and schooner, helped himself to the Scotsman's supply of goods, and held the merchant's son and the captain and crew of the vessel as prisoners. The men were being held prisoner aboard the schooner *Chance* by Ambrister's men even as Jackson's forces captured the vessel.[40]

The British reacted bitterly to Jackson's invasion and to the executions of Ambrister and Arbuthnot. Not surprisingly, the Nassau press was especially caustic, because Ambrister was the nephew of the governor of that island and Arbuthnot a respected merchant. Moreover, the Nassau press did not limit its condemnation to the executions, but also complained vehemently about the Americans' inhumane treatment of the Indians. They accused the Americans of a deliberate campaign to exterminate the natives. That same press viewed the executions not only as harsh and unjustified punishment but also as entirely illegal, since they took place in Spanish territory. The editor of the *Royal Gazette and Bahama Advertiser*, in addition to condemning the act, insisted that the British government punish those responsible.[41]

The London press was no less angry over the executions and probably stimulated widespread demand in Britain that measures be taken. The Houses of Parliament also had numerous bitter debates about the "unwarranted executions." British Minister Charles Bagot, however, after seeing the court-martial records, advised his superiors that any action would be unwarranted and that the publication of the information would greatly embarrass the government. His references were to Arbuthnot's journal and several of his letters, which, by Bagot's own admission, did make it appear that he was an official British agent. Actually, Bagot believed that Arbuthnot and Ambrister both used the British name and prestige without having been given any governmental authority. He concluded from this evidence that the United States could easily deduce that the men were British agents. Lord Castlereagh, after examining the records, agreed that the two had acted improperly, thus making any official intervention unjustified interference.[42] As a result of this stand, the

London government took no action on the case, a crisis was averted, and peaceful relations were maintained.

The executions of Ambrister and Arbuthnot appear to put a permanent end to British influence in Florida. Woodbine continued to operate with MacGregor until the latter returned to Europe. The adventurer eventually settled in Mexico, where he was murdered in Campeche in 1837.[43] The records show no evidence of any other British subjects filibustering in the area, or of any further activities of British merchants trading in Florida. The Forbes Company, which at one time was a British firm, became almost Americanized and rapidly abandoned the Indian trade as a major function. Despite the loss of that trade, the company continued to operate a number of mercantile and other diversified businesses until the 1840s.

Soon after the executions, Jackson, leaving a detachment at St. Marks, returned with most of his forces to Fort Gadsden at Apalachicola. The American retreat to Fort Gadsden gave the appearance that Jackson planned to end his Florida campaign. Shortly after arriving at the bastion, he received a note from the Spanish governor at Pensacola protesting his invasion and threatening force to expel the Americans. This letter supposedly angered Jackson and prompted him to move against Pensacola. His wrath, however, was almost certainly a pretense for what he had intended to do all along—invade and annex Florida. Furthermore, since the Spanish were harboring at least 550 hostile Indians at Pensacola, he believed his advance on the settlement would be justified.[44]

Jackson articulated a more succinct explanation for his actions when he reported to Secretary of War Calhoun that there would never be peace with the Indians in the region until all foreign influences, including the Spanish, were removed. Using this official rationale for his actions, Jackson proceeded against Pensacola, the main center of support for Indian animosity against the United States. He argued that the Spanish were using the settlement to arm hundreds or perhaps even thousands of Indians for an attack.

Jackson departed Fort Gadsden with more than a thousand men and easily captured Pensacola on 28 May 1818. Governor Colonel José Masot fled the city, taking refuge in Fort Carlos of Barrancas, but it too was soon captured. Jackson accused the Spanish of encouraging Indian attacks against the United States and threatened punishment. Actually, Jackson's real demand was for the Spanish to control the Indians within the region, and he planned to occupy Florida unless they provided enough troops to do so. No doubt, he realized that Spain could never garrison the entire region and that U.S. occupation would be permanent, probably ending Spanish rule east of the Mississippi River. Jackson's operations in 1818 did not end Spain's control over Florida, but they did hasten negotiations that ultimately resulted in the region's final transfer to the United States in 1821.[45]

Although American public opinion concerning the executions of Ambrister and Arbuthnot was divided, the capture of Pensacola was viewed more harshly. The *New York Evening Post* bitterly opposed the attack and considered Jackson a perfidious aggressor. The Republican mouthpiece *National Intelligencer* took a more moderate view, although it could hardly be said to have supported the general. Even *The Georgian* of Savannah, while approving of most of the general's acts as necessary, condemned Jackson for his ruthlessness in the whole affair.[46]

These papers represented their regions well. The anti-expansionist views of the East Coast were often illustrated in the *Post*. The *National Intelligencer,* though a Republican paper, was wavering and unwilling to support Jackson, just as the party was divided on this issue. Many Republicans expected to obtain Florida through diplomacy soon and believed that the general's actions jeopardized those negotiations. The Georgia paper, while supportive of annexation, was more moderate than the others.

Jackson, expecting that he would have to account for his actions, did sincerely believe the administration would support his stand. With this in mind, he returned to Nashville, remaining until January 1819, when he traveled to Washington to be present at the congressional hearings investigating his invasion. He no doubt assumed his presence would strengthen his case, especially since there was considerable opposition to his actions. In the end Congress exonerated Jackson from any wrongdoing.[47]

Many Republicans, including Jackson, were clearly interested in expansion and the inevitable annexation of Florida. Yet with the general's withdrawal, Florida reverted to Spanish control for the last phase of foreign dominion. In the period following the Treaty of Ghent there had been many protests concerning the Indian raids into American territory. The Spanish representative in Washington, Don Luis de Onís, consistently denied that the raids had been encouraged by his government. In fact, he too constantly complained of the American encroachments and aggression against Spanish territory. The minister's list of grievances included the occupation of Baton Rouge and Mobile, the failure of the Madison administration to prevent organized filibustering expeditions against Texas by Álvarez de Toledo and others, and lastly, the facilities granted in U.S. ports to rebel privateers such as Jean Laffite.[48] These same protests had been presented on the local level by both the Spanish governor of West Florida and the American governor of Georgia, yet to no avail.[49]

Even before Jackson's punitive expedition, this conflict had reached a point where Spanish officials realized some action had to be taken. The Spanish-American empire was crumbling, and some within the Madrid government realized that U.S. annexation of Florida was inevitable. At the time of the invasion, Onís had already entered into negotiations with Secretary of State John Quincy Adams over the cession of Florida, negotiations that had reached a critical point. In a letter dated 24 January 1818, Onís had proposed to Adams that Spain would cede Florida in exchange for a promise by the United States to relinquish all claims to Texas and to agree on the Texas-Louisiana boundary. Other conditions for the cession included that the United States eliminate American privateering against Spanish territory, that the United States pay damages for spoliations against Spanish commerce, that American citizens stop arming Spanish enemies, and that the government prohibit filibusters from operating on American soil.[50]

Although Jackson's expedition temporarily delayed Spanish-

John Quincy Adams. Portrait by Asher B. Durand after Gilbert Stuart (Courtesy of
the National Archives)

American negotiations, the mediation did continue. Eventually
the cession was made with the provisions mentioned. It is interesting to note that Onís seemed, throughout his correspondence,
to be more concerned with Jean Laffite's privateers and American filibusters in Texas than with the situation in Florida. Even
though most people were unaware of it, Laffite was actually working for the Spanish at this time, as we will explore in more depth
in the next chapter. It seems likely that the Florida cession would
have soon occurred regardless of Jackson's invasion, and that the
concessions regarding Texas made by the United States in the
Transcontinental Treaty were in the beginning no more than a
gesture to Spain. Soon after the treaty, Mexico became indepen-

dent and the agreement with Spain regarding Texas became ir-
relevant.

Actually, Onís and probably most other Spanish officials did
not expect to hold Florida by military power. Onís had opposed
using force to defend Florida during the War of 1812, preferring
to regain Spanish territory with British help at the peace table.
The hope of recovering the lost territory in Florida was not without foundation, since Castlereagh had strongly hinted to Count
Fernán-Núñez, Spanish minister to England, that the British government would help restore Spain's lost Florida lands. The apparent Spanish delays and posturing during the negotiations and
ratification of the Transcontinental Treaty were because they expected British aid at any moment, but it never came.[51]

With the cession of Florida, the great southern push of American expansion was complete—thereafter, further expansion
moved westward. The War of 1812, combined with the annexation of Florida, destroyed the free black settlements that threatened slavery and the plantation system. This acquisition also isolated the southern Indians from further foreign assistance and
broke their power as a meaningful military force. Within a few
years, the U.S. government moved not only the Creeks but most
of the other southern Indians to lands west of the Mississippi
River. Though this move appeared inevitable, it seems probable
that the war and settlement of the Florida question accelerated
the process considerably. What becomes apparent is that the sub-
jugation of the free black communities and the southern Indians
ultimately encouraged Manifest Destiny as well as the westward
movement.[52]

CHAPTER NINE

"Taking Advantage of Propitious Circumstances": The Struggle for Texas

WITHIN JAMES MONROE's administration after 1816, a change occurred in either style or policy, if not both, toward U.S. expansion. At least part of this change can be attributed to the transition from James Monroe to John Quincy Adams as secretary of state; their styles clearly differed. Monroe often used filibusters and revolution, even finding excuses to employ regular U.S. military forces in his efforts to gain new territory. Adams, though sometimes taking advantage of the activities of filibusters and revolutionaries, much preferred to accomplish his objectives through diplomatic efforts.[1]

These differences are especially apparent in the events that took place in Florida and Texas. The Magee-Gutiérrez expedition in 1812 had obviously been supported, and to some degree planned, by the U.S. government. The "patriot war" in Florida had been, for all practical purposes, a regular operation of the American government. The occupation of Amelia Island and activities in East Florida by MacGregor had not been opposed by the administration, although there is no evidence that the government did more than observe these movements. Although American citizens and business interests took part in these operations, the Washington establishment provided neither official nor unofficial support. Only after Amelia Island became a major center of the illegal slave trade and had been claimed for Mexico by Luis Aury did the U.S. government take action.

164

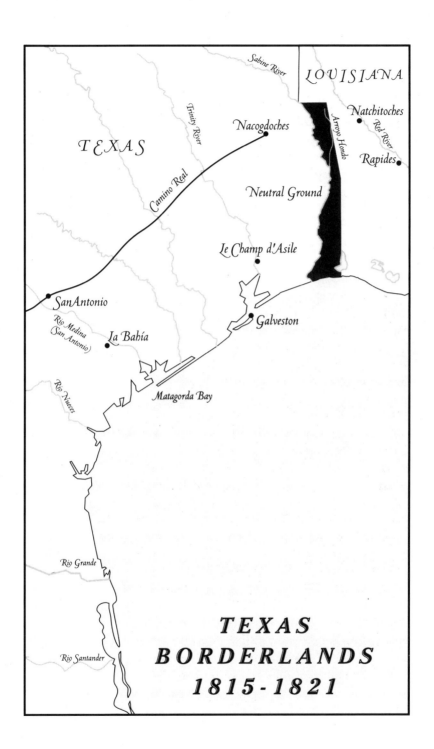

LOUISIANA

Sabine River

Natchitoches

Red River

TEXAS

Trinity River

Nacogdoches

Arroyo Hondo

Rapides

Camino Real

Neutral Ground

Le Champ d'Asile

SanAntonio

Rio Medina
(San Antonio)

La Bahía

Galveston

Matagorda Bay

Rio Nueces

Rio Grande

Rio Santander

TEXAS
BORDERLANDS
1815-1821

The period after 1815 saw a substantial amount of activity in Texas directed against the Spanish, but, as in the case of Amelia Island, the American government offered no planning or coordination. Following the defeat of the Magee-Gutiérrez expedition at the Battle of Medina, several of the movement's former leaders attempted to form a new force. Toledo fled to the United States, eventually making his way to Nashville. Once in the States, he tried to persuade Monroe and others to provide material support for a new expedition. His efforts were unsuccessful, as no government official agreed to grant his petition for support. He also asked Andrew Jackson for an army commission, but the general never acted on the request.[2]

President Madison probably did not want to initiate additional activity in Texas until the war with England had ended. Since the Battle of Medina had been such a disaster, the government likely had no desire to repeat the Texas fiasco. Moreover, the country was badly divided over the War of 1812, and expansionist efforts were certainly not popular in the Northeast, an area already largely disaffected.[3] The United States had always appeared to maintain an official position of neutrality.

John Hamilton Robinson's mission to Mexico had promised U.S. neutrality to Spanish officials. Yet the Claiborne order to stop the Magee-Gutiérrez invasion, carefully timed to reach Natchitoches after the expedition had left the country, was part of this pretended neutrality, a deception needed for political reasons as well as to prevent English intervention. Another view of this activity was offered by Matthew Lyon to Andrew Jackson: "This nation [is] destined to civilize & Govern this Continent. The Spaniards in Europe are in a State of Barbarous Superstitious dependence on an Ignorant bigoted Clergy, those in America are worse." Lyon further argued that Americans alone "are capable of spreading [to] them [Spanish-speaking inhabitants of North America] more than English civilization—this must be a work of time conducted by a wise & Energetic American government taking advantage of propitious circumstances: not by a mob like those now gone or going to Mexico." He informed Jackson that "we took good Stride toward this by getting hold of the mouth [of the] Mississippi and your late labors have a tendency [to continue] that." The Kentucky resident and former Jeffersonian Republican congressman very likely shared this opinion with western moderates—he obviously agreed with the idea of Manifest Destiny, yet he abhorred the unorthodox methods used to achieve it.[4]

At least three new expeditions attempted to retake Texas during the War of 1812. Toledo succeeded to some extent in raising men and money and, above all, in gaining support from the Americans, but he never launched a new invasion of Texas. Also during this period, several French patriots tried to seize part of Texas as a refuge for Napoleon Bonaparte.[5] War with England notwithstanding, the Washington government likely did not want to delay any new action, because any conquest of Texas by an outsider at this time might give the territory to France or some European ally. Many also feared that any land Spain lost to form an independent Mexico would be more difficult for the United States to obtain in the future. It should be noted that in 1819 the Adams-Onís Treaty recognized Spanish, not Mexican, control of Texas. Spain, after all, had not lost Mexico, but was still declining as an imperial power.[6]

A French expedition formed by the two old Napoleonic generals, Jean Joseph Amable Humbert and Ironée Amélot de Lacroix, became one of the many activities continuously rumored in the Louisiana and Philadelphia hotbeds for French refugees. General Humbert claimed to have two thousand French and Irish recruits ready to invade Texas. The revolutionary Juan Mariano Bautista de Picornell Gomila worked with Humbert and other French filibusters. Following the Medina defeat Picornell apparently allied himself with Humbert, but in reality he had no true loyalties, a fact attested to by his proclamation supporting a French expedition into Texas on the one hand, and then his secretly joining the Spanish royalists. Picornell probably relented to the entreaties of Father Antonio de Sedella, a New Orleans resident who had close ties with the Spanish government. Sedella persuaded Picornell to rejoin the royalists with the expectation of winning a royal pardon for his past offenses.

Jean Joseph Amable Humbert. Artist unknown (Courtesy of The Historic New Orleans Collection, Museum/Research Center, accession no. 1974.25.27.194)

Ultimately, nothing came of any of these French activities. Although the U.S. government officially announced a position of neutrality, there was little effort to halt these actions and nothing to assist the filibusters. This lack of full governmental support probably prevented any real unity among various groups and likely provided a major cause for their failures.[7]

Dr. Robinson, who had already led one mission into Texas, arrived at Natchez near the end of 1813. Claiming to have money and arms, Robinson, as well as Humbert, probably intended to assist the Magee-Gutiérrez expedition. But their plans crumbled on 18 August when the Battle of Medina ended any hope for immediate action. Moreover, these leaders anticipated finding a large pool of potential recruits for another invasion of Texas

168

from the ranks of these survivors. Competition for resources, however, among Robinson, Humbert, and Toledo prevented them from achieving the unity they needed to launch a later successful invasion into Spanish territory. In addition, Robinson died of yellow fever in 1819.[8]

The U.S. government had given its unofficial blessing to the Magee-Gutiérrez expedition, but there is no evidence to prove that any of these later efforts received special backing. When Governor Claiborne asked Monroe whether or not he should support the new expeditions, the president informed him that the administration would have no part in these activities. Claiborne responded by issuing an order to stop the invasion, but he did relatively little to enforce it—a few people were arrested, but no one was prosecuted.[9]

In another effort, the adventurers, filibusters, and expansionists sought to recruit Laffite and the Baratarians, whose main interest had been privateering against Spanish commerce. Barataria had emerged before the War of 1812 as a major smuggling and commerce-raiding center that threatened governmental stability along the Louisiana Gulf Coast. It became so troublesome to U.S. officials that in September 1814 a raiding party led by Colonel George T. Ross of the 44th Regiment and Naval Master-Commandant Daniel Todd Patterson captured most of the privateers' ships and eliminated their operational base at Barataria. Despite helping Jackson at the Battle of New Orleans, Laffite was never able to regain his property.[10] After an unsuccessful plot to seize Tampico, the Baratarians established a new base at Matagorda Bay to work in cooperation with renewed land attacks by the Mexican revolutionaries, including possibly General Humbert and/or some of the other French leaders. The British attack on New Orleans cut short all of this activity.[11]

Prior to the attempted invasion of Louisiana, the British had sought unsuccessfully to recruit Jean Laffite and his cohorts.*

*Jean Laffite was the best known of the adventurers along the Gulf Coast. The youngest of eight children, Jean was born 22 April 1782 at Santo Domingo to a French father and a Spanish-Jewish mother. An older brother, Alexander, was the well-known adventurer who later called himself Dominique You (Youx). An

Laffite rejected their offer in part because he would have been unable to continue raiding Spanish commerce since Britain had tacitly allied with Spain. Additionally, most of the Baratarians and filibusters had more or less pro-American loyalties. Certainly they did not want Britain, Spain, or, in most cases, even France to control the area.[12] Laffite wanted to remain on good terms with the U.S. government, if for no other reason than because he probably planned eventually to retire and remain in this country. Whether or not these were his plans in 1813 and 1814, Laffite did retire in the United States some years later.[13]

The British attack on New Orleans in December 1814–January 1815 temporarily ended these activities, as most of the filibusters, along with Laffite's followers from Barataria, joined Andrew Jackson to defend the Crescent City. Laffite's cohorts manned artillery at the Rodriguez Canal and also furnished additional crews for Daniel Patterson's naval forces on the West Bank. The Kemper brothers, Joseph Savary's black Haitian troops, General Humbert and his followers, and Álvarez de Toledo also helped defend the city.[14]

Laffite and the Baratarians received pardons from the U.S. government for their participation at New Orleans, and virtually all of these adventurers received American appreciation. Just how advantageous this gratitude proved to be in their later activities is difficult to judge, but none appeared to have ever been seriously prosecuted or otherwise restrained by U.S. authorities until after the Adams-Onís Treaty in 1819. But at the same time,

---

uncle, Reyne, was invited to accept a high French military rank by Napoleon Bonaparte before 1800. Jean and his brother Pierre became quite famous privateers, holding letters of marque from various South American governments. Besides their effort as privateers, they were best known for assisting Jackson at the Battle of New Orleans. After the war they moved to Galveston, where they remained until March 1821; they burned the town as they left. They continued their success as privateers until 1825, at which time they faded from public view. Rumors of Laffite's demise are as abundant as those about his early life. One story claims that he moved to the Yucatán Peninsula in 1821 and died there of fever in 1826. Another account, however, charges that Laffite, alias John Lafflin, traveled extensively in the United States and Europe and lived a long life in the American Midwest, supposedly dying in 1854 in Alton, Illinois.

Jean Laffite. Reproduced by C. M. Luria from an original drawing (Courtesy of The Historic New Orleans Collection, Museum/Research Center, accession no. 1959.2.347)

it appears that none of these adventurers ever received the kind of support from Washington that had been given to earlier operations against Texas.[15]

After the war, Bernardo Gutiérrez de Lara and several other leaders, including Toledo and Humbert, devised a plan to capture the Spanish arsenal at Pensacola. Rumor had it that the city's armory contained twenty thousand muskets, stores, and other supplies. The Mexican revolutionaries and filibusters planned to capture the weapons for future operations against Texas and Mexico.[16] Actually, it is unlikely that Pensacola possessed any quantity of supplies in 1815 and 1816, certainly nothing like twenty thousand muskets. Only a short time before, the Spanish garrison in West Florida could barely arm itself.[17]

The New Orleans Association, supposedly composed of filibusters, merchants, and lawyers representing numerous prominent citizens of the city, supported the actions against Pensacola, Texas, and Mexico. The association's proposed expedition, planned in the summer of 1815, would collect two armies: one at Belle Island was largely coordinated by Colonel Henry Perry, who intended to establish a landing and base at Matagorda Bay; a second army, led by Gutiérrez, would invade Texas by land from Natchitoches. A group of ships would also launch a simultaneous sea attack on Tampico. Apparently the government offered some unofficial support, as Governor Claiborne remained conveniently absent from his post, while Daniel Patterson seems to have been strangely blind to the entire episode. Though there is no hard evidence, there is strong suspicion that Patterson may have been involved in the plot.[18]

Filibuster and revolutionary activity against Texas increased after 1815. This factor alone complicates any scholarly study of these activities, because it becomes almost impossible to determine who supported a given campaign and what that expedition's objectives were. The revolutionary government in Mexico sent José Manuel de Herrera to New Orleans to secure aid for the independence movement. Herrera was promptly taken into the devious underground activities in New Orleans and eventually lost most of his funds. His activities became even more of a puzzle when Spanish agents working for Don Luis de Onís and more directly for the Spanish consul gathered at New Orleans. Diego Morphy, Jr., Spanish vice-consul at New Orleans, hired, bribed, or otherwise obtained the services of many people who supposedly supported Herrera. Thus, by 1816 it became nearly impossible to tell who supported whom. This infiltration, linked with a campaign of disinformation, probably prevented organization or central direction of any filibuster movement against Texas.[19]

Although local Americans such as Claiborne, Patterson, and Livingston may have given support to these activities, these leaders were unsuccessful simply because there were too many of them. Had all the groups organized behind a single leader, they likely could have succeeded. There was, however, no single leader or even a single objective, since some wanted Mexican independence while others preferred U.S. or even French occupation. This general state of disarray ended any serious efforts to secure Texas from Spain, with the result that many of the filibusters, including Toledo, much to the delight of Onís and the Laffite brothers, secretly turned their coats and joined the Spanish.[20]

The loss of the loyalty of these men and possibly that of General Humbert greatly undermined the effectiveness of any effort to take Texas, either for the United States or for Mexico. In the midst of this confusion, Luis Aury emerged with considerable force. He arrived at Barataria in the fall of 1816 and almost immediately sailed for Galveston. After a series of problems, including a mutiny, he established a base at Galveston for the Mexican independence movement rather than for an American effort to seize Texas. He soon received reinforcements of men and supplies from New Orleans. Though he supposedly had the support of the New Orleans Association, not all of these reinforcements were true allies; Toledo and the Laffite brothers by this time, as already noted, worked for the Spanish.[21]

Aury experienced difficulty during his tenure at Galveston. He struggled for command to such an extent that at times only force or the threat of it maintained his authority. His success in controlling Galveston likely depended on the enduring loyalty of Joseph Savary and his detachment of black soldiers. Savary's battalion of "Free Men of Color" had served with distinction at the Battle of New Orleans. This time they remained loyal to Aury.[22]

Perhaps the most extensive undertaking at Galveston resulted from the arrival of Francisco Xavier Mina, a former Spanish patriot and liberal who had distinguished himself during the recent Peninsular War with France. Mina, bringing supplies and a sub-

Francisco Xavier Mina (Courtesy of Fototecha Instituto Nacional de Antropología e Historia, Pachuca, Hidalgo, México)

stantial number of troops for the invasion and liberation of all Mexico, had received support for his expedition in England, the United States, and numerous other places. His effort represents the most ambitious attempt to dislodge the Spanish from Mexico. Although Mina's expedition gained considerable support from individual American leaders, no record exists showing that he received any money or supplies from the U.S. government. On the other hand, there was absolutely no effort made to hinder his activities. Mina purchased supplies and moved his expedition out of New Orleans with complete freedom. Ignoring strong official Spanish protest, the U.S. government permitted General Mina to recruit a number of Americans, including Colonel Henry Perry, an army officer who had served with Jackson at New Orleans. Arriving at Galveston on 16 March 1817, Mina remained there only briefly before leaving on 7 April for his chosen landing place at the mouth of the Santander River. Despite all his careful preparations, the expedition fragmented and eventually suffered defeat by Spanish royalists.[23]

Whatever motives the United States had for allowing Mina to operate so freely remain unclear, but one can only assume that any effort to alleviate Spain's stranglehold on Mexico would aid the American cause, whether or not it resulted in U.S. occupation of Texas. Perhaps Spain's impending loss of Mexico would stimulate negotiation between Adams and Onís for the cession of Florida and a settlement of the western boundary. The subsequent Adams-Onís Treaty did call for the United States to give up its claim on Texas in exchange for the acquisition of Florida. There may have been significant internal political reasons for the government's failure to stop Mina. In any event, the U.S. government had much more interest in acquiring Florida, even though Mina's activities would have greatly weakened Spanish defenses along the whole Gulf Coast.

Aury went on to an active career of raiding Spanish commerce and also seized Amelia Island, as noted in chapter 7. In fact, he held both Amelia Island and Galveston simultaneously for a short time. But eventually his good fortune turned to bad and he felt himself the victim of dishonest people. Aury died on 30 August 1821 as the result of being thrown from a horse near his island home on Old Providence, off the Mosquito Coast. Laffite, secretly working for Spain, gained complete control of Galveston. Filibusters made some other aborted attempts to seize Texas, but none enjoyed any success. Moreover, the U.S. government openly opposed some efforts.[24]

A group of French exiles launched one of the more ambitious plans against Spanish Texas. As has already been explained, considerable French activity was occurring during the same time that the U.S. government supported the Magee-Gutiérrez expedition in 1812. After the fall of Napoleon, a number of French officers resettled in the United States, plotting to rescue their exiled leader and establish him in a country to be created from New Spain. Some of this group founded the "Vine and Olive Colony" on the Tombigbee River in the Mississippi Territory, and others hoped to seize and develop a colony in Texas. There appears to be no evidence that any of these people attempted to capture American territory, but they did intend to use the United States as an operational base, hoping to recruit settlers in this country.[25]

Under the leadership of brothers Charles François Antoine and Henri Lallemand, the French exiles established the settlement of Le Champ d'Asile on the Trinity River. Traveling by way of Galveston, the Lallemand group arrived at the port on 14 January 1818. Two months later they departed Galveston for a destination about eighteen miles from the mouth of the Trinity, where the group intended to establish its colony. Settlement commander Charles Lallemand organized it as a military unit with rigorous discipline, and constructed two forts. The French settlement possessed ample supplies and appeared to have a good chance to succeed. Yet this optimism was short-lived, as it soon experienced the threat of Spanish attack. The French, believing that a sizable Spanish contingent supplemented by naval forces intended to attack Champ d'Asile, evacuated the place and retreated to Galveston in July 1818. This ended any French attempt to settle in Texas at that time. It is interesting to note that the French fell victim to unfounded rumors. The Spanish could barely keep the Indians in line, much less assemble a large force to attack anyone.[26]

Perhaps the most unusual event occurred when President Monroe sent former secretary of war George Graham to Galveston to negotiate with the French and Jean Laffite for the American annexation of the Texas coast as far as the Rio Grande. Graham, unaware that Laffite was working for the Spanish, tried to persuade all the various groups at Galveston to unite against Spain and seize the coastal positions. He claimed that the United States would intervene with a show of force to occupy the positions and protect the territory from a "lawless" occupation. The United States would then keep the territory, while the property of the filibusters would be respected. There is even evidence that Graham promised rewards from the United States. Although he reported that the French and Laffite agreed to the plan, nothing came of it.[27]

The real objective of the Graham mission is not entirely clear. The U.S. government did fear that a French settlement might become strong enough to establish a permanent presence in Texas, a situation that would complicate future dealings in the region. The French might also join the Spanish or the Mexican Revolution and thereby pose a real threat to the United States in Louisiana. It is likely that Graham primarily intended to determine both the strength and the objectives of the French. For him, gaining control of the Texas coast would appear to have been a secondary goal and might have even been an afterthought.[28]

In any case, the French had already withdrawn to Galveston when Graham arrived. He told Laffite and Lallemand that the United States claimed all of the coastal territory as far as the Rio Grande. Part of the French expedition departed from Galveston in September 1818 and the remainder left in October, thus leaving the port completely under Laffite's control. By insisting to Laffite that Galveston and the Texas coast belonged to the United States, Graham was apparently using the filibusters to secure the territory and thereby avoid a direct confrontation with Spain. Little did he know that Laffite was a Spanish spy and that his effort was doomed from the onset.[29]

Adams, not entirely pleased with this action, wrote in his diary that Graham had probably exceeded his instructions. He was apparently very uncomfortable over Graham's negotiations with Laffite and Lallemand, neither of whom occupied any legal position. Adams expressed concern not only about the character and legality of the French actions but also about Laffite himself. Even so, he did certainly agree that the United States should immediately take possession of Galveston.[30]

Had the U.S. government seized Galveston at this time, it could have used the same justification as when it took Amelia

Island from Aury. Aury and Laffite had the same authority, namely, Mexico. Laffite supposedly acted under Aury's authority at Galveston, and the U.S. government had already seized Amelia Island. The Spaniards had the same claim on Amelia Island as they had on Galveston, even though they controlled neither. Filibusters claiming loyalty to the Mexican Revolution occupied both. In addition, both Galveston and Amelia Island served as points from which to smuggle captured cargoes of Spanish goods and slaves into the United States. Since the government offered this as the reason to seize Amelia Island, one would wonder why it did not take Galveston with the same rationale.

John Quincy Adams calculated that the act of seizing Galveston would not in itself bring enough pressure on Spain to settle claims to the territory. Furthermore, the Adams-Onís negotiations, under way for some time, were nearing completion. Adams may well have thought that diplomatic pressure at this time would hasten the conclusion of a satisfactory settlement. Spain, not surprisingly, did agree to the Adams-Onís Treaty, which was signed on 22 February 1819.[31]

The following summer, James Long made the last American effort to capture Texas. Long had considerable support from old frontier filibusters such as John Sibley, Stephen Barker, and Joshua Child. This force, the largest and best-equipped to invade Texas since the Magee-Gutiérrez expedition of 1812, included several people who desperately wanted to establish themselves in Texas and settle the place. The Long expedition lasted off-and-on from the summer of 1819 until the fall of 1821. Long finally surrendered at that time and was taken to Mexico City, where a soldier supposedly accidentally shot and killed him. It has been charged that "Long's death marked the end of the early filibustering era in Texas and Mexico."[32]

This effort had considerable support from western leaders and settlers unhappy with the Adams-Onís Treaty. Many felt betrayed by the government's surrender of Texas. In any event, they supplied a considerable amount of support for Long. Historian Harris G. Warren argues that the expedition would have succeeded in gaining control of Texas had Long received even a fraction of the support given to the Magee-Gutiérrez force in 1812 and 1813. Certainly the Spanish were even weaker in 1819 than they had been in 1812, and Long's expedition had the potential to be one of the strongest ever launched. As examples of Spanish weakness, Commandant General Joaquín de Arredondo faced attack from the revolutionary armies of Mexico and had neither troops nor supplies to send to Texas. Governor Antonio Martínez had only limited troops stationed at La Bahía del Espíritu Santo and San Antonio de Béxar. These small, underfunded, ill-equipped, dispirited, unpaid, and poorly trained garrisons also had questionable loyalty. Even more dangerous and probably more immediate, these troops often faced warlike Indians who seemed more of a threat than the Americans. From the correspondence of Governor Martínez, it would appear feasible that any American or French expedition entering Texas at this time could have, with the expenditure of real effort, easily defeated the Spanish.[33]

Long's failure can be attributed to a change in enforcing governmental policy. In a surprise move, government officials, especially the army, actually prevented supplies and reinforcements from being shipped to Long; this was the first time American troops had actually tried to stop an effort to seize Texas. Long was forced to divide his army into small groups to forage for supplies, thus making them vulnerable to almost any Spanish attack. No doubt Long and western leaders were surprised at the government's opposition. Many in the West, already unhappy with the Adams-Onís Treaty, probably experienced shock when the army's actions caused the expedition to fail. This clearly represented a complete reversal in policy. Adams actually insisted on compliance with the terms of the treaty.[34]

There may have been several reasons for this change of attitude. First, the Adams-Onís Treaty had in effect relinquished any U.S. claim on Texas in exchange for a clear title to Florida and a defined western boundary. Usually a man of his word, Adams, once he negotiated the treaty, supported it. However, there seems to be more than a promise here. Onís had been given the authority to cede Texas to the United States, but Adams appears to have lost interest. Had he pressured Onís at all, the Spanish minister would have almost certainly handed over Texas. Moreover, had the government simply remained aloof from the whole operation, Long would have likely succeeded.

A second issue—and a very volatile one—namely, slavery, may have had considerable effect on the situation. The conflict over slavery, having already manifested itself in the Missouri Controversy, became a major political issue. Texas was considered a major addition to the power of the states holding slaves. Many supporters of annexation probably thought little about the slavery question, but the Northeast, Adams's home, became increasingly aware of it.[35]

It is easy to be suspicious of the slavery issue at this time because it offered a very convenient excuse to gain support for the Northeast's general opposition to any territorial expansion. The original willingness to close the Mississippi River in exchange for trade concessions as proposed in the Jay-Gardoqui Treaty, the disagreement over the Louisiana Purchase, the resistance to the War of 1812, and even the protest against the annexation of Florida—all continued as significant issues in opposition to expansion. From the start, the Northeast recognized that every new western state weakened its power in the Union. The Hartford Convention attempted to offset this threat, but the southern and western alliance became even stronger. With the Missouri Controversy a new issue emerged—slavery. Not only did the slavery question give the Northeast a moral issue that it could use to oppose expansion, but it also provided an issue that would weaken and perhaps destroy the southern and western alliance. Should this happen, the old power of the Northeast would be restored. Texas, probably not a major factor in the struggle at this time, would certainly have been part of the plan. Although John Quincy Adams may not have been as concerned about restoring power for the Northeast, old Federalists, including John Adams, would have been delighted.[36]

CHAPTER TEN

A Jeffersonian Leviathan:
Manifest Destiny Succeeds

THE INTERNATIONAL STRUGGLE for North America was not new. This contest, with England, France, and Spain as the antagonists, had begun in the seventeenth century and endured throughout the eighteenth century and well into the nineteenth. After 1763, however, France withdrew from the conflict, leaving a considerable number of French-speaking settlers in North America to fend for themselves. These Frenchmen found limited protection from the British enemy in Canada and the Spanish ally in the South and Southwest. The apparent lack of concern for French settlers was partly offset by the British desire to win their support in Canada. But the problems suffered by the ethnic French in Spanish-controlled Louisiana were not caused entirely by Spain's indifference. Spain was declining during this period and was also encountering great difficulties maintaining its own South and Central American colonies in the face of an expanding English and later American empire.

English-speaking Americans, though independent of and frequently antagonistic toward their mother country, nevertheless renewed the expansionist pattern established by Britain. Americans aggressively settled uninhabited lands, as had been characteristic of residents in the English colonies. And although the flags may have changed, the people's attitude toward expansion remained much the same. This scenario continued well into the nineteenth century, and though some of the actors appeared to be new, the script remained the same.

During the Revolutionary War, the United States had accepted aid from both France and Spain, England's traditional enemies. French interests, not only in North America but even in the entire Western Hemisphere, had lessened after 1763 to such an extent that friendship between the United States and France became possible on a reasonably sound basis. Both the United States and France, now rivals of England, accomplished some of their goals during the American Revolution: the United States gained its independence; equally important, France, it seemed, had weakened its archrival, England.

The Franco-American relationship remained in place in the years following 1783 initially because no new rivalry developed to muddy the water. But the beginning of the French Revolution in 1789 presented a new ideological element that reintroduced issues tangentially related to liberty. Thereafter, the struggle to maintain liberty or for Americans to maintain neutrality during the 1790s ultimately brought the two countries to an undeclared naval war, the Quasi-War (1798–1801). Though brief in duration, the Quasi-War nonetheless initiated a fourteen-year epoch in which the relationship between the two countries greatly changed. Neutral rights regarding maritime issues, capricious French enforcement of the Continental System (Napoleon's counterblockade of the British), and the unpredictable treatment of American ships in French ports only exacerbated the difficulties between Napoleonic France and Jeffersonian America. Moreover, Napoleon's deliberate vagueness regarding the boundaries of West Florida and some relatively small or short-lived French activities in Mexico further complicated relations between the two countries. Finally, in 1812 the United States declared war, not on France, but rather on France's most irksome enemy—Great Britain. Although there had been ruffled feathers on the diplomatic front, the United States and France continued in somewhat harmonious accord against the greater British enemy.[1]

Spain, on the other hand, faced an entirely different situation.

The weakening Spanish empire acted as a magnet to expansionists in the United States. Latin American revolutions appeared as an opportunity for those pursuing wealth and, perhaps above all else, adventure. This troubled water offered an excellent occasion for employment to anyone interested in seeking his fortune as a soldier, privateer, pirate, or filibuster. The borderlands between the United States and the crumbling Spanish empire became a prime target for American expansionists. Spain had sparsely settled and left virtually undefended the entire area extending from Amelia Island to the Pacific Ocean in northern California.[2]

The Federalist administrations of George Washington and John Adams busily established a new government and fortunately possessed sufficient western lands to satisfy their immediate needs. But the Jeffersonians who were elected in 1800 differed from their Federalist counterparts and quickly became interested in expansion. Moreover, sectional and ideological differences within the United States that had manifested themselves in the failed 1785 Jay-Gardoqui Treaty demonstrated that the Northeast had developed into an urban society with trade and manufacturing as its main concern, while the South and West remained agrarian.[3]

Thomas Jefferson, unlike his predecessors, represented the views of this southern-western group. It should, therefore, come as no surprise that under the Jeffersonian government, the young and aggressive United States often supported the activities of expansionists and adventurers seeking to possess the Spanish borderlands. The administrations of Thomas Jefferson, James Madison, and James Monroe felt little or no remorse for seizing this territory, and in many instances they actually encouraged the schemes of filibusters and adventurers along Spanish borders. Certainly government officials made no effort to curtail the actions of these people. Annexation of all the lands of North America thus appeared to be the very real objective of the Jeffersonians. These presidents and other major leaders seldom stated their policy publicly, but members of Congress, local leaders, and the press never made any secret of their expansionist designs on the entire continent. Why should they? Was not Manifest Destiny the God-given right for this new democratic republic to control and settle the wilderness of all North America?[4]

The eighteenth century had seen an increased fear of large groups of relatively undisciplined people—especially the city "mob." This trepidation greatly accelerated as a result of the Reign of Terror during the French Revolution. New England Federalists, who controlled the United States during the first years of the Republic, had supported a strong central government with restrictions on suffrage. The Jeffersonian Republicans, though not fearing the mob as much, proposed a more democratic solution; Jefferson favored creating a nation of educated, landowning small farmers. This would, after all, coincide with the pursuit of happiness, or landownership, sought by most people. The president believed that "happy," educated, landowning small farmers were all-important to the formation of a democratic society. They would create a stable electorate that would make unnecessary the need to restrict the franchise. There would be no mob to fear. Yet to make this dream possible the country had to have available vast quantities of cheap land. This translated into Spanish land, Indian land, and any other land the country could obtain from weaker neighbors.[5]

Some American politicians were eager to annex Canada, and at times adventurers and filibusters attempted actions to obtain this vast real estate. But Great Britain, the superpower of the nineteenth century, governed Canada, and neither the U.S. government nor American filibusters, try as they might, had success against that formidable country. Not only did Britain possess a great and growing power, but Canada wanted no part of the United States. Most of that country's inhabitants were satisfied with a reasonably tolerant British rule. Moreover, eastern Canada, heavily settled with loyalists who had fled the American Revolution, still loved or at least respected their king. Farther to the west, central Canada was populated by French Catholics who, even with no great love for England, still felt far more secure as a substantial part of the population under the rule of a tolerant monarchy than they would have as a small minority in a country controlled by aggressive English-speaking Protestants. In other words, French Canadians wanted no part of the United States.[6]

A volatile sectional conflict became another factor undoubtedly affecting American concerns in Canada. Agricultural interests of the southern and western states emerged as a moving force behind territorial expansion; the southern, southwestern, and central areas of the continent offered the best and most easily accessible land. This excluded Canada, where little attractive agricultural acreage seemed to be available. The great grain belts of western Canada had not yet been developed and were likely unknown to citizens of the United States. Americans still had not settled most of the grain belt of the western part of their own country, and there was no pressure to expand into the colder northern plains. Thus, the idea of taking Canada represented merely an ideological dream in the early nineteenth century. If proof were needed as to the utter futility of such efforts, the United States had only to look at the tremendous energy unsuccessfully expended during the War of 1812. The country had learned a lesson when a militia force defended Canada and fought the armies of the United States to a standstill. The War of 1812, though little studied in Great Britain, became Canada's war for independence, in this case independence from the United States.[7]

A major ingredient in this continental power struggle was the Native American. The Indians, though the original settlers, appeared as fairly primitive people who usually offered no match for the white man's superior weapons or technology. Yet at the same time, the Indians had some very capable leaders. Many of the Indian nations soon realized that their survival depended not on themselves but rather on alliances with the various powers. In general it was the white English-speaking American encroachers—with their explosive birthrates and incessant appetite for unlimited supplies of land—rather than governments who represented the Indian's true adversary. English settlers were intolerant, narrow minded, aggressive, and unwilling to allow Indians to live their own lives and have their own culture. Additionally, the white invaders wanted to slaughter the game, cut down the trees, and either kill the Indians or shape them into white men, particularly by tying them to a plow. This policy of assimilation, later implemented by both the Washington and the Jeffersonian administrations, tried to convert the Indians from a hunting culture to agriculture. After the War of 1812, this policy changed as the federal government concentrated on removing the Indians to the West. Although difficult at best, the policy appeared much kinder than extermination, an action that would have pleased many frontier settlers.[8]

Except in cases where the Indian nations had ruthless enemies among their own people whom they believed more dangerous than the settlers, the natives would not consider any alliance with the English-speaking inhabitants. The only exception to this was when some individual Indians and tribes allied themselves with Americans in the erroneous belief that the whites would show their gratitude by allowing them to keep their land. White settlement following the Creek War shattered this illusion.[9]

In colonial times, most Indians had allied themselves with the French and Spanish in North America. There were relatively few French settlers, and they often remained scattered. Many lived in the woods much like the Indians, with whom they even intermarried. These Frenchmen might not have been friends of the Indians, but neither were they enemies, and they did help keep out the English. Another factor was that many Indians came to like the guns and goods of the white man, soon becoming dependent on this commerce. Even though they actually traded with both the British and the French, they felt more comfortable and safer with the latter group.[10]

The Spanish presented no problem, at least to the eastern woodland Indians. Spain, never bringing a significant number of settlers to Florida, had little in North America except for missions and a few isolated military posts, usually located near a very small town. The government not only traded with the Indians but also presented them with gifts in order to protect their settlements and to ensure that they retained the Native Americans' friendship. That Spain did not covet their land meant much to these people, and as long as the Spanish held Florida, the hated

English-speaking people could not overrun them. But the Indians eventually found two problems with this alliance: Spain had become a weakened power, and Spanish trade goods were very expensive.[11]

After the expulsion of France in 1763, the English completely controlled eastern America, no doubt provoking great fear among the Native Americans. Soon thereafter, British merchants learned the profitability of the Indian trade and entered into an effort to protect them from white settlers. The British government decreed the Proclamation Line of 1763, at least in part, to protect the Indians and their trade. This naturally pleased the Indians, and since they had no alternative, they allied themselves with British government agents, who differed from the dangerous settlers. This also was the first time the Indians, as a whole, had made any distinction between the British government and English-speaking settlers.[12]

As a result of this new friendship of necessity with the British Crown, most of the North American Indians sided with the British government against the rebels during the American Revolution. Even though this loyalty cost them dearly, they maintained it even after peace. During the War of 1812 many of these Native Americans again allied themselves with the British and in the South with the Spanish, who were more or less allied with Great Britain. Siding with England and Spain proved to be an even greater disaster in 1812 than it had been during the Revolution. The British retained Canada and temporarily offered some refuge for the Indians in that northern area, but in the South the story differed.[13]

The ever-aggressive American frontiersmen, continuously pressing into Indian territory, always encroached on the weakly held Spanish borderlands. After the Revolutionary War, Spain attempted to hold back American expansion by diplomacy, intrigue, bribery, and, of course, alliances with European powers and the Indians. These efforts offered moderate success, considering Spanish weaknesses. Nevertheless, Spain's long, poorly defended border with the United States provided a tempting target for American expansion.

Between 1796 and the outbreak of the War of 1812, the United States steadily gained in both territory and influence. The Pinckney Treaty provided a major American diplomatic victory and clearly indicated a change in Spanish policy—from a position of relative strength to one of defending its territories from a posture of great weakness. Prior to the treaty, Spain had sought to close the Mississippi River and other waterways to the Gulf Coast in an effort to deter further westward expansion. This would surely prevent restless Americans from moving west and thereby endangering Spanish holdings in Florida and Texas. But the pressure of war in Europe, especially the French threat to Spain proper, rendered this once-great power unable to provide the necessary forces to maintain control of its North American frontier.[14]

Spanish defensive diplomacy provided moderate success in the Florida territory, and even more in Texas as long as distance could be maintained. Even though they were further removed from the United States, Spanish officials in Texas still viewed the spread of ideas from the French Revolution and American expansion with great alarm. In fact, before losing Louisiana the Spanish were likely more agitated about the possibility of insurrectionist beliefs coming from France—and certainly French agents were hard at work everywhere—than they were with the threat of American expansion.[15] The murder of horse trader Philip Nolan was certainly an exception to this.[16]

The Louisiana Purchase represented a great loss made possible only because Napoleon dominated Spain. Although Spain feared French power too much to resist any transfer of land, it did protest the violation of its treaty with France. Neither Spain nor any other country in Europe, with the exception of France and its puppets, recognized the transfer of Louisiana. The presumed illegality of this exchange made during the course of the European war later prompted the British to refuse to recognize the validity of the Louisiana Purchase. In fact, Britain did not consider Louisiana and New Orleans to be included in the Treaty of Ghent. The U.S. government considered the ownership of Louisiana settled, whereas the British believed no overall peace settlement had been made because the war with the United States in 1812 was part of the Napoleonic Wars. The British, therefore, viewed any territorial transfer made during the war as not final, and certainly not an illegal transfer like Louisiana.[17]

The additional lands of the Louisiana Territory did not completely satisfy land-hungry Americans, and as a result they still supported further incursions into Texas. Although carried out under the general title of filibuster expeditions, they were often carefully observed and supported by agents of the U.S. government. American agents attentively watched as adventurers seized Baton Rouge in 1810, and the U.S. government quickly annexed the territory. The same group of rebels and filibusters also made an effort to annex Mobile in 1810, but this time local U.S. authorities stopped the action. This check on expansion occurred not because of any desire to protect Spanish holdings but rather because negotiations were under way that might lead Spain to cede the territory voluntarily. Early in 1812, American filibusters attempted to take East Florida, but the War of 1812 temporarily ended activity in that area. Attacks on West Florida and Texas continued despite the war.[18]

The United States blamed the Spanish in Florida for encouraging the Creek War and for allowing British agents and military forces to use Florida as a base. In reality, Spain lacked the power to keep peace or to prevent a British landing. When Americans pressured Spain, local commanders reluctantly joined Britain. Thus, as a de facto British ally and friend of the hostile Indians, Spain had to face, without support, the military might of the United States. This usually occurred at times and in places where the British offered either no help or too little aid too late. Spanish losses in the War of 1812 greatly enriched the United States and led Americans to view that conflict as a significant victory. The war succeeded in gaining both British and general European recognition of the American claim on Louisiana and Mobile. Perhaps the only effective, albeit unintentional, British aid given to the Spanish during the war was the unsuccessful attack on New Orleans. When Andrew Jackson's intelligence sources informed him that a British expedition intended to attack New Orleans, he evacuated Pensacola, which he had captured the day before. Had Britain's attack not come when it did, Jackson likely would have remained in Pensacola, and, like Mobile, that city would have become part of the United States during the War of 1812.[19]

The War of 1812, which included the defeat of a Spanish army at Pensacola and the capture of that city, so weakened Spain in the Floridas that its holdings soon collapsed. Spain simply did not have the power to maintain law and order in its own provinces. In addition to the weakness produced by Napoleon's conquest and subsequent occupation, Spain faced revolution in its colonies throughout the Western Hemisphere, conflicts that allowed the United States to complete the annexation of Florida and lay the groundwork for American possession of Texas and California.

After Spain vacated North America, the United States soon resumed its crusade of expansion against the former Spanish colony of Mexico. The Texas Revolution (1836) and the Mexican War (1846–48) provide better-known examples than the earlier activities, with the exception of the Louisiana Purchase. Nonetheless, the methods employed by the United States during the later territorial annexations resembled those used in the Jeffersonian period. By the 1840s the only real difference in the way the United States dealt with Mexico and Spain was that this country possessed more power and could afford to use force of arms.

The objective of this study has been to describe the manner in which this U.S. expansion occurred. Along the way there were accounts of adventurers, filibusters, expansionists, government officials, patriots, privateers, bandits, Indians, and others who played out their roles in this conflict. Special emphasis has been placed on detailing the more obscure activities rather than studying well-known events such as the Louisiana Purchase and the seizure of Baton Rouge. This study has examined the varied but relentless efforts of the Jeffersonians to extend the borders of the United States by any means possible. These leaders, convinced that American settlers had not a God-given right but a natural right to all of North America, could not seize Canada from Britain. They did, however, enjoy tremendous success against the weakly held Spanish territories in the Gulf South.

The Jeffersonians, possibly influenced by the French Revolution and its rejection of royalty, did not take seriously European claims to lands in North America. Britain could defend its claims despite what American leaders might plan; fortunately Spain, on the other hand, could not. In the view of the frontiersmen and apparently the Jeffersonians, land belonged to those who inhabited and farmed it. Claims to uninhabited land were worthless and need not be respected if the land could be seized and occupied. Native American land likewise was declared open, not only because the Indians did not actually live on most of it, but also because they were not "civilized" and thus represented a threat to American settlers and property.

New England Federalists usually and justifiably opposed expansion for many reasons, including politics, power, and economics. Federalists believed that a majority of the new western settlers would support the Jeffersonians, and they did. Each new western state, therefore, undermined the northeastern power base and had a deleterious effect on their politics and power. Moreover, the movement of much of the potential workforce to the West made labor both scarce and expensive in the Northeast, or so that section's leaders believed. Although not everyone from the Northeast opposed expansion, most leaders did, with John Quincy Adams as a rare exception.[20]

Were the fears of the Northeast justified? From an economic viewpoint, the area probably lost little, if anything. The West may have drained off labor, resulting in increased costs, but it also created vast new markets. These workers were also eventually replaced with massive immigration. Therefore, this fear remained largely unwarranted. In the area of power and politics, the Northeast did lose greatly. The United States became increasingly dominated by the South and West, and not until the introduction of the slavery controversy was this agrarian alliance interrupted; even then the two regions cooperated on most issues. On the whole, this alliance lasted until the Civil War, making impossible the Northeast's domination of the country's political power.[21] A good case can be made that American expansion during the Jeffersonian period embodied the rural-urban struggle that was not eventually settled until the slavery controversy and Civil War split southern and western agrarian interests. Only this division restored the power of the urban Northeast, thus ending the dominance of the Jeffersonian agrarian expansionists and changing forever the character of the United States.

Notes

INTRODUCTION

1. Albert K. Weinberg, *Manifest Destiny: A Study of Nationalist Expansion in American History* (Baltimore: Johns Hopkins University Press, 1935), 11.

2. Frederick Jackson Turner, "The Significance of the Frontier in American History," originally presented at the American Historical Association's annual meeting in 1893; reprinted in Turner, *The Frontier in American History* (New York: Henry Holt, 1921), 1.

3. Norman Graebner, "Concrete Interests and Expansion," in *Major Problems in American Foreign Policy: Vol. 1: to 1914,* ed. Thomas G. Paterson, 3rd ed. (Lexington, Mass.: Heath, 1989), 276–87.

1. "A SPECIAL KIND OF STATE MAKING":
JEFFERSONIAN MANIFEST DESTINY

1. Henry Adams, *History of the United States of America during the Administrations of Thomas Jefferson and James Madison,* 2 vols. (1891; reprint, New York: Literary Classics of the United States, 1986), 2:214; Joseph Burkholder Smith, *The Plot to Steal Florida: James Madison's Phony War* (New York: Arbor House, 1983), 64; James A. Padgett, ed., "Official Records of the West Florida Revolution and Republic," *Louisiana Historical Quarterly* 21 (1938): 719–21; Stanley Clisby Arthur, *The Story of the West Florida Rebellion* (St. Francisville, La.: St. Francisville Democrat, 1935), 103–7.

2. Padgett, "Official Records," 725–27; Arthur, *West Florida Rebellion,* 112–15; Wanjohi Waciuma, *Intervention in the Spanish Floridas, 1801–1818: A Study of Jeffersonian Foreign Policy* (Boston: Branden Press, 1976), 160–61; H. Adams, *History of the United States,* 2:214–15.

3. James Madison to Thomas Jefferson, 19 October 1810, cited in Irving Brant, *James Madison: The President, 1809–1812* (New York: Bobbs-Merrill, 1956), 182–84; Arthur, *West Florida Rebellion,* 130–35.

4. Brant, *James Madison,* 184–86; James Madison, "Proclamation by the President of the United States," 27 October 1810, in James D. Richardson, ed., *A Compilation of the Messages and Papers of the Presidents, 1789–1897,* 20 vols. (Washington, D.C.: Government Printing Office, 1896–99), 2:465–66.

5. Richardson, *Messages and Papers,* 2:465–66; Brant, *James Madison,* 186; Philip Coolidge Brooks, *Diplomacy and the Borderlands: The Adams-Onís Treaty of 1819* (Berkeley: University of California Press, 1939), 36.

6. Waciuma, *Intervention in the Spanish Floridas,* 166.

7. Graebner, "Concrete Interests and Expansion," 276–78; Weinberg, *Manifest Destiny,* 37.

8. Donald Jackson, *Thomas Jefferson and the Stony Mountains: Exploring the West from Monticello* (Urbana: University of Illinois Press, 1981), 113.

9. Julius W. Pratt, *Expansionists of 1812* (Gloucester, Mass.: Peter Smith, 1957), 14.

10. William Earl Weeks, *John Quincy Adams and American Global Empire* (Lexington: University of Kentucky Press, 1992), 39.

11. Thomas Jefferson, "First Inaugural Address," 4 March 1801, in Richardson, *Messages and Papers,* 1:311.

12. Robert W. Tucker and David C. Hendrickson, *Empire of Liberty: The Statecraft of Thomas Jefferson* (New York: Oxford University Press, 1990), 17, 96.

13. William H. Goetzmann, *Exploration and Empire* (New York: Vintage Books, 1966), 37–66; Ray A. Billington, *Westward Expansion: A History of the American Frontier* (New York: Macmillan, 1949), 370–89; Robert E. Riegel and Robert G. Athearn, *America Moves West* (New York: Holt, Rinehart and Winston, 1964), 151–61; Paul A. Varg, *New England and Foreign Relations, 1789–1850* (Hanover: University Press of New England, 1983), 43–44; Pratt, *Expansionists of 1812,* 126–52.

14. Merrill D. Peterson, *Thomas Jefferson and the New Nation: A Biography* (Oxford: Oxford University Press, 1970), 745–46; Pratt, *Expansionists of 1812,* 60–61; Wesley P. Newton, "Origins of United States–Latin American Relations," in *United States–Latin American Relations, 1800–1850: The Formative Generations,* ed. T. Ray Shurbutt (Tuscaloosa: University of Alabama Press, 1991), 9–10.

15. Frederick Merk, *Manifest Destiny and Mission in American History: A Reinterpretation* (New York: Knopf, 1963), 6–7.

16. Robert E. May, "Young American Males and Filibustering in the Age of Manifest Destiny: The United States Army as a Cultural Mirror," *Journal of American History* 78 (1991): 862.

17. Dumas Malone, *Jefferson the President: First Term, 1801–1805* (Boston: Little, Brown, 1970), 275–76; Mary P. Adams, "Jefferson's Reaction to the Treaty of San Ildefonso," *Journal of Southern History* 21 (1955): 184–85; Weeks, *John Quincy Adams,* 26.

18. Brooks, *Diplomacy and the Borderlands,* 43; Harris G. Warren, *The Sword Was Their Passport: A History of American Filibustering in the Mexican Revolution* (Baton Rouge: Louisiana State University Press, 1943), 33–51.

19. Merk, *Manifest Destiny and Mission,* 6–7.

20. William B. Skelton, *An American Profession of Arms: The Army Officer Corps, 1784–1861* (Lawrence: University Press of Kansas, 1992), 333.

21. Harry Ammon, *James Monroe: The Quest for National Identity* (New York: McGraw-Hill, 1971), 412–14.

22. Ibid., 416–17.

2. "TO CONQUER WITHOUT WAR": THE PHILOSOPHY OF JEFFERSONIAN EXPANSION

1. Merk, *Manifest Destiny and Mission*, 24.

2. Jefferson to A. Stewart, 25 January 1786, in *The Writings of Thomas Jefferson*, ed. H. A. Washington, 8 vols. (Washington, D.C.: Taylor and Maury, 1853–54), 1:518.

3. Jefferson to John Jacob Astor, 24 May 1812, in ibid., 6:55.

4. Jefferson to Gov. James Monroe, 24 November 1801, in *The Writings of Thomas Jefferson*, ed. Andrew A. Lipscomb and Albert Ellery Bergh, 20 vols. (Washington, D.C.: Thomas Jefferson Memorial Association, 1903–4), 10:296.

5. Garrett Ward Sheldon, *The Political Philosophy of Thomas Jefferson* (Baltimore: Johns Hopkins University Press, 1991), 95; Weeks, *John Quincy Adams*, 39.

6. Robert Middlekauf, *The Glorious Cause* (Oxford: Oxford University Press, 1982), 586–87; Samuel Flagg Bemis, *Jay's Treaty: A Study in Commerce and Diplomacy* (1923; reprint, New Haven: Yale University Press, 1962), 23–26.

7. Weinberg, *Manifest Destiny*, 31.

8. Peterson, *Jefferson and the New Nation*, 746; Jefferson to William Carmichael, 27 May 1788, in *Writings of Thomas Jefferson*, ed. Washington, 2:398.

9. Jefferson to James Madison, 30 January 1787, in *Writings of Thomas Jefferson*, ed. Washington, 2:105–6.

10. Jefferson to Madison, 20 June 1787, in ibid., 2:153; Tucker and Hendrickson, *Empire of Liberty*, 95–96.

11. Jefferson to John Brown, 26 May 1788, in *Writings of Thomas Jefferson*, ed. Washington, 2:395.

12. Jefferson to William Short, 10 August 1790, in ibid., 3:178–79.

13. Weinberg, *Manifest Destiny*, 27–28.

14. Peterson, *Jefferson and the New Nation*, 457. Peterson claims that "thus was the venerable doctrine of natural rights mustered into the service of American expansion, making manifest the territorial destiny of the nation as it had earlier made manifest its freedom."

15. Samuel Flagg Bemis, *Pinckney's Treaty: America's Advantage from Europe's Distress, 1783–1800* (1926; reprint, New Haven: Yale University Press, 1960), 281–84.

16. Marshall Smelser, *The Democratic Republic, 1801–1815* (New York: Harper and Row, 1968), 85.

17. Jefferson to Robert R. Livingston, 18 April 1802, in *Writings of Thomas Jefferson*, ed. Washington, 4:431–34.

18. Jefferson to Dupont de Nemours, 25 April 1802, in ibid., 4:436.

19. Jefferson to Archibald Stuart, 25 January 1786, Thomas Jefferson Papers, Virginia Historical Society, Richmond.

20. Robert Ferrell, *American Diplomacy*, 3rd ed. (New York: Norton, 1982), 105–7; Malone, *Jefferson the President: First Term*, 264.

21. Jefferson to Chancellor Livingston, 3 February 1803, in *Writings of Thomas Jefferson*, ed. Washington, 4:460.

22. H. Adams, *History of the United States*, 1:291–92; Malone, *Jefferson the President: First Term*, 269; Jefferson to James Monroe, 13 January 1803, Thomas Jefferson Papers, Library of Congress [LC].

23. John Smith to Jefferson, 15 January 1803, Jefferson Papers, LC.

24. Jefferson to James Monroe, 13 January 1803, in *The Writings of Thomas Jefferson*, ed. Lipscomb and Bergh, 10:344–45; H. Adams, *History of the United States*, 1:292–94.

25. Gene A. Smith, *"For the Purposes of Defense": The Politics of the Jeffersonian Gunboat Program* (Newark: University of Delaware Press, 1995), 24–25.

26. Arthur Preston Whitaker, *The Mississippi Question: 1795–1803* (New York: D. Appleton-Century for the American Historical Association, 1934), 231–32; Jefferson to Sir John Sinclair, 30 June 1803, Jefferson Papers, LC.

27. H. Adams, *History of the United States*, 1:334–35. Adams chronicles the Mississippi question and the Louisiana Purchase on 337–92; Malone, *Jefferson the President: First Term*, 284. Malone's coverage of the same topic is on 262–363; Tucker and Hendrickson, *Empire of Liberty*, 96–97.

28. Jefferson to Thomas Mann Randolph, 5 July 1803, Jefferson Papers, LC.

29. Madison to Jefferson, 20 August 1784, in *The Works of James Madison*, ed. Gaillard Hunt, 9 vols. (New York: Putnam, 1900–1910), 2:73.

30. *Annals of the Debates and Proceedings of Congress*, 7th Cong., 2nd sess., 371–74; Pratt, *Expansionists of 1812*, 64–66.

31. Arthur Styron, *The Last of the Cocked Hats: James Monroe and the Virginia Dynasty* (Norman: University of Oklahoma Press, 1945), 284–85.

32. Jefferson to Washington, 2 April 1791, in *Writings of Thomas Jefferson*, ed. Washington, 3:235.

33. Malone, *Jefferson the President: First Term*, 287; "Extract from Mr. Livingston letter to Mr. Pinckney," 1803, ca. May–June, Monroe Papers, LC.

34. James Monroe to Robert R. Livingston, 23 May–June 7 1803 (letter not sent), Monroe Papers, LC.

35. H. Adams, *History of the United States,* 1:474–79.

36. Malone, *Jefferson the President: First Term,* 342–47; Jefferson's Proclamation of 20 May 1804, in Richardson, *Messages and Papers,* 1:357.

37. George E. Buker, *Jacksonville: Riverport-Seaport* (Columbia: University of South Carolina Press, 1992), 8–24; George Morgan, *The Life of James Monroe* (1921; reprint, New York: AMS Press, 1969), 270–71.

38. Tucker and Hendrickson, *Empire of Liberty,* 158–59.

39. Draft of a letter from Jefferson to the U.S. Commissioners to Spain [Carmichael and Short], 23 March 1793, in *The Writings of Thomas Jefferson,* ed. Paul Leicester Ford, 10 vols. (New York: Putnam, 1892–99), 6:206.

40. James Monroe to John Quincy Adams, 10 December 1815, in *The Writings of James Monroe,* ed. Stanislaus Murray Hamilton, 7 vols. (New York: Putnam, 1898–1903), 5:381.

41. Buker, *Jacksonville,* 30–31; Jefferson to Wilson Cary Nicholas, 25 October 1805, Thomas Jefferson Papers, Manuscripts Division, Special Collections, University of Virginia Library, Charlottesville.

42. Jefferson to John Wayles Eppes, 5 January 1811, Jefferson Papers, University of Virginia Library.

43. Thomas D. Clark and John D. W. Guice, *Frontiers in Conflict: The Old Southwest, 1795–1830* (Albuquerque: University of New Mexico Press, 1989), 51.

44. Frank L. Owsley, Jr., *Struggle for the Gulf Borderlands: The Creek War and the Battle of New Orleans, 1812–1815* (Gainesville: University Presses of Florida, 1981), 20–21.

45. Buker, *Jacksonville,* 29–31.

46. Jefferson to Mr. [James] Bowdoin, 10 July 1806, in *Writings of Thomas Jefferson,* ed. Washington, 5:18.

47. Jefferson to the President of the United States [James Madison], 27 April 1809, in ibid., 5:444; Jefferson to James Monroe, 18 January 1819, in *Writings of Thomas Jefferson,* ed. Ford, 10:122–23; James Monroe to Albert Gallatin, 26 May 1820, in *Writings of James Monroe,* ed. Hamilton, 6:131.

48. Jefferson to James Monroe, 9 July 1786, in *Writings of Thomas Jefferson,* ed. Washington, 1:587–88.

49. Jefferson to William Carmichael, 11 December 1787, in ibid., 2:325; Sheldon, *Political Philosophy of Thomas Jefferson,* 141–45.

50. Jefferson to Dr. [Joseph] Priestley, 29 January 1804, in *Writings of Thomas Jefferson,* ed. Washington, 4:525–26.

51. Jefferson to François Barbé-Marbois, 14 June 1817, Jefferson Papers, LC. Cited in Jackson, *Jefferson and the Stony Mountains,* 298–99; Jefferson to George Clinton, 31 December 1803, Jefferson Papers, University of Virginia Library. Jefferson also disagreed with Montesquieu's

theory in a letter to Nathaniel Niles on 22 March 1801 (*Writings of Thomas Jefferson*, ed. Ford, 8:24).

52. Confidential Message on Expedition to the Pacific, 18 January 1803, in *Writings of Thomas Jefferson*, ed. Ford, 8:192–202. Instructions to Meriwether Lewis are on pages 194 n–199 n; Dumas Malone, *Jefferson the President: Second Term, 1805–1809* (Boston: Little, Brown, 1974), 172–73; Malone, chapter 11, pp. 171–94, deals with Jefferson's role as the patron of the Lewis and Clark expedition.

53. Jefferson to the Secretary of War [Henry Dearborn], 22 June 1807, in *Writings of Thomas Jefferson*, ed. Washington, 5:110–11; Weeks, *John Quincy Adams*, 26.

54. Jefferson to the Secretary of War [Henry Dearborn], 22 June 1807, in *Writings of Thomas Jefferson*, ed. Washington, 5:111.

55. Madison to Jefferson, 30 August 1784, in *The Papers of James Madison*, ed. Robert A. Rutland et al., 17 vols. to date (Chicago: University of Chicago Press, 1962–), 8:107–8.

56. Drew R. McCoy, *The Last of the Founding Fathers: James Madison and the Republican Legacy* (Cambridge: Cambridge University Press, 1989), 180–81; Adrienne Koch, *Jefferson and Madison: The Great Collaboration* (1950; reprint, New York: Oxford University Press, 1964), 58–59.

57. Drew R. McCoy, *The Elusive Republic: Political Economy in Jeffersonian America* (Chapel Hill: University of North Carolina Press, 1980), 121–23.

58. Ernest R. May, *The Making of the Monroe Doctrine* (Cambridge: Belknap Press of Harvard University Press, 1975), 19.

59. James Monroe to James Madison, 8 September 1804, in *Writings of James Monroe*, ed. Hamilton, 4:272–73.

60. Styron, *Last of the Cocked Hats*, 243–44.

61. Tucker and Hendrickson, *Empire of Liberty*, 18; Arthur Preston Whitaker, *The United States and the Independence of Latin America* (New York: Russell and Russell, 1962), 35.

3. FOLLOWERS OF THE GREEN FLAG: REVOLUTION IN THE TEXAS BORDERLANDS

1. T. Harry Williams, Richard N. Current, and Frank Freidel, *A History of the United States to 1877* (New York: Knopf, 1959), 269–73; Samuel Flagg Bemis, *John Quincy Adams and the Foundation of American Foreign Policy* (New York: Norton, 1949), 132, 306.

2. Malcolm D. McLean, ed., *Papers Concerning Robertson's Colony in Texas*, vol. 1 (Fort Worth: Texas Christian University Press, 1974), xxxi.

3. Francis S. Philbrick, *The Rise of the West, 1754–1830* (New York: Harper and Row, 1965), 224–33.

4. Julia K. Garrett, *Green Flag Over Texas* (New York: Cordova Press, 1939), 11–12.

5. Odie B. Faulk, *The Last Years of Spanish Texas, 1778–1821* (The Hague: Mouton, 1969), 111–12; Mattie Hatcher, *The Opening of Texas to Foreign Settlement, 1801–1821* (Philadelphia: Porcupine Press, 1976), 60–206; Nemesio Salcedo to Bernardo Bonavia, 22 June, 21 August 1809, documents numbered 16–18, in appendix to Hatcher, *Opening of Texas*, n.p.

6. Abraham P. Nasatir, *Borderlands in Retreat from Spanish Louisiana to the Far Southwest* (Albuquerque: University of New Mexico Press, 1976), 127–29; Villasana Haggard, "The Neutral Ground between Louisiana and Texas," *Louisiana Historical Quarterly* 28 (1945): 1001–1128.

7. Thomas Maitland Marshall, *A History of the Western Boundary of the Louisiana Purchase* (Berkeley: University of California Press, 1914), 27–30.

8. John Shaw to the Men of his Squadron, 9 October, to Commanders Read and Patterson, 24 October, and to the Secretary of the Navy, 22 August, 10, 31 October 1806, in Letters Received by the Secretary of the Navy from Commanders, 1804–86, RG 45, M147, National Archives [NA], Washington, D.C. (hereafter cited as Commanders' Letters).

9. James Ripley Jacobs, *Tarnished Warrior: Major-General James Wilkinson* (New York: Macmillan, 1938), 230–31; Félix D. Almaráz, *Tragic Cavalier: Governor Manuel Salcedo of Texas, 1808–1813* (Austin: University of Texas Press, 1971), 14–17; Faulk, *Last Years of Spanish Texas*, 124–25.

10. Faulk, *Last Years of Spanish Texas*, 120–28.

11. Thomas D. Clark, *Frontier America: The Story of the Westward Movement* (New York: Scribner, 1959), 254.

12. Faulk, *Last Years of Spanish Texas*, 127; William H. Goetzmann, *New Lands, New Men: America and the Second Great Age of Discovery* (New York: Viking Press, 1986), 117–19.

13. Goetzmann, *Exploration and Empire*, 36–44.

14. Almaráz, *Tragic Cavalier*, 95; Donald E. Chipman, *Spanish Texas, 1519–1821* (Austin: University of Texas Press, 1992), 216–17.

15. Faulk, *Last Years of Spanish Texas*, 108–19; Hugh M. Hamill, Jr., *The Hidalgo Revolt: Prelude to Independence* (Gainesville: University of Florida Press, 1966), 53–54.

16. Timothy E. Anna, *The Fall of the Royal Government in Mexico City* (Lincoln: University of Nebraska Press, 1978), 64–76; Chipman, *Spanish Texas*, 218–22.

17. Almaráz, *Tragic Cavalier*, 108–9.

18. Ibid., 108–25; Hamill, *The Hidalgo Revolt*, 204–9; Chipman, *Spanish Texas*, 232–33.

19. Almaráz, *Tragic Cavalier*, 96; Garrett, *Green Flag Over Texas*, 36–45.

20. Brooks, *Diplomacy and the Borderlands*, 42–43; Warren, *The Sword Was Their Passport*, 4–10.

21. Garrett, *Green Flag Over Texas*, 85–87; Warren, *The Sword Was Their Passport*, 4–10; Brooks, *Diplomacy and the Borderlands*, 43.

22. Warren, *The Sword Was Their Passport,* 7; John Sibley to William Eustis, 14 October 1811, 24 June 1812, in "John Sibley and the Louisiana Texas Frontier, 1803–1814," *Southwestern Historical Quarterly* 49 (1945–1946): 402–17, 417 n.

23. Garrett, *Green Flag Over Texas,* 97–108.

24. Warren, *The Sword Was Their Passport,* 8–9; John Sibley to William Eustis, 28 November 1812, in "John Sibley," 412–18.

25. Brooks, *Diplomacy and the Borderlands,* 43; Garrett, *Green Flag Over Texas,* 97–100.

26. Warren, *The Sword Was Their Passport,* 12–16.

27. Garrett, *Green Flag Over Texas,* 97–108; James P. Baxter III, ed., "Diary of José Bernardo Gutiérrez de Lara, I," *American Historical Review* 34 (1928): 73–75.

28. John Sibley to William Eustis, 24 June 1812, in "John Sibley," 407–10; Roy F. Nichols, *Advance Agents of American Destiny* (Philadelphia: University of Pennsylvania Press, 1956), 83–85; Warren, *The Sword Was Their Passport,* 20–36.

29. Warren, *The Sword Was Their Passport,* 19–26; Garrett, *Green Flag Over Texas,* 104–8; Richard W. Gronet, "The United States and the Invasion of Texas," *The Americas* 25 (1969): 281.

30. Brooks, *Diplomacy and the Borderlands,* 43; Nichols, *Advance Agents,* 98.

31. Warren, *The Sword Was Their Passport,* 37–42, 73–77.

32. James Monroe to Dr. John H. Robinson, 1 July 1812, in Correspondence Relating to the Filibustering Expeditions against the Spanish Government of Mexico, 1811–16, RG 59, T286, NA (hereafter cited as Filibustering Expedition); Gronet, "The United States and the Invasion of Texas," 294; Warren, *The Sword Was Their Passport,* 37–41.

33. Warren, *The Sword Was Their Passport,* 41–42.

34. James Monroe to Dr. John H. Robinson, 1 July 1812, and Robinson to Monroe, 20 July 1813, Filibustering Expedition.

35. A. Curtis Wilgus, "Spanish American Patriot Activity along the Gulf Coast of the United States, 1811–1822," *Louisiana Historical Quarterly* 8 (1925): 197–98; Harry McCorry Henderson, "The Magee-Gutiérrez Expedition," *Southwestern Historical Quarterly* 55 (1951): 43–45, 43 n; Garrett, *Green Flag Over Texas,* 140–47; Warren, *The Sword Was Their Passport,* 44–45.

36. Warren, *The Sword Was Their Passport,* 19; Onís to James Monroe, 18 July 1814, Notes from the Spanish Legation in the United States to the Department of State, 1790–1906, vol. 3, RG 59, M59, NA (hereafter cited as Notes from the Spanish Legation); Garrett, *Green Flag Over Texas,* 138–39, 153–55; John Sibley to William Eustis, 14 July 1812, in "John Sibley," 410–12.

37. William C. C. Claiborne to William Shaler, 17 April 1812, Despatches from Special Agents of the Department of State, RG 59, M37, NA.

38. Garrett, *Green Flag Over Texas*, 143–44; John Sibley to William Eustis, 18 August 1812, in "John Sibley," 415–17.

39. Henderson, "Magee-Gutiérrez Expedition," 44–46.

40. Faulk, *Last Years of Spanish Texas*, 139–40; Henderson, "Magee-Gutiérrez Expedition," 46; Thomas Linnard to General John Mason, 1 February, 15 August 1813, Letterbook of the Natchitoches Sulphur Fork Factory, RG 75, T1029, NA.

41. Garrett, *Green Flag Over Texas*, 150–53; John Sibley to [William Eustis], 1 March 1813, in "John Sibley," 422–23 and note.

42. Henderson, "Magee-Gutiérrez Expedition," 48–50; Warren, *The Sword Was Their Passport*, 42–46; Antonio Menchaca, *Memoirs* (San Antonio: Yanaguana Society Publications, 1937), 14; Ted Schwarz, *Forgotten Battlefield of the First Texas Revolution: The Battle of Medina, August 18, 1813* (Austin: Eakin Press, 1985), 27.

43. Faulk, *Last Years of Spanish Texas*, 139; John Sibley to William Eustis, 21 March 1813, 422–23; John Sibley to General John Armstrong, Secretary of War, 7 May 1813, in "John Sibley," 424–26; Henderson, "Magee-Gutiérrez Expedition," 52–53; Henderson Yoakum, *History of Texas from Its First Settlement in 1685 to Its Annexation to the United States in 1846* (New York: J. S. Redfield, 1855), 167.

44. Warren, *The Sword Was Their Passport*, 52–53; Garrett, *Green Flag Over Texas*, 182–83.

45. Garrett, *Green Flag Over Texas*, 183–85.

46. Warren, *The Sword Was Their Passport*, 53–55.

47. Garrett, *Green Flag Over Texas*, 190–91.

48. Ibid., 184–91; Henderson, "Magee-Gutiérrez Expedition," 54–55; Warren, *The Sword Was Their Passport*, 56–57.

49. Garrett, *Green Flag Over Texas*, 192–93; Warren, *The Sword Was Their Passport*, 58–59.

50. Garrett, *Green Flag Over Texas*, 196–201; Henderson, "Magee-Gutiérrez Expedition," 55–56; Henry P. Walker, ed., "William McLane's Narrative of the Magee-Gutiérrez Expedition, 1812–1813," *Southwestern Historical Quarterly* 66 (1963): 467.

51. John Robinson to James Monroe, 20 July 1813, Filibustering Expedition; Warren, *The Sword Was Their Passport*, 18–20.

52. Warren, *The Sword Was Their Passport*, 19; Owsley, *Struggle for the Gulf*, 263–64.

53. Onís to James Monroe, 18 July 1814, Notes from the Spanish Legation, vol. 3.

54. Warren, *The Sword Was Their Passport*, 50–65; Garrett, *Green Flag Over Texas*, 192–94.

55. Garrett, *Green Flag Over Texas*, 220–21; Almaráz, *Tragic Cavalier*, 174–82; John Sibley to William Eustis, 10 June, 14 July 1813, in "John Sibley," 427–29.

56. Chipman, *Spanish Texas*, 236–37; Garrett, *Green Flag Over Texas*, 202, 216–19.

57. Almaráz, *Tragic Cavalier*, 176–78; Warren, *The Sword Was Their Passport*, 160–69.

58. Warren, *The Sword Was Their Passport*, 66–67; Garrett, *Green Flag Over Texas*, 223–24.

59. Henderson, "Magee-Gutiérrez Expedition," 57–61.

60. Warren, *The Sword Was Their Passport*, 66–72; John Sibley to General John Armstrong, 4 September, 6 October 1813, in "John Sibley," 599–603; Thomas Linnard to General John Mason, 6 October 1813, Letterbook of the Natchitoches Sulphur Fork Factory.

61. Onís to Pedro Labrador, 8 October 1813, Estado, Legajo 5639, letter 110, Archivo Histórico Nacional, Madrid, Spain (hereafter cited as AHN) (photostats in the Library of Congress, Washington, D.C.).

62. Chipman, *Spanish Texas*, 238.

63. Garrett, *Green Flag Over Texas*, 220–21.

4. THE FIRST SPANISH-AMERICAN WAR:
PATRIOT EFFORTS TO ANNEX FLORIDA

1. John Shaw to Paul Hamilton, 25 July 1811, in K. Jack Bauer, ed., *The New American State Papers: Naval Affairs*, vol. 2 (Wilmington, Del.: Scholarly Resources, 1981), 12.

2. James P. Silver, *Edmund Pendleton Gaines: Frontier General* (Baton Rouge: Louisiana State University Press, 1949), 8–17.

3. Isaac J. Cox, *The West Florida Controversy, 1798–1813* (1918; reprint, Gloucester, Mass.: Peter Smith, 1967), 89–101, 388–486; Juan Ventura Morales, "Juan Ventura Morales to Alexandro Ramírez, November 3, 1817," *Boletín del Archivo Nacional* (Cuba) 13 (1941): 9–21; Weeks, *John Quincy Adams*, 24.

4. Nichols, *Advance Agents*, 83.

5. Silver, *Edmund Pendleton Gaines*, 10–16.

6. Jacobs, *Tarnished Warrior*, 209–40.

7. Clement Eaton, *History of the Old South* (New York: Macmillan, 1975), 180; Thomas P. Abernethy, "Aaron Burr in Mississippi," *Journal of Southern History* 15 (1949): 9–21; Cox, *West Florida Controversy*, 188–221.

8. Arthur, *West Florida Rebellion*, 112–15, 130–35.

9. Cox, *West Florida Controversy*, 415–69; Albert J. Pickett, *History of Alabama, and Incidentally of Georgia and Mississippi, from the Earliest Period*, vol. 2 (Charleston: Walker and James, 1851), 505–9; Philbrick, *The Rise of the West*, 231.

10. Varg, *New England and Foreign Relations*, 43–44; James M. Banner, Jr., *To the Hartford Convention: The Federalists and the Origins of Party Politics in Massachusetts, 1789–1815* (New York: Knopf, 1970), 27–28.

11. Cox, *West Florida Controversy*, 213–14; Silver, *Edmund Pendleton Gaines*, 20–25.

12. Rembert W. Patrick, *Florida Fiasco: Rampant Rebels on the Georgia-Florida Border, 1810–1815* (Athens: University of Georgia Press, 1954), 4, 11–35; Vizente Folch to President James Madison, 2 December 1810, in Walter Lowrie et al., eds., *The American State Papers: Foreign Relations* (Washington, D.C.: Gales and Seaton, 1832), 3:398 (hereafter cited as *ASP:FR*); Cox, *West Florida Controversy*, 422, 512–19. For background of Spanish buffer policy, see chapter 5 of Bernard E. Bobb, *The Viceregency of Antonio María Bucareli in New Spain, 1771–1779* (Austin: University of Texas Press, 1962), 128–55.

13. Vizente Folch to President James Madison, 2 December 1810, *ASP:FR*, 3:398; Cox, *West Florida Controversy*, 471–72.

14. Silver, *Edmund Pendleton Gaines*, 23–25.

15. Pratt, *Expansionists of 1812*, 78–80; Cox, *West Florida Controversy*, 523.

16. James Monroe to George Mathews, 26 January 1811, 4 April 1812, East Florida Papers, transcript in Alabama Department of Archives and History, Montgomery.

17. A. H. Phinney, "The First Spanish-American War," *Florida Historical Quarterly* 4 (1926): 116–19.

18. Arthur Preston Whitaker, *Documents Relating to the Commercial Policy of Spain in the Floridas* (Deland, Fla.: Florida State Historical Society, 1931), iii; Brooks, *Diplomacy and the Borderlands*, 30–34.

19. Patrick, *Florida Fiasco*, 19; J. Leitch Wright, *William Augustus Bowles, Director General of the Creek Nation* (Athens: University of Georgia Press, 1967), 142–48.

20. James Monroe to George Mathews, 26 January 1811, East Florida Papers; Weeks, *John Quincy Adams*, 28–29.

21. Weeks, *John Quincy Adams*, 29; Pratt, *Expansionists of 1812*, 80.

22. Phinney, "The First Spanish-American War," 118–19; Brooks, *Diplomacy and the Borderlands*, 32–33.

23. Phinney, "The First Spanish-American War," 118–20; Patrick, *Florida Fiasco*, 70–82.

24. James Monroe to Governor David B. Mitchell, 10 April 1812, East Florida Papers.

25. Hugh Campbell to Secretary of the Navy Paul Hamilton, 1 March, and to Sailing Master Bartran G. Hopkins, 29 March 1812, in William S. Dudley, ed., *The Naval War of 1812: A Documentary History*, vol. 1 (Washington, D.C.: Naval Historical Center, Department of the Navy, 1985), 86–90; Phinney, "The First Spanish-American War," 118.

26. D. C. Corbitt, "The Return of Spanish Rule to the St. Marys and the St. Johns, 1813–1821," *Florida Historical Quarterly* 20 (1941): 47–49.

27. Justo López to Luis Onís, 19 March, enclosure in Onís to James Monroe, 14 April 1812, Notes from the Spanish Legation, vol. 3; Report and Dispatch of Pedro Labrador, Secretary of State, 31 December 1812, to the Deputy Secretaries of the General and Extraordinary Cortes, East

Florida Papers; Spencer C. Tucker, *Jefferson's Gunboat Navy* (Columbia: University of South Carolina Press, 1993), 99–100.

28. Hugh Campbell to the Secretary of the Navy, 11 April 1812, Letters Received by the Secretary of the Navy: Captains' Letters, 1805–85, RG 45, M125, NA (hereafter cited as Captains' Letters).

29. G. I. F. Clarke to O'Reilley, 19 March 1812, in "The Surrender of Amelia, March 1812," *Florida Historical Quarterly* 4 (1925): 91; Phinney, "The First Spanish-American War," 120–21; Report of Pedro Labrador to General Cortes, 31 December 1812, East Florida Papers.

30. Hugh Campbell to Secretary of the Navy Paul Hamilton, 12 March, and Hamilton to Campbell, 8 April 1812, in Dudley, *Naval War of 1812*, 1:86–90; Luis Onís to James Monroe, 4 April 1812, Notes from the Spanish Legation, vol. 3; Virginia Bergman Peters, *The Florida Wars* (Hamden, Conn.: Archon Books, 1979), 38–39.

31. Patrick, *Florida Fiasco*, 103–6.

32. Phinney, "The First Spanish-American War," 120–21; Brooks, *Diplomacy and the Borderlands*, 33.

33. James Madison to Thomas Jefferson, 24 April 1812, in *Works of James Madison*, ed. Hunt, 8:187; "James Monroe to General George Mathews, April 4, 1812," *Florida Historical Quarterly* 6 (1928): 235–37.

34. H. Adams, *History of the United States*, 2:764–68; Pratt, *Expansionists of 1812*, 209–10.

35. Weeks, *John Quincy Adams*, 27–28.

36. Patrick, *Florida Fiasco*, 108–21; Pratt, *Expansionists*, 53, 57, 109–10.

37. Patrick, *Florida Fiasco*, 93–98; Hugh Campbell to Secretary of the Navy Hamilton, 21 March 1812, in Dudley, *Naval War of 1812*, 1:87–88.

38. Secretary of the Navy Hamilton to Hugh Campbell, 8 April 1812, in Dudley, *Naval War of 1812*, 1:90.

39. John McKee to James Innerarity, 18 April 1812, Greenslade Papers, Florida Historical Society, University of South Florida, Tampa.

40. H. Adams, *History of the United States*, 2:766–67; Buker, *Jacksonville*, 30–31.

41. James Monroe to David Mitchell, 10 April 1812, East Florida Papers.

42. Report of Pedro Labrador to the Deputy Secretaries of the General and Extraordinary Cortes, 31 December 1812, East Florida Papers; Patrick, *Florida Fiasco*, 179–94.

43. Weeks, *John Quincy Adams*, 29; Pratt, *Expansionists of 1812*, 109–10; Brooks, *Diplomacy and the Borderlands*, 33.

44. Thomas P. Abernethy, "Florida and the Spanish Frontier," in *The Americanization of the Gulf Coast, 1803–1850*, ed. Lucius Ellsworth (Pensacola: Historic Pensacola Preservation Board, 1972), 96–99.

45. John Floyd to David Mitchell, 5 March 1813, Creek Letters, Talks and Treaties, 1705–1839, Georgia Department of Archives, Atlanta (here-

after cited as Creek Letters); Pratt, *Expansionists of 1812*, 189–207; Patrick, *Florida Fiasco*, 179–94.

46. Frances K. Harrison, "The Indians as a Means of Spanish Defense of West Florida" (M.A. thesis, University of Alabama, 1950), passim; Clem Lanier to David Mitchell, 13 September 1813, Creek Letters; Luis Onís to James Monroe, 30 December 1812, Notes from the Spanish Legation, vol. 3.

47. Ruíz Apodaca to the Governor of East Florida, 10 December 1813, Papeles Procedentes de Cuba, Legajos 1856, Archivo General de Indias, Seville, Spain (hereafter cited as PC Legajos, AGI) (photostats in the Library of Congress, Washington, D.C.); Ruíz Apodaca to the Minister of War Juan O. Donoju, 18 November 1813, 26 April 1814, PC Legajos 1856, AGI; Patrick, *Florida Fiasco*, 184–94.

48. Abernethy, "Florida and the Spanish Frontier," 98–99.

49. Pratt, *Expansionists of 1812*, 190–97.

50. Ibid., 207–8; Jane Landers, "Jorge Biassou, Black Chieftain," *El Escribano: The St. Augustine Journal of History* 25 (1988): 88–89.

51. John K. Mahon, *History of the Second Seminole War, 1835–1842* (Gainesville: University of Florida Press, 1967), 21; Patrick, *Florida Fiasco*, 199–207.

52. Patrick, *Florida Fiasco*, 191–94, 207–27.

53. Thomas Flournoy to William Crawford, 8 February 1813, Letters Received by the Secretary of War, Registered Series, 1801–70, RG 107, M221, NA (hereafter cited as Letters to the Secretary of War); Robert V. Remini, *Andrew Jackson and the Course of American Empire, 1767–1821* (New York: Harper and Row, 1977), 171–77; Peters, *The Florida Wars*, 42–46; Pratt, *Expansionists of 1812*, 219–29.

54. David Holmes to James Wilkinson, 19 October 1812, in Clarence Carter, ed., *The Territory of Mississippi*, vol. 6 of *The Territorial Papers of the United States*, 27 vols. (Washington, D.C.: Government Printing Office, 1934–69), 328–29; Pratt, *Expansionists of 1812*, 214–29; Albert Gallatin to James Monroe, 2 May 1813, Monroe Papers, LC.

55. Brooks, *Diplomacy and the Borderlands*, 33–34.

56. Pratt, *Expansionists of 1812*, 100–118; Peters, *The Florida Wars*, 37–45.

57. Pratt, *Expansionists of 1812*, 228–37.

5. "PACIFIED BY PATERNAL SOLITUDE": INDIAN WARS AS AN EXPANSIONIST MOVEMENT

1. Steven Watts, *The Republic Reborn: War and the Making of Liberal America, 1790–1820* (Baltimore: Johns Hopkins University Press, 1987), 95; J. C. A. Stagg, *Mr. Madison's War* (Princeton: Princeton University Press, 1983), 352.

2. For a historiographical essay on Indian policy during the Jeffersonian period see Tucker and Hendrickson, *Empire of Liberty*, 304–6, n. 102.

3. Pratt, *Expansionists of 1812*, 9–15.

4. Margaret K. Latimer, "South Carolina—A Protagonist of the War of 1812," *American Historical Review* 61 (1956): 914–29.

5. Donald R. Hickey, *The War of 1812: A Forgotten Conflict* (Urbana: University of Illinois Press, 1989), 11–12; Christopher McKee, *A Gentlemanly and Honorable Profession: The Creation of the U.S. Naval Officer Corps, 1794–1815* (Annapolis: Naval Institute Press, 1991), 100–101.

6. Reginald Horsman, "British Indian Policy in the Northwest, 1807–1812," *Mississippi Valley Historical Review* 45 (1958): 51–67; Pratt, *Expansionists of 1812*, 21, 66–67.

7. Stagg, *Mr. Madison's War*, 475–83.

8. Hickey, *The War of 1812*, 303–4.

9. Frank L. Owsley, Jr., "Ambrister and Arbuthnot: Adventurers or Martyrs for British Honor?" *Journal of the Early Republic* 5 (Fall 1985): 289–308.

10. George Washington to the Cherokee Nation, 29 August 1796, in *The Writings of George Washington*, ed. John Fitzpatrick, 33 vols. (Washington, D.C.: Government Printing Office, 1931–41), 15:193–98; Thomas Jefferson to Benjamin Hawkins, 14 March 1800, 16, 18 February 1803, in *Writings of Thomas Jefferson*, ed. Lipscomb and Bergh, 10:160–62, 357–60, 360–65; Bernard Sheehan, *Seeds of Extinction: Jefferson Philanthropy and the American Indian* (Chapel Hill: University of North Carolina Press, 1973), 3–12, 213–79; Frank L. Owsley, Jr., "Benjamin Hawkins, the First Modern Indian Agent," *Alabama Historical Quarterly* 30 (Summer 1968): 7–13.

11. George Stiggins, "History of the Creek Nation Written by One of the Tribe," MS in the Lyman Draper Papers, State Historical Society of Wisconsin, Madison, 44–60; John Cottier and George Wasalkov, "The First Creek War: Twilight of Annihilation," in *Clearings in the Thicket: An Alabama Humanities Reader*, ed. Jerry E. Brown (Macon, Ga.: Mercer University Press, 1985), 21–38; Mary Jane McDaniels, "Tescumseh's Visit to the Creeks," *Alabama Review* 33 (1980): 9–12.

12. Gregory Evans Dowd, *A Spirited Resistance: The North American Indian Struggle for Unity, 1745–1815* (Baltimore: Johns Hopkins University Press, 1992), 154–57; R. David Edmunds, *Tecumseh and the Quest for Indian Leadership* (Boston: Little, Brown, 1984), 20–22, 135–60.

13. Reginald Horsman, *Expansion and American Indian Policy, 1783–1812* (East Lansing: Michigan State University Press, 1967), 166–73; R. David Edmunds, *The Shawnee Prophet* (Lincoln: University of Nebraska Press, 1983), 110–16.

14. Owsley, *Struggle for the Gulf*, 180–83; Hickey, *The War of 1812*, 303–4; Reginald C. Stuart, *United States Expansionism and British North America, 1775–1871* (Chapel Hill: University of North Carolina Press, 1988), 75–76.

15. Owsley, *Struggle for the Gulf,* 6–7; Dowd, *A Spirited Resistance,* 156–57.

16. Jefferson to Hawkins, 14 March 1800, 18 February 1803, Jefferson to Andrew Jackson, 16 February 1803, in *Writings of Thomas Jefferson,* ed. Lipscomb and Bergh, 10:160–62, 360–65, 357–60; Bernard Sheehan, "Indian-White Relations in Early America," and Francis Paul Prucha, "Andrew Jackson's Indian Policy," in *The Indian in American History,* ed. Francis Paul Prucha (New York: Rinehart and Winston, 1971), 51–66, 62–74; M. Adams, "Jefferson's Reaction," 182–83.

17. Jefferson to Andrew Jackson, 16 February 1803, in *Writings of Thomas Jefferson,* ed. Lipscomb and Bergh, 10:357–60; Frank L. Owsley, Jr., "The Fort Mims Massacre," *Alabama Review* 24 (July 1974): 192–204.

18. Owsley, *Struggle for the Gulf,* 8–11.

19. Thomas Perkins Abernethy, *The South in the New Nation, 1789–1819* (Baton Rouge: Louisiana State University, 1961), 44, 367; H. Adams, *History of the United States,* 1:613.

20. H. S. Halbert and T. H. Ball, *The Creek War of 1813 and 1814,* ed. Frank L. Owsley, Jr. (Tuscaloosa: University of Alabama Press, 1969), 58–104; Stagg, *Mr. Madison's War,* 348–49; Owsley, *Struggle for the Gulf,* 6–17; Henry deLeon Southerland, Jr., and Jerry Elijah Brown, *The Federal Road through Georgia, the Creek Nation, and Alabama, 1806–1836* (Tuscaloosa: University of Alabama Press, 1989), 33–50.

21. J. Leitch Wright, *Britain and the American Frontier, 1783–1815* (Athens: University of Georgia Press, 1975), 157, 161–62.

22. Mauricio Zúñiga to Ruíz Apodaca, 18 April 1813, Ruíz Apodaca to the Minister of War, 1 October 1813, 23 March 1814, PC Legajos 1856, AGI.

23. H. Adams, *History of the United States,* 2:456–57.

24. Pratt, *Expansionists of 1812,* 75–76; Owsley, *Struggle for the Gulf,* 21.

25. Brady to Harry Toulmin, 2 October, Toulmin to James Wilkinson, 6 October, Toulmin to Cayetano Pérez, 5 October, Pérez to Toulmin, 5 October, enclosures in Wilkinson to Secretary of War William Eustis, 6 October 1812; Secretary of War John Armstrong to Wilkinson, 16 February, 27 May 1813, Letters to the Secretary of War.

26. James Wilkinson to Commanding Officer of the Spanish Garrison in the town of Mobile, Mississippi Territory, 12 April, and Articles of Capitulation for Mobile, enclosures in Mauricio Zúñiga to Ruíz Apodaca, 2 May 1813, PC Legajos 1794, AGI; Owsley, *Struggle for the Gulf,* 21–24.

27. Luis de Onís to James Monroe, 4 June 1813, Notes from the Spanish Legation, vol. 3; Onís to Labrador, 8 October 1813, Legajo 5639, AHN; Onís to San Carlos, 16 September 1814, Expediente 25, Legajo 5557, AHN; Charles Carroll Griffin, *The United States and the Disruption of the Spanish Empire, 1810–1822: A Study of the Relations of the United States with Spain and with the Rebel Spanish Colonies* (New York: Columbia University Press, 1937), 29–36, 40–41.

28. Onís to James Monroe, 4 June 1813, Notes from the Spanish Legation, vol. 3; Onís to Pedro Labrador, 8 October 1813, Legajo 5639, AHN.

29. Ruíz Apodaca to Minister of War, 1 October 1813, 24 March 1814, PC Legajos 1856, AGI.

30. González Manrique to Ruíz Apodaca, 15 May, 18 December 1813, PC Legajos 1794, AGI; Owsley, *Struggle for the Gulf,* 24.

31. Letter to the Editor, 18 April 1813, in *Niles Weekly Register,* 29 May 1813, 4:209–10; González Manrique to Ruíz Apodaca, September 1813, and Alva to González Manrique, 30 September 1813, PC Legajos 1794, AGI; Deposition of David Tait, 2 August 1813, Claiborne Letterbook "F," Claiborne Papers, Mississippi Department of Archives and History, Jackson.

32. González Manrique to Ruíz Apodaca, 18 May, 23 July, 16 August 1813, PC Legajos 1794, AGI.

33. Pratt, *Expansionists of 1812,* 247; Owsley, "The Fort Mims Massacre," 192–204.

34. González Manrique to the Creek Indians, 29 September 1813, in Claiborne Letterbook "F," Claiborne Papers.

35. Owsley, *Struggle for the Gulf,* 106–24.

36. Ibid., 86–92; Joel W. Martin, *Sacred Revolt: The Muskogee's Struggle for a New World* (Boston: Beacon Press, 1991), 165–66.

37. Secretary of War to Andrew Jackson, 24 May, Jackson to the Secretary of War, 13 June, Harry Toulmin to Jackson, 22 June 1814, in *Correspondence of Andrew Jackson,* ed. John S. Bassett, 6 vols. (Washington, D.C.: Carnegie Institution, 1926–33), 2:4–5, 6–8, 9–11.

38. Owsley, *Struggle for the Gulf,* 99–107.

39. Ruíz Apodaca to the Minister of War, 6 June, 24 September 1814, PC Legajos 1856, AGI.

40. Edward Nicolls to Alexander Cochrane, Report, 12 August to 17 November 1814, MS 2328, The Papers of Admiral Alexander Forrester Inglis Cochrane, National Library of Scotland, Edinburgh (hereafter cited as Cochrane Papers).

41. Owsley, *Struggle for the Gulf,* 109–19.

42. González Manrique to Ruíz Apodaca, 14 November 1814, PC Legajos 1795, AGI; James Gordon to Alexander Cochrane, 18 November 1814, Public Record Office, Admiralty Office 1, vol. 505 (hereafter cited as PRO, Adm.).

43. Owsley, *Struggle for the Gulf,* 118–19; William S. Coker, "How General Andrew Jackson Learned of the British Plans *before* the Battle of New Orleans," *Gulf Coast Historical Review* 3 (1987): 85–95.

44. Owsley, *Struggle for the Gulf,* 106–24; Alexander Cochrane to John W. Croker, 9 December 1814, PRO, Adm. 1/508; Ventura Morales, "Juan Ventura Morales to Alexandro Ramírez," 15–16; González Man-

28. Duncan Clinch to R. Butler, 2 August 1816, "Operation, Negro ort."

29. Ibid.; Knox, "Forgotten Fight in Florida," 512–13; Covington, "Ne-o Fort," 83, 86–87. Covington gives the date of the attack as 25 July, hereas Knox in the article cited above gives the date as 27 July; Dowd, Spirited Resistance, 188.

30. Coker and Watson, Indian Traders, 304–5, 307; Edward Nicolls to ritish Chargé d'Affairs, 12 June 1815, and Alexander Arbuthnot to harles Cameron, 10 January 1817, PRO, FO 5/127.

31. Coker and Watson, Indian Traders, 308–9; Duncan Clinch to Butler, 2 August 1816, "Operation, Negro Fort"; Boyd, "Events at Pros-ct Bluff," 81; Mulroy, Freedom on the Border, 15; Patrick, Aristocrat in Uni-rm, 33.

32. Duncan Clinch to R. Butler, 2 August 1816, "Operation, Negro rt"; Patrick, Aristocrat in Uniform, 32–33; Coe, Red Patriots, 19.

33. Duncan Clinch to R. Butler, 2 August 1816, "Operation, Negro rt"; Patrick, Aristocrat in Uniform, 32–33.

34. Boyd, "Events at Prospect Bluff," 81–82; John Innerarity to John orbes, 13 August 1816, Forbes Papers; Duncan Clinch to R. Butler, 2 Au-ust 1816, "Operation, Negro Fort"; Knox, "Forgotten Fight in Florida," 2; Daniel Patterson to the Secretary of the Navy, 15 August 1816, Cap-ins' Letters.

35. Duncan Clinch to R. Butler, 2 August 1816, "Operation, Negro rt"; Knox, "Forgotten Fight in Florida," 512.

36. Knox, "Forgotten Fight in Florida," 512–13; Covington, "The Ne-o Fort," 87–88.

37. Boyd, "Events at Prospect Bluff," 81–82; John Innerarity to John orbes, 13 August 1816, Forbes Papers.

38. Ventura Morales, "Juan Ventura Morales to Don Alexandro amírez," 16–17.

39. Edward Nicolls to John W. Coker, 15 August 1815, PRO, WO 143.

40. Robert Spencer to Alexander Cochrane, 17 February, Cochrane Earl of Bathurst, 12 March 1816, PRO, WO 1/144; Edward Nicolls to orier, 16 November 1815, John Croker to Henry Goulburn, 11 Novem-r 1815, PRO, WO 1/143.

41. Henry Bunbury to John Barrow, 7 September 1815, PRO, FO 140; Edward Nicolls to Alexander Cochrane, 1 March, Robert Spencer Cochrane, 17 February, Cochrane to Earl of Bathurst, 12 March 1816, RO, WO 1/144.

42. Edward Nicolls to Henry Goulburn, 15 January, and to exander Cochrane, 15 August 1816, PRO, WO 1/144.

43. "Estimate of Agricultural and Household Instruments for the reek Indian Chief Hidlis Hadjo and Estimate of Clothing," enclosed in colls to Goulburn, 15 January, 8 October 1816, PRO, WO 1/144.

rique to Cochrane, 5 December 1815, Forbes Papers, Mobile Public Li-brary, Mobile, Alabama; Memorandum and Petition from Citizens of East Florida, 6 March 1815, Public Record Office, War Office 1, vol. 144 (here-after cited as PRO, WO).

45. Alexander Cochrane to John Lambert, 3 February 1815, PRO, WO 1/143; Cochrane's Journal, Admiral's Journals 5, 10, 18, 1815, PRO, Adm. 50/122.

46. Pultney Malcolm to Edward Nicolls, 5, 29 March 1815; Alexander Cochrane to Nicolls, 9 March 1815; Ratification of Article Nine of the Treaty of Ghent signed by the Chiefs of the Muscogee Nation, 2 April 1815, all in Public Record Office, Foreign Office 5, vol. 139 (hereafter cited as PRO, FO).

47. Bartholomew to Alexander Cochrane, 31 January 1815, MS 2328, Cochrane Papers.

48. Alexander Cochrane to John Lambert, 17 February 1815, PRO, WO 1/143.

49. Alexander Cochrane to Pultney Malcolm, General Instructions, 17 February 1815, PRO, WO 1/141.

50. Pultney Malcolm to Edward Nicolls, 29 March 1815, PRO, FO 5/139; Nicolls to John W. Croker, 15 August 1815, PRO, WO 1/143; Nicolls to Alexander Cochrane, 1 March 1816, PRO, WO 1/144.

51. Secretary of War Alexander J. Dallas to Jackson, 12 June 1815, Letters to the Secretary of War; Remini, Andrew Jackson, 324–26.

52. Marquis James, The Life of Andrew Jackson (Indianapolis: Bobbs-Merrill, 1938), 190.

53. Edward Nicolls to his Bms Chargé d'Affairs, 12 June 1815, PRO, FO 5/139; Robert Spencer to Alexander Cochrane, 17 February, Nicolls to Cochrane, 1 March, Cochrane to Bathurst, 12 March 1816, PRO, WO 1/144.

54. Benjamin Hawkins to Edward Nicolls, 24 March, 28 May, Nicolls to Hawkins, 12 May 1815, in Niles Weekly Register, 24 June 1815, 8:285–87; Nicolls to Hawkins, 28 April 1815, PRO, WO 1/143.

55. Edmund P. Gaines to Andrew Jackson, 22 May 1815, Letters to the Secretary of War.

56. Augusta (Ga.) Chronicle, 3 November 1815.

57. Dowd, A Spirited Resistance, 190.

58. Ibid., 187–90; Rembert Patrick, Aristocrat in Uniform: General Dun-can Clinch (Gainesville: University of Florida Press, 1963), 24–36.

6. A LEFTOVER OF WAR: NEGRO FORT

1. Narrative of a Voyage to the Spanish Main, in the Ship "Two Friends" (Gainesville: University of Florida Press, 1978), passim.

2. Kevin Mulroy, Freedom on the Border: The Seminole Maroons in Flor-ida, the Indian Territory, Coahuila, and Texas (Lubbock: Texas Tech Univer-

sity Press, 1993), 14–15; William S. Coker and Thomas D. Watson, *Indian Traders of the Southeastern Spanish Borderlands: Panton, Leslie and Company, and John Forbes and Company, 1783–1847* (Pensacola: University of West Florida Press, 1986), 297–300.

3. James Leitch Wright, "A Note on the First Seminole War as Seen by the Indians, Negroes, and Their British Advisors," *Journal of Southern History* 34 (1968): 568–69; Frank L. Owsley, Jr., "Prophet of War: Josiah Francis and the Creek War," *American Indian Quarterly* 9 (1985): 284–90.

4. Wright, "A Note on the First Seminole War," 569; Eugene P. Southall, "Negroes in Florida Prior to the Civil War," *Journal of Negro History* 19 (1934): 82–83; Kenneth Wiggins Porter, *The Negro on the American Frontier* (New York: Arno Press, 1971), 216.

5. Deposition of Samuel Jarvis, 9 May 1815, enclosure Gaines to the Secretary of War, Letters of the Secretary of War. There is no doubt that Jarvis's report is accurate. It is probably not possible to give an exact count of the arms sent to Prospect Bluff by the British or to determine how many had already been distributed to the Indians, but the memorandum cited below as an enclosure from Bathurst to Ross, 10 September 1814, states that 3,000 muskets, 1,000 carbines, 500 rifles, and 1,000 swords were shipped from England for the attack on New Orleans. Prior to this shipment, 2,000 muskets were shipped aboard HMS *Orpheus* and landed at Apalachicola by Captain Hugh Pigot. There were apparently other shipments as well, but the records are not as clear and detailed. Listed below are references that document these arms shipments: Cochrane to Nicolls, 28 December 1814, PRO, Adm. 1/505; Bathurst to Ross, 10 August, and memorandum enclosed in Bathurst to Ross, 10 September 1814, PRO, WO 6/2; "Expedition against New Orleans," PRO, WO 1/142; Charles Cameron to Cochrane, 2 August 1814, MS 2328, Cochrane Papers; Hugh Pigot to Cochrane, 8 June 1814, PRO, Adm. 1/506.

6. Junius P. Rodriguez, "Ripe for Revolt: Louisiana and the Tradition of Slave Insurrection, 1803–1865" (Ph.D. diss., Auburn University, 1992), 87–111.

7. Conde de Fernán-Núñez to Vizconde Castlereagh, 8 December 1815, PRO, FO 72/180.

8. Petition of the Pensacola Citizens to his Excellency the Governor of West Florida, March 1815, MS 2328, Cochrane Papers; González Manrique to Alexander Cochrane, 5 December 1814, José Urcerllo to Manrique, 23 January 1815, Forbes Papers; Cochrane to Manrique, 10 February 1815, Cruzat Papers, Florida Historical Society, University of South Florida, Tampa; Ruíz Apodaca to the Minister of War, 6 May, 15 June 1815, PC Legajos 1856, AGI; Mulroy, *Freedom on the Border*, 13.

9. John Innerarity to James Innerarity, 10 May 1815, Forbes Papers.

10. Mark F. Boyd, "Events at Prospect Bluff on the Apalachicola River, 1808–1818," *Florida Historical Quarterly* 14 (1937): 75–76.

11. Hawkins to Jackson, 5 May, Gaines to Jacks[...] ters to the Secretary of War.

12. Dowd, *A Spirited Resistance*, 188; James W. [...] Fort," *Gulf Coast Historical Review* 5 (Spring 1990): [...] in Florida," 83; Charles H. Coe, *Red Patriots: The S[...] (1898; reprint, Gainesville: University of Florida P[...] Duncan Clinch to R. Butler, 2 August 1816, "Oper[...] 45: HJ Box 181, 1816, NA (hereafter cited as "Op[...]

13. Porter, *The Negro on the American Frontier*, 2[...] in Florida," 83; Gaines to the Secretary of War, 22 [...] the Secretary of War; Thomas Freeman to Josiah [...] Carter, *Territorial Papers*, 6:677–78; Covington, "Th[...]

14. Boyd, "Events at Prospect Bluff," 75; Coke[...] *Traders*, 304.

15. Peter Early to Sebastian Kindelan, 24 May [...] terbook, 18 May 1814 to 30 October 1827, Georgi[...] chives, Atlanta.

16. Juan José de Estrada to Peter Early, 14 Jun[...]

17. Estrada to Early, 11 September 1815, ibid. [...]

18. Luis de Onís to Monroe, 28 August, 30 D[...] from the Spanish Legation, vol. 3.

19. Remini, *Andrew Jackson*, 344.

20. Patrick, *Aristocrat in Uniform*, 27; Boyd, "E[...] Bluff," 77; Duncan Clinch to R. Butler, 2 August 1[...] gro Fort."

21. Covington, "The Negro Fort," 80–81; Dur[...] 2 August 1816, "Operation, Negro Fort."

22. Patrick, *Aristocrat in Uniform*, 28–29; Covi[...] Fort," 83–84.

23. Dudley W. Knox, "A Forgotten Fight in Fl[...] *val Institute Proceedings* 62 (1936): 510; Covington, [...]

24. Duncan Clinch to R. Butler, 2 August 181[...] Fort"; Silver, *Edmund Pendleton Gaines*, 62–63; Boy[...] Bluff," 78; Covington, "The Negro Fort," 84; Kno[...] Florida," 510; Porter, *The Negro on the American Fr[...]

25. Duncan Clinch to R. Butler, 2 August 181[...] Fort"; James Grant Forbes, *Sketches, Historical and [...] *das: More Particularly of East Florida* (1821; reprint[...] of Florida Press, 1964), 200–205; Patrick, *Aristocr[...]

26. Boyd, "Events at Prospect Bluff," 74–80.

27. Duncan Clinch to R. Butler, 2 August 181[...] Fort"; Knox, "A Forgotten Fight in Florida," 522; [...] Fort," 85.

44. Edward Nicolls to Henry Goulburn, 7 January 1817, ibid.

45. Edward Nicolls to Earl of Bathurst, 23 September 1817, ibid.

46. Boyd, "Events at Prospect Bluff," 89.

47. Edmund Doyle to John Innerarity, 17 June 1817, in "The Panton, Leslie Papers: Continuing the Letters of Edmund Doyle, Trader," *Florida Historical Quarterly* 18 (1939): 61–63.

48. Henry Goulburn to William Hamilton, 17 May 1816, 2 April 1817, Public Record Office, Colonial Office 138, vol. 146 (hereafter cited as PRO, CO).

49. J. Plantasto to John Bidwell, 14 September, Bidwell to William Hamilton, 17 September 1818, PRO, FO 5/140.

50. William Hamilton to John Croker, 14, 15 September 1818, PRO, FO 5/140.

51. Stuart, *United States Expansionism*, 79–80.

52. Porter, *The Negro on the American Frontier*, 235–36; Dowd, *A Spirited Resistance*, 190; Hickey, *The War of 1812*, 303–4.

53. Skelton, *An American Profession of Arms*, 333.

7. "A SET OF DESPERATE AND BLOODY DOGS": THE ACQUISITION OF AMELIA ISLAND

1. Jefferson to John Jacob Astor, 24 May 1812, in *Writings of Thomas Jefferson*, ed. Washington, 6:55.

2. Bemis, *John Quincy Adams*, 251–61; Don E. Fehrenbacher, *The Era of Expansion: 1800–1848* (New York: Wiley, 1969), 26–30.

3. Fernán Núñez to Count Castlereagh, 8 December 1815, PRO, FO 72/180; González Manrique to Juan Ruíz de Apodaca, 18 November, 5 December 1814, PC Legajos 1795, AGI; T. Frederick Davis, *MacGregor's Invasion of Florida, 1817: Together with an Account of His Successors, Irwin, Hubbard, and Aury on Amelia Island, East Florida* (Jacksonville, 1928), 8–9, 19–30.

4. Davis, *MacGregor's Invasion*, 9–19.

5. Brooks, *Diplomacy and the Borderlands*, 86–87.

6. Davis, *MacGregor's Invasion*, 8–11; Belton Copp to John Quincy Adams, Secretary of State, 1 April 1818, in "The Patriot War: A Contemporary Letter," *Florida Historical Quarterly* 5 (1927): 162.

7. Belton Copp to John Quincy Adams, 1 April 1818, in "The Patriot War," 166; Jane Lucas de Grummond, ed., *Caracas Diary, 1835–1840: The Journal of John G. A. Williamson* (Baton Rouge: Camellia Publishing Company, 1954), 307–8; Sir Leslie Stephen and Sir Sidney Lee, eds., *The Dictionary of National Biography*, 43 vols. (London: Oxford University Press, 1949–50), 12:539.

8. Davis, *MacGregor's Invasion*, 2–4; "Sir Gregor Macgregor," *Dictionary of National Biography*, 12:539.

9. Abernethy, "Florida and the Spanish Frontier," 111–12; Davis, *MacGregor's Invasion*, 4–7.

10. Rufus Kay Wyllys, "The Filibusters of Amelia Island," *Georgia Historical Quarterly* 12 (1928): 302–3; Davis, *MacGregor's Invasion*, 2–4; de Grummond, *Caracas Diary*, 307–8.

11. Davis, *MacGregor's Invasion*, 4–5; Gregor Macgregor's Commission, 31 March 1817, *ASP:FR*, 4:415; Wyllys, "Filibusters of Amelia Island," 302–3.

12. Abernethy, "Florida and the Spanish Frontier," 111–12.

13. Davis, *MacGregor's Invasion*, 4–6; John Skinner to Secretary of State John Quincy Adams, 30 July 1817, "Letters Relating to MacGregor's Attempted Conquest of East Florida, 1817," *Florida Historical Quarterly* 18 (1939): 655–57.

14. Charles Bagot to Castlereagh, 25 April 1817, PRO, FO 5/122; Herbert Bruce Fuller, *The Purchase of Florida: Its History and Diplomacy* (1906; reprint, Gainesville: University of Florida Press, 1964), 226–27.

15. Abernethy, "Florida and the Spanish Frontier," 111; Fuller, *Purchase of Florida*, 278–79; Charles Bagot to Castlereagh, 25 April 1817, PRO, FO 5/122; Wilgus, "Spanish American Patriot Activity," 207 n.

16. Charles Bagot to Castlereagh, 25 April 1817, PRO, FO 5/122.

17. Abernethy, "Florida and the Spanish Frontier," 111–12.

18. Davis, *MacGregor's Invasion*, 6–8.

19. Ibid., 11–15; Wyllys, "Filibusters of Amelia Island," 303–4; *Niles Weekly Register*, 30 August 1817, 13:12.

20. Fuller, *Purchase of Florida*, 232–36; *Niles Weekly Register*, 6 September 1817, 13:28.

21. Wilgus, "Spanish American Patriot Activity," 207 n.

22. Davis, *MacGregor's Invasion*, 12–19.

23. Belton Copp to John Quincy Adams, 1 April 1818, in "The Patriot War," 162.

24. Davis, *MacGregor's Invasion*, 18–19; Wyllys, "Filibusters of Amelia Island," 304–5.

25. Fuller, *Purchase of Florida*, 233–34; Patrick, *Aristocrat in Uniform*, 39.

26. Abernethy, "Florida and the Spanish Frontier," 112–13.

27. *Niles Weekly Register*, 18 September 1817, 13:62; 4 October 1817, 13:95; 8 November 1817, 13:175; 22 November 1817, 13:207.

28. *Niles Weekly Register*, 11 October 1817, 13:111.

29. Davis, *MacGregor's Invasion*, 22–25; Wyllys, "Filibusters of Amelia Island," 307; Abernethy, "Florida and the Spanish Frontier," 113–16.

30. Fuller, *Purchase of Florida*, 234; Abernethy, "Florida and the Spanish Frontier," 113–14.

31. Brooks, *Diplomacy and the Borderlands*, 94; Wilgus, "Spanish American Patriot Activity," 207 n; Bemis, *John Quincy Adams*, 307.

32. Brooks, *Diplomacy and the Borderlands*, 94; Duke of San Carlos to Castlereagh, 16 April 1818, PRO, FO 72/16; Davis, *MacGregor's Invasion*, 66–68.

33. Secretary of the Navy Benjamin W. Crowninshield to John Elton of the USS *Saranac*, 24 July 1817, *Niles Weekly Register*, 24 January 1818, 14:340.

34. Davis, *MacGregor's Invasion*, 24–25.

35. Wilgus, "Spanish American Patriot Activity," 207–8; Abernethy, "Florida and the Spanish Frontier," 114.

36. *Charleston News and Courier*, 13, 16, 18, 19 September 1817; *Savannah Republican*, 16 September 1817.

37. *Charleston News and Courier*, 19, 22, 26 September 1817; *Narrative of a Voyage in the Ship "Two Friends,"* 99; *Niles Weekly Register*, 27 September 1817, 13:79.

38. *Niles Weekly Register*, 6 September 1817, 13:28; Davis, *MacGregor's Invasion*, 24–30.

39. *Charleston News and Courier*, 13 October 1817.

40. Beverly Chew to William Crawford, 17 October 1817, *ASP:FR*, 4:136–37; *Annals of Congress*, 15th Cong., 2nd sess., 409; Warren, *The Sword Was Their Passport*, 119.

41. Davis, *MacGregor's Invasion*, 46; Harris G. Warren, "The Origin of General Mina's Invasion of Mexico," *Southwest Historical Quarterly* 42 (1938–39): 1–20.

42. Beverly Chew to Customs Office, New Orleans, 30 August 1817, Despatches from the U.S. Consuls in Galveston, Texas, 1832–46, RG 59, T151, NA (hereafter cited as Despatches from the U.S. Consuls). (It should be noted that this microfilm, although dated as 1832–46, actually starts at the much earlier time of 1817 or before. The record also contains an extensive account of smuggling from Galveston to New Orleans, which was collected by the New Orleans customs authorities.)

43. Stanley Faye, "The Great Stroke of Pierre Laffite," *Louisiana Historical Quarterly* 23 (1940): 762–63.

44. Davis, *MacGregor's Invasion*, 29–38; Wyllys, "Filibusters of Amelia Island," 307–9.

45. *Niles Weekly Register*, 11 October 1817, 13:111.

46. Davis, *MacGregor's Invasion*, 32–38.

47. *Charleston News and Courier*, 29 September 1817.

48. Warren, *The Sword Was Their Passport*, 143, 166; Roland C. McConnell, *A History of the Battalion of Free Men of Color* (Baton Rouge: Louisiana State University Press, 1968), 77, 87–88.

49. *Savannah Republican*, 25 September 1817; Beverly Chew to William Crawford, 1 August 1817, in Report of Secretary of Treasury to Secretary of State, 10 January 1818, *ASP:FR*, 6:133–35; *Charleston News and Courier*, 25, 29 September 1817.

50. Wyllys, "Filibusters of Amelia Island," 311–14; *Times* (London), 10 June 1818; Beverly Chew to Customs Office, New Orleans, 30 August 1817, Despatches from the U.S. Consuls.

51. Belton Copp to John Quincy Adams, 1 April 1818, in "The Patriot War," 162; Harris Gaylord Warren, "Louis-Michel Aury," in *The Handbook of Texas,* ed. Walter Prescott Webb, vol. 1 (Austin: Texas State Historical Association, 1952), 78–79.

52. J. B. Wait, *State Papers and Publick Documents of the United States* (Boston: T. B. Wait, 1819), 396–97; Weeks, *John Quincy Adams,* 62–63.

53. *Charleston News and Courier,* 29 September, 4 October 1817; *Times* (London), 5, 13 December, 1817.

54. Secretary of War John C. Calhoun to Edmund P. Gaines, 26 December 1817, in Walter Lowrie et al., eds., *The American State Papers: Military Affairs* (Washington, D.C.: Gales and Seaton, 1832), 1:690 (hereafter cited as *ASP:MA*).

8. DESTINY BECOMES MANIFEST: ANDREW JACKSON INVADES FLORIDA

1. H. Adams, *History of the United States,* 2:1331–33; George Dangerfield, *The Awakening of American Nationalism, 1815–1828* (New York: Harper and Row, 1965), viii; Stuart, *United States Expansionism,* 76.

2. Stuart, *United States Expansionism,* 5.

3. Edmund P. Gaines to the Secretary of War, 14 October 1815, Letters to the Secretary of War.

4. Kendall Lewis to C. Limbaugh, 6 August 1815, ibid.

5. James Parton, *Life of Andrew Jackson,* 3 vols. (New York: Mason Brothers, 1861), 2:409–12; Boyd, "Events at Prospect Bluff," 82–83.

6. Hawkins to the Secretary of War, 8 December 1815, Letters to the Secretary of War.

7. *Royal Gazette and Bahama Advertiser,* 8 February 1817.

8. Boyd, "Events at Prospect Bluff," 83.

9. *Royal Gazette and Bahama Advertiser,* 17 June 1818.

10. Parton, *Life of Andrew Jackson,* 2:453; *Columbia Museum and Savannah Daily Gazette,* 17 December 1818; Wright, "Note on the First Seminole War," 573.

11. Arbuthnot's Journal, 8 November 1817, copy in "Papers relative to Arbuthnot and Ambrister communicated by Richard W. Rush, 12 January 1819," PRO, FO 5/146.

12. Arbuthnot to Nicolls, 20 August 1817, PRO, FO 5/140; Parton, *Life of Andrew Jackson,* 2:414–16; Arbuthnot to Charles Cameron, Governor of Bahamas, n.d., *ASP:MA,* 1:722.

13. Sworn statement of John Forbes, 11 October 1815, Fernán-Núñez to Castlereagh, 13 December 1816, PRO, WO 1/144; Coker and Watson, *Indian Traders,* 301.

14. George Woodbine to Hugh Pigot, 25 May 1814, MS 2328, Cochrane Papers; Edmund Doyle to John Innerarity, 11 July 1817, in *Florida Historical Quarterly* 18 (1939): 135–38; Parton, *Life of Andrew Jackson*, 2:415–21; Wright, "Note on the First Seminole War," 570–71; information concerning Woodbine, enclosure in Charles Cameron to Henry Goulburn, 12 November 1817, PRO, CO 23/65.

15. Ammon, *James Monroe*, 412; Belton A. Copp to John Q. Adams, 1 April 1818, in *Florida Historical Quarterly* 5 (1927): 162–67.

16. Parton, *Life of Andrew Jackson*, 2:421–23.

17. Memorandum from Governor Charles Cameron, 1 February, enclosure in Admiral Sir Home Popham to Earl Bathurst, 12 April 1818, PRO, Adm. 1/219.

18. Sworn Statement of Robert Christie Ambrister before T. Mathews, New Providence, 16 October 1815, PRO, WO 1/144.

19. Duke of San Carlos to Castlereagh, 16 April 1818, PRO, FO 72/16; Davis, *MacGregor's Invasion*, 65–66.

20. Davis, *MacGregor's Invasion*, 66–68.

21. Memorial of Ambrister to Munnings, 29 June 1818. Another copy of this memorial, which provided some information concerning James Ambrister, is contained in the *Mobile Gazette*, 3 November 1818; see also, Wright, "Note on the First Seminole War," 573.

22. Parton, *Life of Andrew Jackson*, 2:478–79; James, *Life of Andrew Jackson*, 313–14.

23. Boyd, "Events at Prospect Bluff," 83–84; Silver, *Edmund Pendleton Gaines*, 68–72.

24. Mulroy, *Freedom on the Border*, 15–16; Porter, *The Negro on the American Frontier*, 221–22.

25. Boyd, "Events at Prospect Bluff," 83–84; Parton, *Life of Andrew Jackson*, 2:430–31; R. W. Scott to Major General Edmund P. Gaines, 28 November 1817, *ASP:MA*, 1:687–88; Report of U.S. Senate Committee, 24 February, enclosed in Charles Bagot to Viscount Castlereagh, 6 March 1819, PRO, FO 5/142; Fuller, *Purchase of Florida*, 236–39; Porter, *The Negro on the American Frontier*, 224–25; Silver, *Edmund Pendleton Gaines*, 68–69.

26. Silver, *Edmund Pendleton Gaines*, 73–74; Ammon, *James Monroe*, 414.

27. Remini, *Andrew Jackson*, 346.

28. Silver, *Edmund Pendleton Gaines*, 68–74; John C. Calhoun to Andrew Jackson, 26 December 1817, *ASP:MA*, 1:690.

29. Ammon, *James Monroe*, 415–16; John Rhea to Jackson, 12 January 1818, in *Correspondence of Andrew Jackson*, ed. Bassett, 2:345; Monroe to Jackson, 20 October 1818, Monroe Papers, New York Public Library; Remini, *Andrew Jackson*, 346–48.

30. Parton, *Life of Andrew Jackson*, 2:436–45; Jackson to the Secretary of War, 25 March 1818, *ASP:MA*, 1:698–99; Remini, *Andrew Jackson*, 353.

31. Jackson to Rachel Jackson, 26 March 1818, Harvard University Autograph Collection, Houghton Library, Harvard University, Cambridge, Mass.; Jackson to Rachel Jackson, 8 April 1818, in *Correspondence of Andrew Jackson,* ed. Bassett, 2:357; Silver, *Edmund Pendleton Gaines,* 78.

32. Jackson to the Secretary of War, 8 April 1818, *ASP:MA,* 1:699–700; Jackson to G. W. Campbell, 5 October 1818, Andrew Jackson Papers, LC; Jackson to Rachel Jackson, 10 April 1818, Harvard University Autograph Collection; Coe, *Red Patriots,* 21.

33. Parton, *Life of Andrew Jackson,* 2:459–63; Remini, *Andrew Jackson,* 353; Testimony of John L. Fenix, 2 July, enclosure in Munnings to Bathurst, 8 August, and Testimony of John James Arbuthnot, 6 August 1818, PRO, FO 5/133.

34. Silver, *Edmund Pendleton Gaines,* 79–80; James, *Life of Andrew Jackson,* 312–13; Boyd, "Events at Prospect Bluff," 83–90; *Royal Gazette and Bahama Advertiser,* 13 May, 13 June, 1 July 1818. For a complete transcript of the trial see *ASP:MA,* 1:716–30.

35. Sworn statement of John Forbes, 11 October 1815, Fernán-Núñez to Lord Castlereagh, 13 December 1816, PRO, WO 1/44; Coker and Watson, *Indian Traders,* 301.

36. Arbuthnot to Charles Bagot, 19 January 1818, PRO, FO 5/131; Memorial of Mrs. Mary Ann Arbuthnot, widow, to His Honor William Vesey Munnings, 11 July, enclosure in Munnings to Bagot, 20 July 1818, PRO, FO 5/133.

37. *National Intelligencer,* 1 June 1818; Remini, *Andrew Jackson,* 357.

38. Arbuthnot to his Son, 2 April 1818, and unsigned memorandum on letter, Arbuthnot to Charles Bagot, n.d., *ASP:MA,* 1:722–23; Boyd, "Events at Prospect Bluff," 83–84.

39. *National Intelligencer,* 1 June 1818; Remini, *Andrew Jackson,* 357; James, *Life of Andrew Jackson,* 313–14; *ASP:MA,* 1:734; Petition of James Ambrister to His Honor William Vesey Munnings, 19 June, enclosure in Munnings to Bagot, 20 June 1818, PRO, FO 5/133.

40. Statement of John L. Fenix, 13 July, enclosure in Munnings to Bagot, 20 July 1818; statement of John James Arbuthnot, 6 August 1818, both in PRO, FO 5/133.

41. *Royal Gazette and Bahama Advertiser,* 13, 17, 24 June, 1 July 1818.

42. Owsley, *Struggle for the Gulf,* 182–83; Parton, *Life of Andrew Jackson,* 2:486–87; Bagot to Viscount Castlereagh, 3 December 1818, PRO, FO 5/133.

43. Davis, *MacGregor's Invasion,* 68.

44. Parton, *Life of Andrew Jackson,* 2:498–502; *National Intelligencer,* 23 June 1818.

45. Remini, *Andrew Jackson,* 359–63; Parton, *Life of Andrew Jackson,* 2:498–502; *National Intelligencer,* 23 June 1818.

46. *New York Evening Post,* 18 July 1818; *National Intelligencer,* 25 October 1818; *The Georgian,* 29 January 1819.

47. James, *Life of Andrew Jackson*, 314–24; *The Georgian*, 29 January 1819.

48. Onís to Monroe, 18 July 1814, 24 August 1815, Notes from the Spanish Legation, vol. 4; Griffin, *The United States and the Disruption of the Spanish Empire*, 71.

49. Juan José de Estrada to Peter Early, 17 June, 11 September, "East and West Florida Land," and Early to Sebastian Kindelan, 24 May 1815, Governor's Letterbook, 18 May 1814 to 30 October 1827, Georgia Department of Archives, Atlanta.

50. Onís to Adams, 24 January 1818, Notes from the Spanish Legation, vol. 4.

51. Griffin, *The United States and the Disruption of the Spanish Empire*, 40–41, 80–85, 164–66, 207–14.

52. Porter, *The Negro on the American Frontier*, 235–36; Dowd, *A Spirited Resistance*, 190; Hickey, *The War of 1812*, 303–4.

9. "TAKING ADVANTAGE OF PROPITIOUS
CIRCUMSTANCES": THE STRUGGLE FOR TEXAS

1. Castlereagh to Bagot, 10, 11 December 1817, PRO, FO 5/120; Luis de Onís to John Quincy Adams, 7 May, 17 June 1818, Notes from the Spanish Legation, vol. 4; Howard Jones, *The Course of American Diplomacy: Vol. 1: to 1813* (Chicago: Dorsey Press, 1988), 107–8; Bemis, *John Quincy Adams*, 300–340.

2. John C. Calhoun to Major Bankhead, 12 February 1818, Letters Sent by the Secretary of War Relating to Military Affairs, 1800–1869, vol. 10, RG 107, M6, NA; Calhoun to Andrew Jackson, 12 December 1817, ibid., vol. 9; Warren, *The Sword Was Their Passport*, 55–85; Bemis, *John Quincy Adams*, 300–340.

3. Jones, *The Course of American Diplomacy*, 90.

4. Matthew Lyon to Andrew Jackson, 2 June 1814, in *The Papers of Andrew Jackson*, ed. David D. Moser et al., 4 vols. to date (Knoxville: University of Tennessee Press, 1980–), 4:78–79.

5. Warren, *The Sword Was Their Passport*, 73–95.

6. Ferrell, *American Diplomacy*, 157–68.

7. Warren, *The Sword Was Their Passport*, 73–95; Jean Laffite, *The Journal of Jean Laffite* (New York: Vantage Press, 1958), 78–80.

8. Brooks, *Diplomacy and the Borderlands*, 43; Nichols, *Advance Agents*, 98; Warren, *The Sword Was Their Passport*, 238, n. 25.

9. Onís to James Monroe, 18 July 1814, Notes from the Spanish Legation, vol. 3; Warren, *The Sword Was Their Passport*, 77–95.

10. Daniel Patterson to the Secretary of the Navy, 18 July, 20 August 1814, Commanders' Letters.

11. Warren, *The Sword Was Their Passport*, 101–4, 120; Laffite, *Journal*, 53–54.

12. Hugh Pigot to Alexander Cochrane, 8 June 1814, PRO, WO 142; Cochrane to Edward Nicolls, 4 July 1814, PRO, Adm. 1/506; Nicholas Lockyer to William Percy, 4 September 1814, in A. Lacarrière Latour, *Historical Memoir of the War in West Florida and Louisiana in 1814–15* (1816; reprint, Gainesville: University of Florida Press, 1964), appendix 12; Nicolls to Jean Laffite, 31 August 1814, PC Legajos 1795, AGI, in ibid., appendix 19–25; Owsley, *Struggle for the Gulf,* 107–9.

13. Laffite, *Journal,* 50–61; Owsley, *Struggle for the Gulf,* 106–9.

14. Laffite, *Journal,* 53–70; Owsley, *Struggle for the Gulf,* 107–68; Jane Lucas de Grummond, *The Baratarians and the Battle of New Orleans* (Baton Rouge: Louisiana State University Press, 1961), 111–18.

15. De Grummond, *The Baratarians,* 153–58.

16. Warren, *The Sword Was Their Passport,* 119–20.

17. González Manrique to Juan Ruíz Apodaca, 15 May 1813, PC Legajos 1794, AGI; Manrique to Apodaca, 10 June 1814, PC Legajos 1795, AGI; Apodaca to Minister of Indies Miguel de Lardizabah y Uribe, 10 March 1815, PC Legajos 1795, AGI. Although all of these reports appeared at an earlier date, there is no reason to believe that Pensacola had received any large amount of supplies in the following four years.

18. Faye, "The Great Stroke of Pierre Laffite," 761–65; Wilgus, "Spanish American Patriot Activity," 203–7; Warren, *The Sword Was Their Passport,* 119–25.

19. Stanley Clisby Arthur, *Jean Laffite, Gentleman Rover* (New Orleans: Harmanson, 1952), 139–48; Harris Gaylord Warren, "José Alvarez de Toledo's Reconciliation with Spain and Projects for Suppressing Rebellion in the Spanish Colonies," *Louisiana Historical Quarterly* 23 (1940): 827–36; Laffite, *Journal,* 74–88; Warren, *The Sword Was Their Passport,* 119–45.

20. Brooks, *Diplomacy and the Borderlands,* 82.

21. Warren, *The Sword Was Their Passport,* 130–43.

22. *National Intelligencer,* 25 October 1818; Almaráz, *Tragic Cavalier,* 181–82; Warren, *The Sword Was Their Passport,* 143–66.

23. Warren, "The Origin of General Mina's Invasion of Mexico," 8–20; Warren, *The Sword Was Their Passport,* 130–43.

24. Stanley Faye, "Commodore Aury," *Louisiana Historical Quarterly* 24 (1941): 696–97; Weeks, *John Quincy Adams,* 64; Andrew Jackson to John C. Calhoun, 8 November 1818, 21 December 1820, in *Papers of Andrew Jackson,* ed. Moser et al., 4:251, 409–10.

25. Charles Bagot to Lord Castlereagh, 25 April 1817, PRO, FO 5/122; Winston Smith, *Days of Exile: The Story of the Vine and Olive Colony in Alabama* (Tuscaloosa: Drake Printers, 1967), 113, passim; Brooks, *Diplomacy and the Borderlands,* 121.

26. Warren, *The Sword Was Their Passport,* 204–12, 222–23; Brooks, *Diplomacy and the Borderlands,* 121–23; Chipman, *Spanish Texas,* 239.

27. Warren, *The Sword Was Their Passport*, 216–20; Brooks, *Diplomacy and the Borderlands*, 123.

28. George Graham to John Quincy Adams, 9 September, Graham to Charles Lallemand, 26 August, Lallemand to Graham, 26 August, Graham to Jean Laffite, 26 August 1818, all in Despatches from the U.S. Consuls.

29. Jean Laffite to George Graham, 28 August 1818, ibid.; Warren, *The Sword Was Their Passport*, 214–32.

30. Charles Francis Adams, ed., *Memoirs of John Quincy Adams, Comprising Portions of His Diary from 1795–1848*, 12 vols. (Philadelphia: Lippincott, 1874–77), 4:175–76.

31. Weeks, *John Quincy Adams*, 123–24.

32. Warren, *The Sword Was Their Passport*, 233–64; Brooks, *Diplomacy and the Borderlands*, 186; Chipman, *Spanish Texas*, 240.

33. Antonio Martínez to the Commandant General Joaquín de Arrendondo, 4, 7, 11, 15 June 1817, in Virginia Taylor, ed., *The Letters of Antonio Martínez, Last Spanish Governor of Texas, 1817–1822* (Austin: Texas State Library, 1957), v–vi, 3–9.

34. Warren, *The Sword Was Their Passport*, 239–41; Brooks, *Diplomacy and the Borderlands*, 186; Chipman, *Spanish Texas*, 240.

35. Weeks, *John Quincy Adams*, 123–26.

36. Brooks, *Diplomacy and the Borderlands*, 193–96.

10. A JEFFERSONIAN LEVIATHAN: MANIFEST DESTINY SUCCEEDS

1. For a detailed discussion of Franco-American relations during the Federalist era see Albert Hall Bowman, *The Struggle for Neutrality: Franco-American Diplomacy during the Federalist Era* (Knoxville: University of Tennessee Press, 1974); for a discussion during the Jeffersonian period see Clifford L. Egan, *Neither Peace Nor War: Franco-American Relations, 1803–1812* (Baton Rouge: Louisiana State University Press, 1983).

2. Brooks, *Diplomacy and the Borderlands*, 29–53.

3. Goetzmann, *Exploration and Empire*, 37–66; Varg, *New England and Foreign Relations*, 43–44; Pratt, *Expansionists of 1812*, 126–52.

4. Tucker and Hendrickson, *Empire of Liberty*, 17, 157–71, 235–36.

5. Ibid., 30–31; Peterson, *Jefferson and the New Nation*, 256–57.

6. Richard W. Van Alstyne, *The Rising American Empire* (New York: Norton, 1960), 88; Stuart, *United States Expansionism*, 28–53.

7. Edgar McInnis, *Canada: A Political and Social History* (New York: Rinehart and Company, 1947), 192–97. For a more detailed analysis of the Canadian participation in the war see Pierre Berton, *The Invasion of Canada* (Boston: Little, Brown, 1980), and *Flames across the Border* (Boston: Little, Brown, 1981).

8. Sheehan, *Seeds of Extinction*, 243–50, 263–65; Brian W. Dippie, *The Vanishing American: White Attitudes and U.S. Indian Policy* (Middletown, Conn.: Wesleyan University Press, 1982), 5–11.

9. Dippie, *The Vanishing American*, 7–9; Dowd, *A Spirited Resistance*, 118–20.

10. Gary B. Nash, *Red, White, and Black: The Peoples of Early North America*, 3rd ed. (Englewood Cliffs, N.J.: Prentice Hall, 1992), 104–11.

11. Ibid., 111–16; Pratt, *Expansionists of 1812*, 66–67.

12. Middlekauf, *The Glorious Cause*, 148; Dowd, *A Spirited Resistance*, 25–27.

13. Dowd, *A Spirited Resistance*, 47–64; Dippie, *The Vanishing American*, 7–9.

14. Cox, *West Florida Controversy*, 60–63; Van Alstyne, *The Rising American Empire*, 89–91.

15. Weeks, *John Quincy Adams*, 70–77; Alexander DeConde, *This Affair of Louisiana* (New York: Scribner, 1976), 55, 78–79; Chipman, *Spanish Texas*, 216–17.

16. Jackson, *Jefferson and the Stony Mountains*, 100–101; Peterson, *Jefferson and the New Nation*, 588–89.

17. Owsley, *Struggle for the Gulf*, 192–93; Robin Reilly, *The British at the Gates: The New Orleans Campaign in the War of 1812* (New York: Putnam, 1974), 344–46; Remini, *Andrew Jackson*, 306–7.

18. Arthur, *West Florida Rebellion*, passim; Abernethy, "Florida and the Spanish Frontier," 88–100; Cox, *West Florida Controversy*, 437–668; Warren, *The Sword Was Their Passport*, 33–118.

19. Owsley, *Struggle for the Gulf*, 187, Hickey, *The War of 1812*, 205–6.

20. Pratt, *Expansionists of 1812*, 163–64; Hickey, *The War of 1812*, 269–70; Varg, *New England and Foreign Relations*, 43–44.

21. Owsley, *Struggle for the Gulf*, 194–95.

Bibliography

MANUSCRIPT COLLECTIONS

Alabama Department of Archives and History, Montgomery
  East Florida Papers
Archivo General de Indias, Seville, Spain
  Papeles Procedentes de Cuba, Legajos 1794–95, 1856 (photostats in
    the Library of Congress, Washington, D.C.)
Archivo Historico Nacional, Madrid, Spain
  Estado, Legajo 5639 (photostats in the Library of Congress, Washing-
    ton, D.C.)
  Estado, Legajo 5557 (photostats in the Library of Congress, Washing-
    ton, D.C.)
Florida Historical Society, University of South Florida, Tampa
  Cruzat Papers
  Greenslade Papers
Georgia Department of Archives, Atlanta
  Creek Letters, Talks and Treaties, 1705–1839, Georgia
  Governor's Letterbook, 28 November 1809 to 10 April 1814, and
    18 May 1814 to 30 October 1827
Houghton Library, Harvard University, Cambridge, Mass.
  Harvard University Autograph Collection
Henry H. Huntington Library, San Marino, Calif.
  Ruíz de Apodaca, "Official Letterbooks, 1816–1821"
Library of Congress, Washington, D.C.
  Andrew Jackson Papers
  Thomas Jefferson Papers
  James Monroe Papers
Mississippi Department of Archives and History, Jackson
  J. F. H. Claiborne Collection, "Letters Relating to the Indian Wars,
    1812–1816," Letterbook F
Mobile Public Library, Mobile, Ala.
  John Forbes Papers
National Archives, Washington, D.C.
  Record Group 45, Department of the Navy
    Letters Received by the Secretary of the Navy: Captains' Letters,
      1805–61, 1866–85. M125

Bibliography

Letters Received by the Secretary of the Navy from Commanders, 1804–86. M147

"Operation, Negro Fort," HJ Box 181, 1816

Record Group 59, Department of State

Correspondence Relating to the Filibustering Expeditions against the Spanish Government of Mexico, 1811–16. T286

Despatches from Special Agents of the Department of State. M37

Despatches from the U.S. Consuls in Galveston, Texas, 1832–46. T151

Notes from the Spanish Legation in the United States to the Department of State, 1790–1906. M59

Record Group 75, Department of the Interior, Records of the Bureau of Indian Affairs

Letterbook of the Natchitoches Sulphur Fork Factory. T1029

Record Group 107, Department of the Army

Letters Received by the Secretary of War, Registered Series, 1801–70. M221

Letters Sent by the Secretary of War Relating to Military Affairs, 1800–1869. M6

Confidential and Unofficial Letters Sent, 1814–47. M7

National Library of Scotland, Edinburgh

The Papers of Admiral Alexander Forrester Inglis Cochrane, MSS 2328.

New York Public Library, New York, N.Y.

James Monroe Papers

Public Record Office, London, England

Admiralty Office 1, vols. 219, 505, 506, 508

Admiralty Office 50, vol. 122

Colonial Office 23, vols. 65, 67

Colonial Office 138, vol. 146

Foreign Office 5, vols. 113, 127, 131–33, 139, 140, 142, 146

Foreign Office 72, vols. 16, 180

War Office 1, vols. 141–44

War Office 6, vol. 2

State Historical Society of Wisconsin, Madison

Lyman Draper Papers

University of Virginia Library, Manuscripts Division, Special Collections, Charlottesville

Thomas Jefferson Papers

Virginia Historical Society, Richmond

Thomas Jefferson Papers

PUBLIC DOCUMENTS AND PUBLISHED COLLECTIONS

Adams, Charles Francis, ed. *Memoirs of John Quincy Adams, Comprising Portions of His Diary from 1795–1848.* 12 vols. Philadelphia: Lippincott, 1874–77.

Bauer, K. Jack, ed. *The New American State Papers: Naval Affairs.* 10 vols. Wilmington, Del.: Scholarly Resources, 1981.

Bibliography

Carter, Clarence Edwin, ed. *The Territorial Papers of the United States.* 27 vols. Washington, D.C.: Government Printing Office, 1934–69.

Dudley, William S., ed. *The Naval War of 1812: A Documentary History.* 2 vols. to date. Washington, D.C.: Naval Historical Center, Department of the Navy, 1985–.

Jackson, Andrew. *Correspondence of Andrew Jackson.* Edited by John S. Bassett. 6 vols. Washington, D.C.: Carnegie Institution, 1926–33.

——. *The Papers of Andrew Jackson.* Edited by David D. Moser et al. 4 vols. to date. Knoxville: University of Tennessee Press, 1980–.

Jefferson, Thomas. *The Writings of Thomas Jefferson.* Edited by Paul Leicester Ford. 10 vols. New York: Putnam, 1892–99.

——. *The Writings of Thomas Jefferson.* Edited by Andrew A. Lipscomb and Albert Ellery Bergh. 20 vols. Washington, D.C.: Thomas Jefferson Memorial Association, 1903–4.

——. *The Writings of Thomas Jefferson.* Edited by H. A. Washington. 8 vols. Washington, D.C.: Taylor and Maury, 1853–54.

Madison, James. *The Papers of James Madison.* Edited by Robert A. Rutland et al. 17 vols. to date. Chicago: Chicago University Press, 1962–.

——. *The Works of James Madison.* Edited by Gaillard Hunt. 9 vols. New York: Putnam, 1900–1910.

McLean, Malcolm D., ed. *Papers Concerning Robertson's Colony in Texas.* 14 vols. Vols. 1–3, Fort Worth: Texas Christian University Press, 1974–76; vols. 4–14, Arlington: University of Texas at Arlington, 1977–88.

Monroe, James. *The Writings of James Monroe.* Edited by Stanislaus Murray Hamilton. 7 vols. New York: Putnam, 1898–1903.

Richardson, James D., ed. *A Compilation of the Messages and Papers of the Presidents, 1789–1897.* 20 vols. Washington, D.C.: Government Printing Office, 1896–99.

Taylor, Virginia, ed. *The Letters of Antonio Martínez, Last Spanish Governor of Texas, 1817–1822.* Austin: Texas State Library, 1957.

U.S. Congress. *The American State Papers: Documents, Legislative and Executive of the Congress of the United States.* Edited by Walter Lowrie and Walter S. Franklin. Washington, D.C.: Gales and Seaton, 1832.

Wait, J. B. *State Papers and Publick Documents of the United States.* Boston: T. B. Wait, 1819.

Washington, George. *The Writings of George Washington.* Edited by John Fitzpatrick. 33 vols. Washington, D.C.: Government Printing Office, 1931–41.

NEWSPAPERS

Augusta (Ga.) Chronicle
Charleston (S.C.) News and Courier
Columbia Museum and Savannah Daily Gazette
The Georgian
Mobile Gazette (Alabama Territory)
National Intelligencer and Washington Advertiser

Bibliography

New York Evening Post
Niles Weekly Register (Baltimore)
Royal Gazette and Bahama Advertiser (Nassau, New Providence)
Savannah Republican

BOOKS, THESES, AND DISSERTATIONS

Abernethy, Thomas P. *The South in the New Nation, 1789–1819*. Baton Rouge: Louisiana State University Press, 1961.

Adams, Henry. *History of the United States of America during the Administrations of Thomas Jefferson and James Madison*. 2 vols. 1891. Reprint, New York: Literary Classics of the United States, 1986.

Almaráz, Félix D. *Tragic Cavalier: Governor Manuel Salcedo of Texas, 1808–1813*. Austin: University of Texas Press, 1971.

Ammon, Harry. *James Monroe: The Quest for National Identity*. New York: McGraw-Hill, 1971.

Anna, Timothy E. *The Fall of the Royal Government in Mexico City*. Lincoln: University of Nebraska Press, 1978.

Arthur, Stanley Clisby. *Jean Laffite, Gentleman Rover*. New Orleans: Harmanson, 1952.

———. *The Story of the West Florida Rebellion*. St. Francisville, La.: St. Francisville Democrat, 1935.

Banner, James M., Jr. *To the Hartford Convention: The Federalists and the Origins of Party Politics in Massachusetts, 1789–1815*. New York: Knopf, 1970.

Bemis, Samuel Flagg. *Jay's Treaty: A Study in Commerce and Diplomacy*. 1923. Reprint, New Haven: Yale University Press, 1962.

———. *John Quincy Adams and the Foundations of American Foreign Policy*. New York: Norton, 1949.

———. *Pinckney's Treaty: America's Advantage from Europe's Distress, 1783–1800*. 1926. Reprint, New Haven: Yale University Press, 1960.

Berton, Pierre. *Flames across the Border*. Boston: Little, Brown, 1981.

———. *The Invasion of Canada*. Boston: Little, Brown, 1980.

Billington, Ray A. *Westward Expansion: A History of the American Frontier*. New York: Macmillan, 1949.

Bobb, Bernard E. *The Viceregency of Antonia María Bucareli in New Spain, 1771–1779*. Austin: University of Texas Press, 1962.

Bolton, Herbert Eugene. *The Spanish Borderlands: A Chronicle of Old Florida and the Southwest*. New Haven: Yale University Press, 1921.

———. *Wider Horizons of American History*. New York: D. Appleton-Century Company, 1939.

Bowman, Albert Hall. *The Struggle for Neutrality: Franco-American Diplomacy during the Federalist Era*. Knoxville: University of Tennessee Press, 1974.

Brant, Irving. *James Madison: The President, 1809–1812*. New York: Bobbs-Merrill, 1956.

Brooks, Philip Coolidge. *Diplomacy and the Borderlands: The Adams-Onís Treaty of 1819*. Berkeley: University of California Press, 1939.

Bibliography

Brown, Charles H. *Agents of Manifest Destiny: The Lives and Times of the Filibusters*. Chapel Hill: University of North Carolina Press, 1980.

Buker, George E. *Jacksonville: Riverport-Seaport*. Columbia: University of South Carolina Press, 1992.

Chipman, Donald E. *Spanish Texas, 1519–1821*. Austin: University of Texas Press, 1992.

Clark, Thomas D. *Frontier America: The Story of the Westward Movement*. New York: Scribner, 1959.

Clark, Thomas D., and John D. W. Guice. *Frontiers in Conflict: The Old Southwest, 1795–1830*. Albuquerque: University of New Mexico Press, 1989.

Coe, Charles H. *Red Patriots: The Story of the Seminoles*. 1898. Reprint, Gainesville: University of Florida Press, 1974.

Coker, Williams S., and Thomas D. Watson. *Indian Traders of the Southeastern Spanish Borderlands: Panton, Leslie and Company, and John Forbes and Company, 1783–1847*. Pensacola: University of West Florida Press, 1986.

Cox, Isaac J. *The West Florida Controversy, 1798–1813*. 1918. Reprint, Gloucester, Mass.: Peter Smith, 1967.

Cullum, George W. *Biographical Register of the Officers and Graduates of the U.S. Military Academy, West Point, N.Y., from Its Establishment March 16, 1802, to the Army Reorganization of 1866–67*. New York: D. Van Nostrand, 1868.

Dangerfield, George. *The Awakening of American Nationalism, 1815–1828*. New York: Harper and Row, 1965.

Davis, T. Frederick. *MacGregor's Invasion of Florida, 1817: Together with an Account of His Successors, Irwin, Hubbard and Aury on Amelia Island, East Florida*. Jacksonville: Florida Historical Society, 1928.

DeConde, Alexander. *This Affair of Louisiana*. New York: Scribner, 1976.

DeVoto, Bernard. *The Course of Empire*. Boston: Houghton Mifflin, 1952.

Dippie, Brian W. *The Vanishing American: White Attitudes and U.S. Indian Policy*. Middletown, Conn.: Wesleyan University Press, 1982.

Dodd, William E. *Expansion and Conflict*. Boston: Houghton Mifflin, 1915.

Dowd, Gregory Evans. *A Spirited Resistance: The North American Indian Struggle for Unity, 1745–1815*. Baltimore: Johns Hopkins University Press, 1992.

Eaton, Clement. *History of the Old South*. New York: Macmillan, 1975.

Edmunds, R. David. *The Shawnee Prophet*. Lincoln: University of Nebraska Press, 1983.

———. *Tecumseh and the Quest for Indian Leadership*. Boston: Little, Brown, 1984.

Egan, Clifford L. *Neither Peace Nor War: Franco-American Relations, 1803–1812*. Baton Rouge: Louisiana State University Press, 1983.

Faulk, Odie B. *The Last Years of Spanish Texas, 1778–1821*. The Hague: Mouton, 1969.

Fehrenbacher, Don E. *The Era of Expansion: 1800–1848*. New York: Wiley, 1969.

Ferrell, Robert. *American Diplomacy*. 3rd ed. New York: Norton, 1982.

Bibliography

Forbes, James Grant. *Sketches, Historical and Topographical of the Floridas: More Particularly of East Florida.* 1821. Reprint, Gainesville: University of Florida Press, 1964.

Fuller, Herbert Bruce. *The Purchase of Florida: Its History and Diplomacy.* 1906. Reprint, Gainesville: University of Florida Press, 1964.

Garrett, Julia K. *Green Flag Over Texas.* New York: Cordova Press, 1939.

Goetzmann, William H. *Exploration and Empire.* New York: Vintage Books, 1966.

———. *New Lands, New Men: America and the Second Great Age of Discovery.* New York: Viking Press, 1986.

Griffin, Charles Carroll. *The United States and the Disruption of the Spanish Empire, 1810–1822: A Study of the Relations of the United States with Spain and with the Rebel Spanish Colonies.* New York: Columbia University Press, 1937.

de Grummond, Jane Lucas. *The Baratarians and the Battle of New Orleans.* Baton Rouge: Louisiana State University Press, 1961.

———, ed. *Caracas Diary, 1835–1840: The Journal of John G. A. Williamson.* Baton Rouge: Camellia Publishing Company, 1954.

Halbert, H. S., and T. H. Ball. *The Creek War of 1813 and 1814.* Edited by Frank L. Owsley, Jr. Tuscaloosa: University of Alabama Press, 1969.

Hamill, Hugh M., Jr. *The Hidalgo Revolt: Prelude to Independence.* Gainesville: University of Florida Press, 1966.

Harrison, Frances K. "The Indians as a Means of Spanish Defense of West Florida." M.A. thesis, University of Alabama, 1950.

Hatcher, Mattie. *The Opening of Texas to Foreign Settlement, 1801–1821.* Philadelphia: Porcupine Press, 1976.

Heidler, David S., and Jeanne T. Heidler. *Old Hickory's War: Andrew Jackson and the Quest for Empire.* Mechanicsburg, Pa.: Stackpole Books, 1996.

Hickey, Donald R. *The War of 1812: A Forgotten Conflict.* Urbana: University of Illinois Press, 1989.

Horsman, Reginald. *Expansion and American Indian Policy, 1783–1812.* East Lansing: Michigan State University Press, 1967.

———. *The Frontier in the Formative Years, 1783–1815.* New York: Holt, Rinehart and Winston, 1970.

Jackson, Donald. *Thomas Jefferson and the Stony Mountains: Exploring the West from Monticello.* Urbana: University of Illinois Press, 1981.

Jacobs, James Ripley. *Tarnished Warrior: Major-General James Wilkinson.* New York: Macmillan, 1938.

James, Marquis. *The Life of Andrew Jackson.* Indianapolis: Bobbs-Merrill, 1938.

Jarratt, Rie. *Gutiérrez de Lara, Mexican-Texas: The Story of a Creole Hero.* Austin: Creole Texana, 1949.

Jones, Howard. *The Course of American Diplomacy: Vol. 1: to 1813.* Chicago: Dorsey Press, 1988.

Koch, Adrienne. *Jefferson and Madison: The Great Collaboration.* 1950. Reprint, New York: Oxford University Press, 1964.

Laffite, Jean. *The Journal of Jean Laffite.* New York: Vantage Press, 1958.

Latour, A. Lacarrière. *Historical Memoir of the War in West Florida and Loui-*

siana in 1814–15. 1816. Reprint, Gainesville: University of Florida Press, 1964.

Mahon, John K. *History of the Second Seminole War, 1835–1842*. Gainesville: University of Florida Press, 1967.

Malone, Dumas. *Jefferson the President: First Term, 1801–1805*. Boston: Little, Brown, 1970.

———. *Jefferson the President: Second Term, 1805–1810*. Boston: Little, Brown, 1974.

Marshall, Thomas Maitland. *A History of the Western Boundary of the Louisiana Purchase*. Berkeley: University of California Press, 1914.

Martin, Joel W. *Sacred Revolt: The Muskogee's Struggle for a New World*. Boston: Beacon Press, 1991.

May, Ernest R. *The Making of the Monroe Doctrine*. Cambridge: Belknap Press of Harvard University Press, 1975.

McConnell, Roland C. *A History of the Battalion of Free Men of Color*. Baton Rouge: Louisiana State University Press, 1968.

McCoy, Drew R. *The Elusive Republic: Political Economy in Jeffersonian America*. Chapel Hill: University of North Carolina Press, 1980.

———. *The Last of the Founding Fathers: James Madison and the Republican Legacy*. Cambridge: Cambridge University Press, 1989.

McInnis, Edgar. *Canada: A Political and Social History*. New York: Rinehart and Company, 1947.

McKee, Christopher. *A Gentlemanly and Honorable Profession: The Creation of the U.S. Naval Officer Corps, 1794–1815*. Annapolis: Naval Institute Press, 1991.

Menchaca, Antonio. *Memoirs*. San Antonio: Yanaguana Society Publications, 1937.

Merk, Frederick. *History of the Westward Movement*. New York: Knopf, 1978.

———. *Manifest Destiny and Mission in American History: A Reinterpretation*. New York: Knopf, 1963.

Middlekauf, Robert. *The Glorious Cause*. Oxford: Oxford University Press, 1982.

Morgan, George. *The Life of James Monroe*. 1921. Reprint, New York: AMS Press, 1969.

Mulroy, Kevin. *Freedom on the Border: The Seminole Maroons in Florida, the Indian Territory, Coahuila, and Texas*. Lubbock: Texas Tech University Press, 1993.

Narrative of a Voyage to the Spanish Main, in the Ship "Two Friends." Gainesville: University of Florida Press, 1978.

Nasatir, Abraham P. *Borderlands in Retreat from Spanish Louisiana to the Far Southwest*. Albuquerque: University of New Mexico Press, 1976.

Nash, Gary B. *Red, White, and Black: The Peoples of Early North America*. 3rd. ed. Englewood Cliffs, N.J.: Prentice Hall, 1992.

Nichols, Roy F. *Advance Agents of American Destiny*. Philadelphia: University of Pennsylvania Press, 1956.

Owsley, Frank L., Jr. *Struggle for the Gulf Borderlands: The Creek War and the Battle of New Orleans, 1812–1815*. Gainesville: University Presses of Florida, 1981.

Bibliography

Parton, James. *Life of Andrew Jackson.* 3 vols. New York: Mason Bros., 1861.

Patrick, Rembert W. *Aristocrat in Uniform: General Duncan Clinch.* Gainesville: University of Florida Press, 1963.

———. *Florida Fiasco: Rampant Rebels on the Georgia-Florida Border, 1810–1815.* Athens: University of Georgia Press, 1954.

Peters, Virginia B. *The Florida Wars.* Hamden, Conn.: Archon Books, 1979.

Peterson, Merrill D. *Thomas Jefferson and the New Nation: A Biography.* Oxford: Oxford University Press, 1970.

Philbrick, Francis S. *The Rise of the West, 1754–1830.* New York: Harper and Row, 1965.

Pickett, Albert J. *History of Alabama, and Incidently of Georgia and Mississippi, from the Earliest Period.* 2 vols. Charleston: Walker and James, 1851.

Porter, Kenneth Wiggins. *The Negro on the American Frontier.* New York: Arno Press, 1971.

Pratt, Julius W. *Expansionists of 1812.* Gloucester, Mass.: Peter Smith, 1957.

Reilly, Robin. *The British at the Gates: The New Orleans Campaign in the War of 1812.* New York: Putnam, 1974.

Remini, Robert V. *Andrew Jackson and the Course of American Empire, 1767–1821.* New York: Harper and Row, 1977.

Riegel, Robert E., and Robert G. Athearn. *America Moves West.* New York: Holt, Rinehart and Winston, 1964.

Rodriguez, Junius P. "Ripe for Revolt: Louisiana and the Tradition of Slave Insurrection, 1803–1865." Ph.D. diss., Auburn University, 1992.

Schwarz, Ted. *Forgotten Battlefield of the First Texas Revolution: The Battle of Medina, August 18, 1813.* Austin: Eakin Press, 1985.

Sheehan, Bernard. *Seeds of Extinction: Jefferson Philanthropy and the American Indian.* Chapel Hill: University of North Carolina Press, 1973.

Sheldon, Garrett Ward. *The Political Philosophy of Thomas Jefferson.* Baltimore: Johns Hopkins University Press, 1991.

Silver, James P. *Edmund Pendleton Gaines: Frontier General.* Baton Rouge: Louisiana State University Press, 1949.

Skelton, William B. *An American Profession of Arms: The Army Officer Corps, 1784–1861.* Lawrence: University Press of Kansas, 1992.

Smelser, Marshall. *The Democratic Republic, 1801–1815.* New York: Harper and Row, 1968.

Smith, Gene A. *"For the Purposes of Defense": The Politics of the Jeffersonian Gunboat Program.* Newark: University of Delaware Press, 1995.

Smith, Joseph Burkholder. *The Plot to Steal Florida: James Madison's Phony War.* New York: Arbor House, 1983.

Smith, Winston. *Days of Exile: The Story of the Vine and Olive Colony in Alabama.* Tuscaloosa: Drake Printers, 1967.

Southerland, Henry deLeon, Jr., and Jerry Elijah Brown. *The Federal Road through Georgia, the Creek Nation, and Alabama, 1806–1836.* Tuscaloosa: University of Alabama Press, 1989.

Stagg, J. C. A. *Mr. Madison's War.* Princeton: Princeton University Press, 1983.

Stephen, Sir Leslie, and Sir Sidney Lee, eds. *The Dictionary of National Biography.* 43 vols. London: Oxford University Press, 1949–50.

Stuart, Reginald C. *United States Expansionism and British North America, 1775–1871*. Chapel Hill: University of North Carolina Press, 1988.

Styron, Arthur. *The Last of the Cocked Hats: James Monroe and the Virginia Dynasty*. Norman: University of Oklahoma Press, 1945.

Tucker, Robert W., and David C. Hendrickson. *Empire of Liberty: The Statecraft of Thomas Jefferson*. New York: Oxford University Press, 1990.

Tucker, Spencer C. *Jefferson's Gunboat Navy*. Columbia: University of South Carolina Press, 1993.

Turner, Frederick Jackson. *The Frontier in American History*. New York: Henry Holt, 1921.

Van Alstyne, Richard W. *The Rising American Empire*. New York: Norton, 1960.

Varg, Paul. *New England and Foreign Relations, 1789–1850*. Hanover: University Press of New England, 1983.

Waciuma, Wanjohi. *Intervention in the Spanish Floridas, 1801–1818: A Study of Jeffersonian Foreign Policy*. Boston: Branden Press, 1976.

Warren, Harris G. *The Sword Was Their Passport: A History of American Filibustering in the Mexican Revolution*. Baton Rouge: Louisiana State University Press, 1943.

Watts, Steven. *The Republic Reborn: War and the Making of Liberal America, 1790–1820*. Baltimore: Johns Hopkins University Press, 1987.

Webb, Walter Prescott, ed. *The Handbook of Texas*. Austin: Texas State Historical Association, 1952.

Weeks, William Earl. *John Quincy Adams and American Global Empire*. Lexington: University of Kentucky Press, 1992.

Weinberg, Albert K. *Manifest Destiny: A Study of Nationalist Expansion in American History*. Baltimore: Johns Hopkins University Press, 1935.

Whitaker, Arthur Preston. *Documents Relating to the Commercial Policy of Spain in the Floridas*. Deland, Fla.: Florida State Historical Society, 1931.

———. *The Mississippi Question: 1795–1803*. New York: D. Appleton-Century Company for the American Historical Association, 1934.

———. *The United States and the Independence of Latin America*. New York: Russell and Russell, 1962.

Williams, T. Harry, Richard N. Current, and Frank Freidel. *A History of the United States to 1877*. New York: Knopf, 1959.

Wright, J. Leitch. *Britain and the American Frontier, 1783–1815*. Athens: University of Georgia Press, 1975.

———. *William Augustus Bowles, Director General of the Creek Nation*. Athens: University of Georgia Press, 1967.

Yoakum, Henderson. *History of Texas from Its First Settlement in 1685 to Its Annexation to the United States in 1846*. New York: J. S. Redfield, 1855.

ARTICLES

Abernethy, Thomas P. "Aaron Burr in Mississippi." *Journal of Southern History* 15 (1949): 9–21.

———. "Florida and the Spanish Frontier." In *The Americanization of the Gulf Coast, 1803–1850*, ed. Lucius F. Ellsworth, 88–120. Pensacola: Historic Pensacola Preservation Board, 1972.

Bibliography

Adams, Mary P. "Jefferson's Reaction to the Treaty of San Ildefonso." *Journal of Southern History* 21 (1955): 173–88.

Baxter, James P., III, ed. "Diary of José Bernardo Gutiérrez de Lara, I." *American Historical Review* 34 (1928): 55–91.

Boyd, Mark F. "Events at Prospect Bluff on the Apalachicola River, 1808–1818." *Florida Historical Quarterly* 14 (1937): 55–96.

Bradley, Jared W. "W.C.C. Claiborne and Spain: Foreign Affairs under Jefferson and Madison, 1801–1811." *Louisiana History* 12 (1971): 297–314; 13 (1972): 5–26.

Coker, William S. "How General Andrew Jackson Learned of the British Plans *before* the Battle of New Orleans." *Gulf Coast Historical Review* 3 (1987): 84–95.

Corbitt, D. C. "The Return of Spanish Rule to the St. Marys and the St. Johns, 1813–1821." *Florida Historical Quarterly* 20 (1941): 47–68.

Cottier, John, and George Wasalkov. "The First Creek War: Twilight of Annihilation." In *Clearings in the Thicket: An Alabama Humanities Reader*, ed. Jerry E. Brown, 21–38. Macon, Ga.: Mercer University Press, 1985.

Covington, James W. "The Negro Fort." *Gulf Coast Historical Review* 5 (Spring 1990): 79–91.

Cox, Isaac Joslin. "The Louisiana-Texas Frontier." *Quarterly of the Texas State Historical Association* 10 (1906): 1–75; 12 (1913): 1–42, 140–75.

Dabney, Lancaster E. "Louis Aury: The First Governor of Texas under the Mexican Republic." *Southwestern Historical Quarterly* 42 (1938): 108–16.

Davis, T. Frederick. "MacGregor's Invasion of Florida, 1817." *Florida Historical Quarterly* 7 (1928): 3–71.

Faye, Stanley. "Commodore Aury." *Louisiana Historical Quarterly* 24 (1941): 611–97.

———. "The Great Stroke of Pierre Laffite." *Louisiana Historical Quarterly* 23 (1940): 733–826.

Graebner, Norman. "Concrete Interest and Expansion." In *Major Problems in American Foreign Policy: Vol. 1: to 1914*, 3rd ed., ed. Thomas G. Paterson, 176–87. Lexington, Mass.: Heath, 1989.

Gronet, Richard W. "The United States and the Invasion of Texas." *The Americas* 25 (1969): 281–306.

Haggard, Villasana. "The Neutral Ground between Louisiana and Texas." *Louisiana Historical Quarterly* 28 (1945): 1001–1128.

Henderson, Harry McCorry. "The Magee-Gutiérrez Expedition." *Southwestern Historical Quarterly* 55 (1951): 43–61.

Horsman, Reginald. "British Indian Policy in the Northwest, 1807–1812." *Mississippi Valley Historical Review* 45 (1958): 51–67.

"James Monroe to General George Matthews, April 4, 1812." *Florida Historical Quarterly* 6 (1928): 235–37.

"John Sibley and the Louisiana Texas Frontier, 1803–1814." *Southwestern Historical Quarterly* 49 (1945–46): 116–19, 290–92, 399–431.

Knox, Dudley W. "A Forgotten Fight in Florida." *United States Naval Institute Proceedings* 62 (1936): 507–13.

Landers, Jane. "Jorge Biassou, Black Chieftain." *El Escribano: The St. Augustine Journal of History* 25 (1988): 85–100.

Bibliography

Latimer, Margaret K. "South Carolina—A Protagonist of the War of 1812." *American Historical Review* 61 (1956): 914–29.

"Letters Relating to MacGregor's Attempted Conquest of East Florida, 1817." *Florida Historical Quarterly* 18 (1939): 655–57.

May, Robert E. "Young American Males and Filibustering in the Age of Manifest Destiny: The United States Army as a Cultural Mirror." *Journal of American History* 78 (1991): 857–86.

McCaleb, Walter F. "The First Period of the Gutiérrez-Magee Expedition." *Texas Historical Association Quarterly* 4 (1900): 218–29.

McDaniels, Mary Jane. "Tescumseh's Visit to the Creeks." *Alabama Review* 33 (1980): 3–14.

Milligan, John D. "Slave Rebelliousness and the Florida Maroon." *Prologue: The Journal of the National Archives* 6 (1974): 4–18.

Newton, Wesley P. "Origins of United States–Latin American Relations." In *United States–Latin American Relations, 1800–1850: The Formative Generations*, ed. T. Ray Shurbutt, 1–24. Tuscaloosa: University of Alabama Press, 1991.

Owsley, Frank L., Jr. "Ambrister and Arbuthnot: Adventurers or Martyrs for British Honor?" *Journal of the Early Republic* 5 (Fall 1985): 289–308.

———. "Benjamin Hawkins, the First Modern Indian Agent." *Alabama Historical Quarterly* 30 (Summer 1968): 7–13.

———. "The Fort Mims Massacre." *Alabama Review* 24 (July 1974): 192–204.

———. "Prophet of War: Josiah Francis and the Creek War." *American Indian Quarterly* 9 (1985): 284–90.

Padgett, James A., ed. "Official Records of the West Florida Revolution and Republic." *Louisiana Historical Quarterly* 21 (1938): 685–805.

———. "The West Florida Revolution of 1810, as Told in the Letters of John Rhea, Fulwar Skipwith, Reuben Kemper, and Others." *Louisiana Historical Quarterly* 21 (1938): 76–202.

"The Panton, Leslie Papers: Continuing the Letters of Edmund Doyle, Trader." *Florida Historical Quarterly* 18 (1939): 61–63.

"The Patriot War: A Contemporary Letter." *Florida Historical Quarterly* 5 (1927): 162–67.

Phinney, A. H. "The First Spanish-American War." *Florida Historical Quarterly* 4 (1926): 114–29.

Prucha, Francis Paul. "Andrew Jackson's Indian Policy." In *The Indian in American History*, ed. Prucha, 67–74. New York: Rinehart and Winston, 1971.

Sheehan, Bernard. "Indian-White Relations in Early America." In *The Indian in American History*, ed. Francis Paul Prucha, 51–66. New York: Rinehart and Winston, 1971.

Smith, F. Todd. "The Kadohadacho Indians and the Louisiana-Texas Frontier, 1803–1815." *Southwestern Historical Quarterly* 95 (1991): 177–204.

Southall, Eugene P. "Negroes in Florida Prior to the Civil War." *Journal of Negro History* 19 (1934): 77–86.

"The Surrender of Amelia, March 1812." *Florida Historical Quarterly* 4 (1925): 90–95.

Bibliography

Ventura Morales, Juan. "Juan Ventura Morales to Alexandro Ramírez, November 3, 1817." *Boletín del Archivo Nacional* (Cuba) 13 (1941): 9–21.

Walker, Henry P., ed. "William McLane's Narrative of the Magee-Gutiérrez Expedition, 1812–1813," *Southwestern Historical Quarterly* 66 (1963): 457–79.

Warren, Harris G. "José Álvarez de Toledo's Reconciliation with Spain and Projects for Suppressing Rebellion in the Spanish Colonies." *Louisiana Historical Quarterly* 23 (1940): 827–36.

———. "Louis-Michel Aury." In *The Handbook of Texas,* vol. 1, ed. Walter Prescott Webb, 78–79. Austin: Texas State Historical Association, 1952.

———. "The Origin of General Mina's Invasion of Texas." *Southwest Historical Quarterly* 42 (1938–39): 1–20.

West, Elizabeth H. "Diary of José Bernardo Gutiérrez de Lara, II." *American Historical Review* 33 (1928): 44–55, 34 (1929): 281–95.

Wilgus, A. Curtis. "Spanish American Patriot Activity along the Gulf Coast of the United States, 1811–1822." *Louisiana Historical Quarterly* 8 (1925): 193–215.

Wright, James Leitch. "A Note on the First Seminole War as Seen by the Indians, Negroes, and Their British Advisors." *Journal of Southern History* 34 (1968): 565–75.

Wyllys, Rufus Kay. "The Filibusters of Amelia Island." *Georgia Historical Quarterly* 12 (1928): 297–305.

INDEX

Adair, General John, 55, 56
Adams, Henry, 21
Adams, John, 183
Adams, John Quincy, 161–62, 164, 175,
    177, 178, 180, 191; appointment as
    secretary of state, 119; portrait, 162
Adams-Onís Treaty, 167, 170, 175, 178–
    79
Admiralty court: Amelia Island, 128
African Americans, 11, 15, 77, 83
Alabama River system, 22
Alazán, Battle of, 56
Alden, Samuel, 56
Almaráz, Félix D., 40
Ambrister, Robert Christie, 132, 143,
    145, 147, 149–50, 155–60
Ambrister-Arbuthnot incident, 133
Amelia Island, 4, 14, 73, 125–30, 137,
    143, 146, 151, 153, 164, 166, 175,
    177; taken by the United States, 140–
    41
American Revolution, 10, 97, 187
Apache Indians, 39
Apadoca, Juan Ruíz, 93, 94, 96; portrait,
    93
Apalachicola River, 14, 22
Appalachian Mountains, 16, 17, 22
Arbuthnot, Alexander, 85, 114, 142,
    144–45, 151, 155–60
Armstrong, John, 91, 100n
Army of the North, 54
Arredondo y Mioño, General José
    Joaquín de, 53, 57–58, 179
Arroyo Hondo, 38
Arthur, Stanley Clisby, 4
Article Nine. See Treaty of Ghent
Astor, John Jacob, 16
Aury, Luis, 6, 137–40, 146, 164, 175,
    178; at Amelia Island, 135; back-
    ground, 136; in Barataria, 173

Bagot, Charles, 115, 125–26, 158
Bankhead, Colonel James, 15, 140
Barataria, 55, 169–70, 173
Baratarians, 169–70
Barbé-Marbois, François, 21
Barker, Stephen, 178
Bassett, James, 111
Bathurst, Earl of, 114
Baton Rouge, 4, 7–8, 13, 25, 63, 190
Battle of Alazán, 56
Battle of Horseshoe Bend, 95
Battle of Medina, 57–59, 166–68
Battle of New Orleans, 55, 138
Battle of Salado Creek, 51
Battle of Tippecanoe, 86
Belle Island, 172
Biassou, Haitian General Jorge, 79
Bibb, Governor William W., 152
Bidwell, John, 115
Billington, Ray Allen, 3
Black troops, 77, 79; training at Amelia
    Island, 138; Battle of New Orleans,
    170
Blount, John (Lafarka), 109
Bolívar, Simón, 122
Bolton, Herbert Eugene, 3
Bonaparte, Joseph, 126
Bonaparte, Napoleon, 12, 19, 31, 36,
    43, 149, 167, 170n, 176, 182. See also
    Bonapartists; Napoleonic Wars
Bonapartists, 36, 43, 56–57, 125–26,
    167–68, 175, 182
Bowlegs, Chief Billy, 77, 144, 147, 150,
    155, 157
Brown, Charles H., 4
Bullard, Henry, 56
Burr, Aaron, 32, 38, 62–63

Caddo Indians, 39
Cadiz, 44

235

Index

Calderón, Don Benigno García, 113
Calhoun, John C., 100n, 140, 151–52, 159
Caller, James, 61
Caller, John, 61
Camella, 130
Cameron, Governor Charles, 147
Camino Real (King's Highway), 50
Campbell, Captain Hugh, 69–76
Camp Crawford (later Fort Scott), 109, 144. *See also* Fort Scott
Captain Isaacs, 110
Carmichael, William, 19
Carr, Judge John, 49
Casas, Juan Bautista, 41
Castlereagh, Lord, 158, 163
Champlin, Samuel, 48n
Chance, 158
Charles IV, 21
Child, Joshua, 178
Choctaw Indians, 111
Chouteau, Auguste, 48n
Civil War, 6, 191
Claiborne, Governor William C. C., 7–8, 42, 44, 53, 60, 166, 169, 172–73; portrait, 45
Clark, William, 12, 27
Clarke, George I. F., 120–21
Clemente, Don Lino de, 124
Clinch, Colonel Duncan, 109–12
Cochrane, Admiral Alexander Inglis, 98–99
Coffee, General John, 97
Coggswell, Nathan, 56–57
Comanche Indians, 39, 51
Continental System, 182
Convention of 1818, 116
Cook, Peter, 143, 155
Coppinger, José, 120–21, 127, 130, 133–34
Cordero: Comanche chief, 51
Coweta Indians, 101
Cox, Isaac Joslin, 4
Craig, Governor-General James, 73
Crawford, Senator William H., 78, 100n, 108, 117
Creek Indians, 14, 25, 74, 84, 88, 99, 101–3, 114, 142, 145, 147. *See also* Lower Creek Indians; Upper Creek Indians

Creek Indian War, 4, 95, 86, 88–89, 186, 189
Creek Nation, 87, 105, 149

Dallas, Alexander J., 100
Dangerfield, George, 141
Daniels, Edward, 110
Davenport, Samuel, 49–50
Davis, T. Frederick, 4, 136
Dearborn, Henry, 27
Declaration of Independence, 2, 26
Deputies of Free America, Resident in the United States of the North, 124
DeVoto, Bernard, 3
Dodd, William E., 4
Doyle, Edmund, 144, 151
Ducoudray-Holstein (agent), 55
Dunbar-Hunter expedition, 27
Duncan, Abner, 136

Early, Governor Peter, 108
East Florida, 13, 121–22, 125, 128–29, 139, 164, 189; haven for runaway slaves, 77
Elguezabal, Juan Bautista, 34, 36
Elizondo, Ignacio, 41, 53, 56–58
Embargo Act of 1808, 39
Empire of liberty, 5, 26
Escambia River, 22
Estrada, Juan José de, 108
Eustis, William, 100n

Federal Alabama, 85, 88
Federalists, 11, 32, 73, 80, 119, 180, 183, 191
Ferdinand VII, 40, 44, 122
Fernandina, 13, 69, 71, 133, 138
Fernán-Núñez, Count, 163
Filibusters, 4–5, 9, 172, 184
Florida, 61–81, 141–63. *See also* East Florida; West Florida
Floyd, General John, 73
Folch, Governor Vincente, 64–66
Forbes Company, 106, 145–46, 151, 156, 159. *See also* John Forbes Company
Fort Barrancas, 97
Fort Bowye, 96
Fort Carlos of Barrancas, 160
Fort Charlotte, 91
Fort Gadsden, 154, 159–60

Fort Hawkins, 153
Fort Jackson, 153
Fort Mims, 95
Fort San Nicholas, 128, 129
Fort Scott (originally Camp Crawford),
    109–10, 144, 149–53
Fort Stoddert, 23, 61–63, 92
Fowltown, 150–51
Francis, Josiah (Hidlis Hadjo), 95, 114–
    15, 145
Freeman expedition, 27
Free men of color, 138; Savary detach-
    ment, 173
French agents, 47, 54
French Revolution, 55, 105, 184, 191

Gaines, General Edmund Pendleton,
    16, 63, 107–9, 140, 149–54; portrait,
    107
Gallatin, Albert, 80
Galveston, 170n, 175, 176, 177
Gardoqui, Don Diego de, 17
Garrett, Julia K., 4
Garson, Chief, 110, 112
Gaul, Pedro, 124
General Pike, 109
Georgian (Savannah), 160
German Coast (Louisiana) insurrec-
    tion, 105
Graebner, Norman, 5
Graham, George, 43–44, 60, 100n, 176–
    77
Grand-Pré, Louis Antonio de, 7
Green Cross of Florida, 127
Gunboat *No. 154*, 109, 111
Gunboat *No. 149*, 109
Gutiérrez de Lara, José Bernardo, 13,
    42–57, 122, 143, 171–72

Hambly, William, 111, 143–44, 151, 156–
    57
Hamilton, Alexander, 32
Hamilton, Paul, 71, 73
Harrison, William Henry, 86
Hartford Convention, 180
Hawkins, Benjamin, 87, 101, 107
Heath, John D., 128, 131
Henry, John: letters, 73, 76
Herrera, José Manuel de, 137, 172
Herrera, Simón de, 37–38, 51

Hidalgo Revolution, 13, 39, 53, 63
Hidalgo y Costilla, Father Miguel, 39–41
Hidlis Hadjo (Josiah Francis), 114. *See
    also* Francis, Josiah
Holmes, Governor David, 7, 90
Horseshoe Bend, Battle of, 95
Horsman, Reginald, 3
Hubbard, Ruggles, 131, 135, 138–39
Humbert, General Jean Joseph Amable,
    55, 167–73; portrait, 168

Impressment, 83
Indian removal, 84
Ingersoll, Charles Jared, 82
Inihamathla, Chief, 150
Innerarity brothers, 74
Iris, 130
Irwin, Colonel Jared, 130–35, 138–39
Isaacs, Captain, 110

Jackson, General Andrew, 4, 10, 14–15,
    55, 80, 95, 100, 107, 138, 142–43,
    145, 147, 149, 151–61, 166, 169–70,
    175, 189; captures Pensacola, 96–97;
    orders reduction of Negro Fort, 108;
    portrait, 143
Jacobo, Jorge, 79
Jarvis, Samuel, 210 (n. 5)
Jay, John, 17
Jay-Gardoqui Treaty, 17, 19, 180, 183
Jay Treaty, 19
Jefferson, Thomas, 2–3, 5, 13, 16–17,
    20–21, 23, 32, 34, 62, 71, 119, 181–84;
    favors expansion, 8–11; extends
    boundaries, 12; acquires New Or-
    leans, 24; beliefs, 26–27; policy of seiz-
    ing Indian lands, 82; favors assimila-
    tion, 87; portrait, 18
Jeffersonian Republicans, 184
Jeffersonians, 2, 3, 5–6, 9–10, 81, 183–
    84, 190–92; administrations, 6; ideas,
    9; expansion, 117, 190, 191, 192
John Forbes Company, 74, 142, 144. *See
    also* Forbes Company
Jupiter, 133

Kemper, Nathan, 61
Kemper, Reuben, 61, 63
Kemper, Major Samuel, 51–52, 56, 61
Kemper brothers, 170

Index

Kennedy, Joseph, 63
Kindelan, Governor Sebastian, 76, 81, 108
King Hatchy, 150, 156
Kingsley, Zephania, 120
Kotchahaijo (Mad Tiger), 110

La Bahía, 50, 51
Lacroix, General Ironée Amélot, 167
Lafarka (John Blount), 109
Laffite, Alexander (Dominique You/Youx), 169n
Laffite, Jean (John Lafflin), 6, 137, 161–62, 169–71, 175–78; biographical sketch, 169n; portrait, 171
Laffite, Pierre, 170n
Laffite, Reyne, 170n
Laffite brothers, 55, 173
Lafflin, John. See Laffite, Jean
Lafon, Bartholomé, 55
Lallemand, Charles François Antoine, 176–77
Lallemand, Henri, 176
Landownership: right of, 11
Lassus, Carlos de, 7
Laval, Major Jacint, 68–70
Leariramis, HMS, 115
Le Champ d'Asile, 176
Lewis, Meriwether, 12, 27
Lewis and Clark expedition, 13
Livingston, Edward, 136, 173
Livingston, Robert R., 12, 21, 23
Lloyd's of London, 139
Long, James, 178–80
Loomis, Jairus, 109, 111, 113
Lopez, John, 110
López, José, 70
Louisiana Purchase, 8, 11, 13, 15, 21–23, 33–34, 62–65, 68, 73, 89, 100, 118, 180, 188, 190
Lovera Bolívar, Doña Josefa Antonia Xeres Aristequienta y, 122
Lower Creek Indians, 67, 88–89, 94, 96, 115
Luffborough, Midshipman, 109, 110
Lyon, Matthew, 10, 166

MacGregor, Gregor, 6, 14–15, 122–34, 136, 139, 143, 146–47, 159, 164; background, 122; portrait, 123; receives commission, 124; recruits, 126; takes Fernandina, 127–28; men desert, 129–31; departs to meet Woodbine, 132; after Amelia Island, 133n
Madison, James, 2–3, 5, 12–14, 17, 22, 27, 29, 60, 62–68, 70–73, 75–77, 80, 82, 99–100, 161, 166, 183; wants expansion, 8–9, 12; pursuit of happiness, 29; cautious, 64; Folch offers Florida, 65–66; differs with Mathews, 67–68; authorizes Mathews's negotiation with Florida, 70–71; makes Mathews scapegoat, 76; policy on seizing Indian Land, 82; portrait, 28
Madison administration, 118; Treaties of Fort Jackson and Ghent, 99, 100
Mad Tiger (Kotchahaijo), 110
Magee, William Augustus, 6, 13, 48, 50–53, 61; biography, 48; made leader, 48; death, 51
Magee-Gutiérrez expedition, 54, 59, 61, 164–65, 168–69, 175, 178–79; reasons for failure, 59
Malcolm, Admiral Pultney, 99
Manifest Destiny, 2–6, 9–10, 15–16, 163, 167, 184; definition of, 10
Manrique, Don Mateo González, 95–97
Margaret, 133
Maria, 113
Martínez, Governor Antonio, 179
Masot, Governor José, 150, 160
Matagorda Bay, 47, 172
Matamoras, Manuel, 7
Mathews, Governor George, 6, 66–76, 139, 153; authorized to negotiate for Florida, 66; interprets Madison's instructions, 67; disagrees with Laval, 69; removed, 71
Maximiliano, 41
McIntosh, General John H., 69, 71
McIntosh, William, 107, 110, 112–13, 155
McKee, John, 66, 74
McKeever, Isaac, 155
McQueen, Peter, 95
Medina, Battle of, 57–59, 166–68
Merk, Frederick, 3, 12
Mexican Revolution, 43–44, 58, 178; final battle, 58
Mexican War (1846–1848), 190

Miccosukee Indians, 154
Mina, Francisco Xavier, 136–37, 173–75; portrait, 174
Miranda, General Francisco de, 122
Mississippi River: right of use, 27–28. *See also* Jay-Gardoqui Treaty
Mississippi Territory, 7, 63, 91; addition of Mobile, 91
Missouri Controversy, 180
Mitchell, Governor David B., 73–79; replaces Mathews, 74; portrait, 75
Mobile Act, 23, 62
Mobile customs district, 62
Mobile district: added to Mississippi Territory, 91, 92
Monroe, James, 2–5, 9, 12, 14, 20–24, 42–44, 46, 55, 62, 69–71, 73–76, 78, 80, 100n, 119, 151–53, 169, 176, 183; expansion, 9; extends boundaries, 12; pursuit of happiness, 29; Robinson's mission, 47; actions during Mexican Revolution, 59–60; policy on seizing Indian lands, 82; using filibusters to add territory, 164; portrait, 72
Monroe Doctrine, 2
Montero, Bernardino, 50
Moosa Creek, 78
Morales, Commander Francisco, 127–28
Morales, Juan Ventura, 20–21
Morgiana, 133
Morphy, Diego, Jr., 172

Nacogdoches, 36, 37, 50
Napoleon. *See* Bonaparte, Napoleon
Napoleonic Wars, 12, 25, 85, 103, 189
Narrative of a Voyage to the Spanish Main in the Ship "Two Friends," 103
Natchitoches, 37, 41, 45, 46, 49, 172
Natchitoches Sulphur Fork Factory, 50
National Intelligencer, 160
Native Americans, 1–2, 5, 10–11, 15, 82, 85, 88, 118, 185. *See also* individual tribes
Natural right, 5, 10, 190
Nava, Pedro de, 34
Negro Fort, 4, 14–15, 103–5, 107–8, 110–13, 115–17, 141, 144, 149, 154; description, 105; destruction, 110–13
Nero (Bowlegs's chief slave), 150
New England, 5, 11, 73

New Orleans, 12, 17, 19
New Orleans Association, 136, 172–73
New York Evening Post, 160
Newnan, Colonel Daniel, 79
Nicolls, Major Edward, 95–96, 104–5, 113–15, 144–45, 147, 149, 151, 157; established base at Prospect Bluff, 94–95; trains Indians and blacks, 98–99
Noah, Samuel, 48n
Nolan, Philip, 33, 34, 188
Nootka Sound, 18
Northeast: against expansion, 5; losing power, 11
Northern Company for South American Emancipation, 135

Onís, Don Luis de, 44, 54–55, 58, 64–65, 78, 92–94, 108, 126, 161–62, 172–73, 175, 179–80
Orleans Territory, 7
O'Sullivan, John L., 9
Overton, Captain John, 42

Patrick, Rembert W., 4, 73
Patriota, 131
Patriot Revolution, 68, 78, 81
Patterson, Daniel Todd, 135–36, 169–70, 172–73; portrait, 135
Peace of Amiens, 20
Peninsular War, 12, 173
Pérez, Cayetano, 92, 97
Perry, Major (Colonel) Henry, 56–57, 172, 175
Perryman, George, 115–16
Philbrick, Francis S., 3
Picornell Gomila, Juan Mariano Bautista de, 167
Pike, Zebulon, 46
Pike expedition (1806–1807), 27, 39
Pinckney, General Thomas, 19, 81
Pinckney Treaty, 20, 61, 188
Point Peter, 68–69
Pratt, Julius W., 4, 83
Prince Regent (Great Britain), 114
Prince Witen, 79
Prophet, the (Tenskwatawa), 86
Prophetstown, 86
Prospect Bluff, 14, 95; becomes Negro Fort, 103
Pursuit of happiness, 26

Index

Quasi-War, 182
Quesada, Nepomuceno de, 23

Rapides, Louisiana, 55–56
Red Sticks, 88, 95
Regnault, M. (probably Regnault St. Jean d'Angey), 125
Reign of Terror, 184
Remini, Robert V., 4, 152
Republic of Florida, 13
Republican Army of the North, 50
Republicans, 11–13, 16, 24, 26, 72–73, 80, 119, 161, 167, 184
Revolutionary War, 1, 182
Rhea, Congressman John, 152
Right of navigation and deposit, 26
Robinson, Dr. John Hamilton, 6, 48, 60, 166–69; mission to Mexico, 46
Rose's Bluff, 69
Ross, Colonel George T., 169
Ross, Major Reuben, 56
Royal Gazette: account of Arbuthnot, 145
Royal Gazette and Bahama Advertiser, 158
Royal Marines, 95
Runaway slaves: trained and armed, 103; British policy on return of, 106
Rush-Bagot Agreement, 116

Salado Creek, Battle of, 51
Salcedo, Governor Manuel, 40–41, 51
Salcedo, Commandant-General Nemesio, 36–37, 39–40, 46
Santo Domingo, 19, 44; uprising, 105
Saranac, 130, 133
Savary, Major Joseph, 138, 170, 173
Scott, Lieutenant Richard W., 151, 154
Sectionalism, 4, 5
Sedella, Father Antonio de, 167
Semilante, 109
Seminole Indians, 25, 67, 74, 77–79, 99, 101, 103, 114, 142, 150
Shaler, Captain William, 45–46, 52–57, 59–60
Shaw, Captain John, 37
Shawnee Indians, 84, 86
Sibley, Dr. John, 27, 49, 53, 178
Sibley expedition, 27
Sketch of the Mosquito Coast, 123
Skinner, John, 124

Smith, Robert: secretary of the navy, 31, 37
Smith, Colonel Thomas A., 71, 76, 78–79
St. Augustine: siege of 1812, 13
St. Joseph, 133–34
St. Marks, 15, 145, 154–55
St. Stephens, 62
Strangeway, Thomas, 123
Sulphur Fork Factory, 50

Tecumseh, 86–87, 89, 95
Tenskwatawa (the Prophet), 86
Territorial expansion, 2–3
Texas, 33–37, 39–44, 46–60, 164–68, 171, 172, 173–80
Texas Revolution (1836), 190
Texas Declaration of Independence, 53
Thirty-first parallel, 1–3, 61–62
Thomas, Philemon, 7
Thompson, Martin, 124
Tippecanoe, Battle of, 86
Toledo y Dubois, José Álvarez de, 13, 44, 53–57, 166–67, 169–71, 173
Toulmin, Judge Harry, 63
Transcontinental Treaty, 15, 162
Treaty of Fort Jackson, 93, 98–100, 104, 107, 116
Treaty of Fort Wayne, 86
Treaty of Ghent, 85, 98, 101, 104, 114–15, 141–42, 145, 156, 161, 188
Treaty of Greenville, 86
Treaty of Neutral Ground, 38
Treaty of Paris, 101n
Treaty of San Ildefonso, 19
Trinity River, 36, 175
Tuckabatchee Indians, 101
Turner, Frederick Jackson, 2
Turreau, General Louis Marie, 31
Twiggs, Major David, 150–51
Two Friends, 131

Upper Creek Indians, 88, 94

Venus, 131
Veracruz, 8
Vine and Olive Colony, 176

War of 1812, 4, 15–16, 64, 83, 88, 103, 119, 149, 163, 167, 169, 180, 184–85, 187, 190

Ward's Bluff, 61
Warren, Harris G., 4, 178
Washington, George, 23, 183
Weinberg, Albert, 2
West Florida, 8, 9, 23
West Indian troops, 99
Wilkinson, General James, 6, 33, 37–38, 42, 46–47, 49, 56, 60, 62, 80; Burr plot, 32; commander at Natchitoches, 37; seized Mobile, 91–92; portrait, 33
Wilkinson, Joseph, 56
Williams, Captain, 79

Wollestoncraft, Captain Charles, 48–49
Woodbine, George, 114, 131, 133n, 143, 145–47, 151, 157, 159

You (Youx), Dominique (Alexander Laffite), 169n
Young, Henry, 120
Yrujo, Marquis de Casa, 23

Zarate, F., 124
Zúñiga, Mauricio de, 94, 108–9

DATE DUE